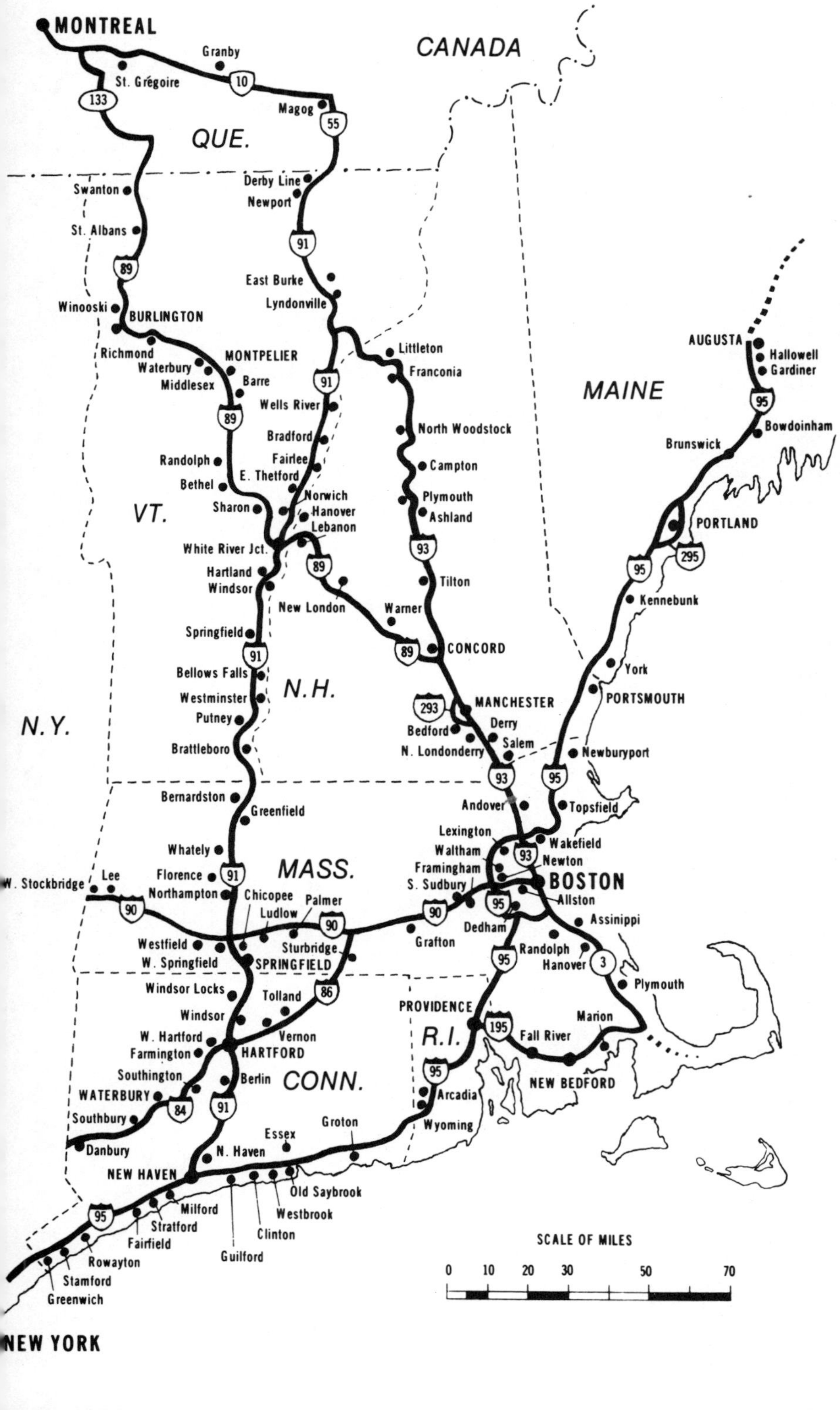
MONTREAL
CANADA
Granby
St. Grégoire
10
133
Magog
55
QUE.
Swanton
Derby Line
Newport
St. Albans
91
89
East Burke
Winooski
BURLINGTON
Lyndonville
AUGUSTA
Hallowell
Gardiner
Richmond
Waterbury
Middlesex
MONTPELIER
Barre
Littleton
Franconia
MAINE
Wells River
North Woodstock
Bowdoinham
Brunswick
Bradford
Randolph
Fairlee
E. Thetford
Campton
Bethel
Norwich
Hanover
Lebanon
Plymouth
Ashland
Sharon
VT.
PORTLAND
295
95
White River Jct.
93
Hartland
Windsor
Tilton
Kennebunk
New London
Warner
Springfield
CONCORD
York
Bellows Falls
N.H.
PORTSMOUTH
Westminster
293
MANCHESTER
Putney
Bedford
Derry
N.Y.
Salem
Brattleboro
N. Londonderry
Newburyport
Bernardston
Andover
Topsfield
Greenfield
Lexington
Waltham
Wakefield
Whately
Framingham
Newton
MASS.
W. Stockbridge
Lee
Florence
S. Sudbury
BOSTON
Northampton
Chicopee
Palmer
Allston
90
Ludlow
Assinippi
Grafton
Dedham
Westfield
Sturbridge
Randolph
W. Springfield
SPRINGFIELD
Hanover
3
Windsor Locks
Tolland
86
Plymouth
PROVIDENCE
Windsor
Marion
R.I.
195
Fall River
W. Hartford
Vernon
Farmington
HARTFORD
Southington
Berlin
CONN.
NEW BEDFORD
WATERBURY
Arcadia
84
Southbury
Groton
Wyoming
Essex
Danbury
N. Haven
NEW HAVEN
Old Saybrook
Milford
Westbrook
Stratford
Clinton
Fairfield
SCALE OF MILES
Guilford
0
10
20
30
50
70
Rowayton
Stamford
Greenwich
NEW YORK

BY THE SAME AUTHORS

The Interstate Gourmet—The Mid-Atlantic States

The Interstate Gourmet—California and the Pacific Northwest

THE INTERSTATE GOURMET

New England

Neal O. Weiner and
David M. Schwartz

SUMMIT BOOKS
NEW YORK

The reader should be aware that the restaurant business is unpredictable. Restaurants change their menus, prices and hours, some even change their names or addresses. While we have made every effort to update this book over the past year, we would be most grateful to hear about any changes you have encountered in your travels so that we may keep future editions up to date.

Published by SUMMIT BOOKS
A Simon & Schuster Division of Gulf & Western Corporation
Simon & Schuster Building
Rockefeller Center
1230 Avenue of the Americas
New York, New York 10020

SUMMIT BOOKS and colophon are trademarks of Simon & Schuster
Designed by Eve Kirch
Map: Robert MacLean
Drawings: Kristin Funkhauser
Manufactured in the United States of America

10 9 8 7 6 5 4 3 2 1

First edition
Library of Congress Cataloging in Publication Data
Weiner, Neal O.
The interstate gourmet—New England.

Includes index.
1. Restaurants, lunch rooms, etc.—New England—Directories. 2. Restaurants, lunch rooms, etc.—Québec (Province)—Directories. I. Schwartz, David M.
II. Title.
TX907.W438 1983 647'.9574 82-19399
ISBN 0-671-44992-3

ACKNOWLEDGMENTS

So many people helped us in so many ways that no list could even remotely do justice to the extent of our appreciation. But from among the multitude we must single out Barbara Yunger, who helped at the most critical periods of infancy; Charlotte Sheedy, who taught the child to walk; and Becky Nordstrom, who helped with the travails of adolescence. And, at every age and crisis, Mary Lou Brozena was there to assist and soothe when called upon.

Frank and Doris Birmingham, Jeanne Holzman, Leo Kretzner, and Jane Levenson all warmed our tired souls when we came in from a very cold road. Jessica Weiner's kindly forbearance left her father free to work out his compulsion.

And our heartfelt thanks to the many others who helped, especially our friends back at the beginning of the road in Brattleboro, Vermont.

CONTENTS

INTRODUCTION

If you've ever been stuck at a chain restaurant, this book is for you.

Perhaps you know the feeling: you've been driving the interstate just over the speed limit for two and a half, maybe three hours. You're bored. Hungry. Maybe your back hurts. It's time for a break.

As the exits fly by, you crane your neck, searching for an inviting restaurant. No luck. Nothing but weeds and an empty road. Or the massive signs of chain restaurants shouting for your dollars. You know their fare: dull food and sharp prices. But you don't have time to go poking up back roads looking for Ma's Diner. Do you press on, or do you give in to Ho-Jo's?

In its early days, motoring was an arduous but colorful adventure. Now, the interstate system has made long trips less grueling, but less interesting too. Superhighways insulate us from the local life and lead us only to mass-meal monsters that lie in ambush at the exits. Inside these chain restaurants, Maine looks—and tastes—just like Arizona, downtown Boston like Butte, Montana.

Gone—or at least hidden—are the diners, the small-town lunchrooms, the ethnic restaurants, and other owner-run establishments that offer good food (or better) at decent prices.

We end up choosing between heroic feats of highway endurance and stops at places that don't quite feel like breaks from the grind. But must we make the choice? If only we knew where to find the *little* restaurants, the ones the local people visit! If only *they* were close to the interstate.

Well, they are. And with this book you'll know how to find them. All kinds of restaurants! In almost every big city of New England—Boston, Hartford, Providence, New Haven—the interstate highway passes within blocks of an old Italian neighborhood. All the restaurants, bakeries, and cafés you could ask for are yours for the stopping. Where the interstate passes over Springfield, Massachusetts, you can actually see a fine old German place (if you know where to look), and in Fall River and New Bedford, Portuguese food awaits your discovery. French, Mexican, Polish, Jewish, Greek, Japanese, Korean, Vietnamese, and the Chinese cooking of every province: they're all within striking distance of the highway. In fact, for those in the know, an overview of New England's interstate highways starts to look like a blown-up dining guide to Manhattan. Well, not quite . . . we didn't find anything Armenian. But we did locate a terrific Hungarian restaurant in Danbury (see p. 17), where the prices were so low they seemed to predate the interstate system, and the chicken paprikash so good it lingers in the mind like memories of an old love.

But not only ethnic restaurants dot the highways. Smithsonian-quality diners, replete with mahogany woodwork, marble counters, mosaic tile floors, and arched ceilings, abound in New England. Many of them date back to the 1920s, hand-crafted products of the Worcester Lunch Car Company, kept spanking clean through the years by their proud owners. The food at these diners is usually decent, sometimes it's actually quite good, and always, it's affordable and prepared with a personal touch no chain restaurant can match.

Diners also come in humble little wood frame buildings hardly bigger than a toolshed (there's a great one in Fairlee, Vermont; see p. 118), and in the "silver bullets" that could be hooked onto an Amtrak Metroliner without being noticed (check out the Orchid, in New Bedford, p. 228).

The diner, by the way, was born as a horse-drawn lunch wagon on the streets of Providence, where you can still find the last remnant of the ancestral form. A pick-up truck does the pulling now, but every night Haven Brothers Diner pulls up next to City Hall and plugs itself into a lamppost. There, it plays host to as odd an assortment of night owls as you'll find anywhere.

In a desperate grab for middle-class respectability, diners sometimes get too dressed up. Suddenly, the corner chow house grows a stone façade; inside, it sports arched columns of ersatz brick, and everything—even the men's room—gets tiled over. When this happens, the prices go up and the food goes down; so, for the most part, we have left out this subspecies. The Aetna, in Hartford, is a spectacular Art Deco exception.

Diners are a slice of Americana, a world in themselves, with an etiquette and ethos all their own. There's a tradition, for instance, of friendly banter, playful insults, and outright pranksterism between owners and regulars (see Miss Newport). Oil paintings have commemorated them and books have been written about them, but we tried not to get too carried away with diners, because there's so much more to dining on the road.

A whole new genus of American café has sprung up in the last decade. Because they are so often decorated in brick, plants, and oak, we call these restaurants B.P.O.'s. Stained glass, mirrors, pressed-tin ceilings, and Tiffany-style lamps also star in B.P.O. decor.

The menus at these places are usually studded with puns, like "Lady Chatterley's Liver" or "Uncle Monte's Cristo." They invariably feature fancy sandwiches, big salads, and quiche. (Quiche, Reuben sandwiches, and spinach salads are so widespread, in fact, that we have nicknamed this the "Q.R.S." menu.) Crepes and omelettes are also big, and these are the restaurants that wrote the book on fried potato skins. Melted cheese is fashionable as a garnish on almost anything, pocket bread is on the rise, and carrot cake seems to be a dessert whose time has come.

Sometimes, brick-plants-and-oak cafés are stunningly beautiful, like Freestone's in New Bedford, where the requisite oak has been upgraded to mahogany. In other cases, they are on the funky side—which, we suspect, is how the type originated. And, as with everything else that catches on, the unbearable clichés crop up like weeds. Where we found sixteen old-style advertising mirrors ganged on a single barnboard wall, or three imitation Tiffany lamps hanging over each table, we tended to look elsewhere for something to report.

Usually frequented by the 25-to-40 set, B.P.O.'s have appeared everywhere since their advent in the late sixties. Often they are found in renovated brick buildings, frequently just a minute or two from an interstate highway. Without question, they have added a welcome variety to the highway dining landscape.

A distant cousin to the B.P.O.'s are the natural foods restaurants so liberally scattered across New England. Check out the worker-owned Common Ground in Brattleboro, Vermont, one of the first of its kind—a survivor of the era of communes and flower children—or the Horn of the Moon Café in Montpelier, Vermont, whose coffee stands as the best we've found. With their reliance on whole grains and previously unheard-of ingredients like tofu and miso, natural foods restaurants have changed the culinary consciousness of a whole generation.

And what about New England's wealth of country inns? They too come in many types. There's the delightful Kennebunk Inn in Maine, the lively Wayside Inn in Massachusetts that was called "old" by Longfellow in 1863, and the ancient Griswold in Connecticut. Unfortunately, some come close to being tourist traps, but because most of the inns have long-standing reputations to protect, their food is almost always good—sometimes gourmet, sometimes quaint, and other times just plain American. We'll tell you which is which.

On and on goes the list: the magnificent and pricey Greenstreet in Greenwich, Connecticut; the chowder houses of the Connecticut coast; Durgin-Park and the No-Name in Boston; the Vermont dairy bar run by a French chef; the pancake house in the White Mountains that stone-grinds four kinds of flour; the Norman Rockwell lunchroom near Plymouth Rock; the bakeries, the delis, the dairies . . .

All of these restaurants have one thing in common: we liked them. Something about each is worth reporting—the food, atmosphere, prices, or perhaps the owner's personality. We leave out the losers—you don't need to be told where not to go. To our minds, that meant leaving out not only the bad examples of good types, but also the monotonous steak-and-lobster places and almost anything with a name like Beef 'n Brew, Burger 'n Bun, or Suds 'n Duds. Of course, we ignored all the chain restaurants and those that wished they were, as well as the Polynesian palaces, the shopping-mall refueling stations, and the cutesy theme restaurants, except when the food was better than the theater. ("Hey!

How 'bout a restaurant based on a golf course? One course after each hole.")

Within these limits, we looked hard for variety, trying to please all palates and purses. In this book, you'll find 80-cent hamburgers reported next to $18 Chateaubriand, all treated with egalitarian respect, though we've borne in mind that most people aren't looking for extravagant fare when on the road. We've tried, when possible, to space out our choices so that whatever your taste and wherever you are, something you like will be no more than thirty minutes down the road.

Occasionally in our travels, we found slim pickin's. When this happened, we put in a few marginal places so that you would have something better than a chain restaurant in which to satisfy a sharp hunger. But don't worry—we'll let you know which ones these are.

We discovered all of these restaurants on a gargantuan, six-state eating odyssey, and we sampled the food in nearly every one (no, we didn't get fat). Unfortunately, some were closed for vacation when we passed through, and frankly, there were a few times we simply couldn't bear the thought of another bite. So there are places (not many) in this book where you are left to your own spirit of adventure. We get you to the front door. Let us hear what you found inside.

But 99 percent of the time, you'll know just what lies beyond the highway signs. Now, long-distance driving can be an adventure in eating. Without sacrificing time, you can experience some of the local life—and taste some of the regional dishes—that you'd otherwise pass by.

Wherever you are when you stop for a roadside lunch, you are not merely buying food. You're also renting space, and for that reason we tell you how a place feels, what it'll be like to pass an hour there. Of course, we also describe the menu, the prices, and the quality of food, without trying to sound as though we're reviewing Lutèce for *The New York Times*. And we provide you with clear directions, stop sign by stop sign, from highway to restaurant. Well we know the distress of aimless searching after a long, hard drive!

We've given prices as we found them when we made our grand tour, and, although they may have changed by the time you visit, they'll still be useful as a relative guide to what you'll spend in each place.

As with any directory, from *Who's Who* to the Yellow Pages, this book will no doubt be challenged about who got in and who was left out. Inevitably, there will be cries of protest, and surely we've missed some very good restaurants, perhaps even "the best in town."

If, in fact, we managed to skip your favorite little gem of a roadside eatery, we ask that you let us know, so that future editions can be even more useful than this one. In the meantime, we hope this book will change your whole perspective on the highway dining dilemma. It is true, certainly, that getting stuck at a chain restaurant is but a minor misfortune, but it is one we have endeavored to cure for good. Perhaps the little evils are the only ones that can be done away with once and for all.

I-84

Connecticut

THE GOULASH PLACE, *Exit 4, Danbury*

One of our all-time best discoveries was made not on our grand tour of New England, but years ago when one of us first began compiling culinary oases along interstate highways. The Goulash Place is everything a find like this should be: an all but unknown ethnic restaurant, owned and operated by people who learned their trade in the mother country, clean but with no decor to speak of, absolutely wonderful food, and rock-bottom prices. It's simply perfection within the genus, and we checked it out on our recent odyssey to make sure nothing had changed.

It hadn't. The piquant mushroom and pork soup with dumplings was still 80 cents, and it still had the flavor that for three years had haunted our memories. The Transylvanian goulash with sauerkraut was equally spectacular, and still just $4.50. The colorful Hungarian bric-a-brac still cluttered the bright white walls, the chairs were still vinyl-covered metal, and the tiny eight-stool counter was still occupied by people speaking Hungarian (as was almost everyone else in the restaurant, for that matter).

One reason the place is not so well known is the location of its Hansel and Gretel building. Actually an addition to the home of Aczel and John Magdola, the restaurant is on a side street in a residential neighborhood.

Like the building, the cooking has its roots in the home. Aczel learned from her parents, who ran a small restaurant in Budapest. Friends on this side of the Atlantic kept saying her food was so good, she ought to open a restaurant too. Unlike most who receive such praise, Aczel did it. After she spent two years experimenting to adapt her recipes to the restaurant business, the Goulash Place opened its doors. The results have been phenomenal, even if the cash flow hasn't overrun Danbury's banks.

On the menu at the Goulash Place you'll find 24 entrées, among them Hungarian stew ($3.35), goulash ($4.80), stuffed cabbage ($3.35), and chicken paprikash ($4.15). There are four strictly-from-scratch soups, and for dessert you can try Aczel's homemade strudel or layer cake at $1. All these dishes are available at lunchtime, but then you'll also find things like sausage grinders ($2.20) and meatloaf ($2.25). No liquor license here; bring your own.

If you have even the faintest taste for this kind of eating, don't miss the Goulash Place. And don't fail to chat with Aczel, whose warm and honest personality is as lovely as her cooking.

HOURS Tue.–Thu. 11 am–9 pm; Fri. & Sat. 11 am–10 pm; Sun. 1–8 pm; Closed Mon.

DIRECTIONS From Exit 4 turn left and go about ¾ mile to the light at Westville. Turn left on Westville and go 1 short block to Roger. Right on Roger and go 2 long blocks to the corner of Highland Ave. You're there; it's on the right at 42 Highland.

THE OASIS, *Exit 4, Danbury*

Quite unlike the Goulash Place, the Oasis is in a large, conspicuous building on a well-traveled road. From the outside it looks like a nightclub, and its cocktail lounge is big enough for the purpose. But once you sit down to eat in the well-separated dining area, and once you have a chance to talk with Abe Haddad, whose family has kept the hummus flowing here for 22 years, you'll realize that the Oasis has the soul of a small family-run restaurant.

In this case, of course, it's Middle Eastern food—Lebanese in particular (Syrian cuisine uses different spices, Abe says). Although Danbury has a sizable population of middle-aged Arabic people who order the house specialties, Abe considers it a personal challenge to educate Danbury's youth about Lebanese cooking. "Today's teenagers were brought up on fast food, and it's tough to get them to take out a date for kibbee."

But if only the teenagers would give it a try! We did, and we now understand Abe's frustration. Kibbee is finely ground fresh lamb and top-round beef mixed with cracked wheat. Here it is baked and served as a dinner entrée with rice and salad for $7.95 ($3.95 at lunch). Or, it is fried and served on a roll—a Middle Eastern hamburger, if you will (only $2.65). After trying it, you'll probably agree with us that it makes a plain ole beefburger seem dull indeed.

At the Oasis you can also get rolled grape leaves stuffed with lamb and rice for $6.95, and the waitresses, who all seem very friendly, will be glad to show you how to eat them with pocket bread and yogurt. The baked squash is stuffed with rice and flavorfully seasoned in the Lebanese style—with cinnamon, nutmeg, allspice, and mint. For $7.25 it is served with a minty salad; if you like food that bites back, try the spicy lemon-and-oil house dressing.

If you simply won't be tempted, Abe offers high-quality American food too. The usual dinner entrées run from $6.50 to $9.50, while sandwiches—including, yes, the plain ole beefburger—are $1.65 to $2.95. Lunch salads and platters go from $1.90 to $5. All meats are fresh, cooked and ground on the premises, and sliced to order.

HOURS Sun., Wed., Thu. 11 am–11 pm; Mon. & Tue. 11 am–3 pm and 4:30–11 pm; Fri. & Sat. 11 am–midnight.

DIRECTIONS From Exit 4 turn left and go about ¼ mile; you'll see it on your left.

BELLA ITALIA, *Exits 5 & 6, Danbury*

* *Untried, but likely*

Once Danbury had a lovely little Italian restaurant with red-checked tablecloths, gracious waiters, low prices, and food so good that *The New York Times* raved and a flood of customers rushed in. And it was just yards from Interstate 84.

But success has changed Bella Italia. It recently moved across the street into far more sumptuous quarters—three separate dining areas, each with a different menu, expensive furniture, imported tile, and parking facilities. Since someone has to pay for these amenities, the prices moved too.

The exclusive formal dining room offers continental cuisine in the $13–$18 range. The old trattoria has been reincarnated as a casual dining area with mostly Italian cuisine, $7–$12 per entrée. Happily, there is also a pizzeria, where travelers can enjoy a grinder or a pizza and still afford to fill the gas tank before hitting the road.

We loved the old place, but haven't yet been to the grown-up version. We await your reports.

HOURS Every day, noon–2:30 pm and 5–10:30 pm or later.

DIRECTIONS See **Tortilla Flat,** below.

TORTILLA FLAT, *Exits 5 & 6, Danbury*

Tales of Tortilla Flat's outstanding margueritas are legion in Danbury, but more important to the traveler are its fine Mexican cooking and an atmosphere that's been described as "funky chic." If you show up in blue jeans, you won't feel any more out of place than do the suited businessmen who come here regularly. The dark-stained rustic look of Tortilla Flat is surely nothing new in American restaurants, but this one has an unexpected presence: huge blow-ups of Mexican revolutionaries whose steely stares join you at your meal. A bit unnerving perhaps, but different.

The food here is spiced to be lively, not deadly. (If you like it searing, there are two types of hot sauce on the table.) Among the entrée choices are tostadas, enchiladas, burritos, and the house specialty, chili rellenos—cheese-stuffed green chili peppers dipped in egg batter and deep-fried, then topped with onions, sauce, and cheese.

Prices are most affordable. Eight out of ten combination plates are under $5; each plate includes two or three main items, rice, and beans. The special combination plate is enough for two if neither is ravenous: a chicken taco, a beef taco, a cheese enchilada, guacamole salad, rice and beans, all for $5.95. Smooth it down with a lovely flan for dessert.

HOURS Mon.–Thu. 11:30 am–10 pm; Fri. & Sat. 11:30 am–11 pm; Sun. 3–9 pm.

DIRECTIONS Eastbound: From Exit 5 go straight to traffic light and cross through light onto North St. In 0.7 mile you reach a light at the North Street Shopping Plaza. ■ For **Bella Italia,** bear left at this light and it's on your left. For **Tortilla Flat,** turn right at this light (Hayestown Ave.). Go 0.3 mile to stop sign at a T. Left at the T, and 0.2 mile to a fork; bear left at fork onto East Pembroke Rd. In 0.3 mile you'll come upon it, on your right.

Westbound: From Exit 6 turn right at the light and go 0.1 mile to the light at the North Street Shopping Plaza. Then, as above from ■.

LORENZO'S TOO, *Exit 15, Southbury*

Lorenzo's Too can be described in pretty much the same words as **Kent Pizza** (p. 31) and **Tolland Pizza** (p. 31)—read about them and you'll have the picture. Perhaps it's a little bit less of a joint and more of a restaurant, with carpeted floors, captain's chairs, and a slightly wider menu including hamburgers ($1.15), lasagne ($5.75), eggplant parmigiana ($5.50), linguine with clam sauce ($4), and baked stuffed manicotti ($5.25). But it's mostly pizza, grinders, and pasted-on decor.

HOURS Tue.–Thu. 11 am–10 pm; Fri. & Sat. 11 am–11 pm; Sun. 5–10 pm; closed Mon.

DIRECTIONS From Exit 15 turn left if eastbound, right if westbound. At the first light, turn left. Go one block and pull into Bennet's Shopping Plaza on your right.

ABOUT WATERBURY

Waterbury's enormous granite cross looks down upon all who drive through on I-84. Those in search of spiritual food can climb Pine Hill to "Holyland," a miniature Bethlehem Village created in 1956, but the traveler in need of more mundane nutrition will have to descend into the bowels of this gritty city, once known as the Brass Center of the World.

DRESCHER'S RESTAURANT, *Exit 22, Waterbury*

All the elements of Waterbury's industrial past—and present—can be seen at Drescher's, where the city's German community has been well fed since 1868. Now everyone goes there. "You can see a millionaire sitting next to a sanitation worker," boasts owner Don Monllos with obvious pride.

Although a few beer steins and a gigantic cuckoo clock adorn the walls, Drescher's does not try to be a museum of Germanica. The Old World feel is not tacked on; it just seems to come naturally.

The brick and stone building is itself a historic landmark, and when urban renewal struck, citizens successfully lobbied to have it preserved. It's hard to believe, but true: the whole building was lifted, moved one block, and set down in its present location. Monllos watched it all happen, wiped off the dust, then went back to his business of serving homemade bratwurst ($4.25 with red cabbage and potatoes), sauerbraten ($4.75, with potatoes), schnitzel ($4.75), and fresh pig's knuckles with sauerkraut, as well as American standbys like scallops, liver and onions, and half a dozen club sandwiches ($3.25–$4). His soups are all homemade—cream of spinach, chicken with rice, and Manhattan clam chowder are the favorites.

We found the sauerbraten to be well prepared and tasty. Upon inquiry we discovered that the dark, rich gravy is thickened with crushed ginger snaps! The sweet-and-sour cabbage was pungent and pleasant.

As we were rising to leave, a woman at a neighboring table leaned over to tell us that the real treat here was Mrs. Monllos's special desserts; but she warned that their availability was unpredictable. We were in luck: the apple cake we were able to sample was delicious—moist, not too sweet, with a lovely nutty flavor.

HOURS Every day 11 am to midnight. Closed holidays.

DIRECTIONS Eastbound: From Exit 22, turn left at light at the end of the ramp. At next light, turn left onto Grand St. and then right at the second light onto Leavenworth. **Drescher's** is on the right, 1½ blocks down.

Westbound: From Exit 22 go straight through the light at the end of the ramp, down the hill into town, and straight through two more lights. Next light is Leavenworth; turn right. **Drescher's** is 1½ blocks down, on right.

ACROSS FROM THE HORSE, *Exit 22, Waterbury*

While Drescher's fits Waterbury like a pair of well-worn dungarees, Across from the Horse is more like designer jeans. But in its own ritzy way, it too is attuned to Waterbury's character as a metalworking town.

Located directly opposite a 2500-pound bronze steed on the city green, this is a high-toned brick-plants-and-oak café of the brassiest sort: outsized curtain rods and handrails, chandeliers, and even an ornate dumbwaiter are all made of the bold metal. So is a most unusual ventilation system consisting of paddles affixed to a rotating 15-foot bar. Add to all of this a silvery tin ceiling, luxuriant hanging plants that cascade over back-lit stained-glass panels, and finely crafted mahogany trim. The result is a very plush eating establishment that falls somewhere between just right and too much.

The menu is a 14-page staple-bound affair, beginning with drinks and ending with desserts. Steaks and seafood are available (in the $7–$12 range), but so are burgers (from $2.75 with lettuce and tomato to $3.25 for some slightly more inspired variations). Not surprisingly, given the restaurant's outstanding credentials as a B.P.O. café, sandwiches are a house specialty, and each has a sobriquet: Stevie's Wonder ($3.50) is batter-dipped chicken topped with bacon and covered with melted cheese; Rosie's Roast Beast ($3.75) is sliced London broil with sautéed onions and melted cheese on rye. We could list more, like Donald W. Delicious and Miss Piggy's, but we think you've got the idea.

HOURS Mon.–Sat. 11:30 am–10 pm; Sun. 11:30 am–3:30 pm.

DIRECTIONS Eastbound: From Exit 22 turn left at the first light, go through three more lights, and it will be on your right, opposite the equestrian statue on the green.

Westbound: From Exit 22 go straight through the light at the end of the ramp, and turn right at the next light (South Main). Go through two lights and you'll see it on your right.

VENICE DINER, *Exit 32, Southington*

The front of the Venice Diner's menu depicts a gondolier poling his craft past the Leaning Tower of Pisa and toward the Colosseum, with Mount Vesuvius erupting in the background. Hmmm! We don't recommend you come to this modern-style diner with its pebbled exterior and ersatz mansard roof for a lesson in Italian geography. It's not even an Italian diner; it's Greek. But we do recommend you come here for the bargains.

Every day from 6 am to 3 pm, you can get three eggs, home fries, and toast for 99 cents. Or, how about two pancakes with two eggs, or four slices of French toast for the same price? After 3 pm, help yourself to all the fried chicken you can eat for $3.95, or gorge yourself on unlimited fish and chips ($3.50), stuffed crab ($4.95), or fried shrimp ($5.95).

Don't expect candles or plush carpets at these prices. The interior is done up in inexpensive paneling, the booth seats have seen better days, and the floor is a little on the grungy side.

Mrs. Christodlis, a sweet-looking little lady, will gladly discuss the Greek dishes on her ever-changing menu. The house favorites are "pastichios," a kind of baked macaroni, Greek style ($2.90 à la carte/$3.90 dinner), and spiced stuffed peppers ($3.50/$4.50). All the soups are homemade (60–70 cents a bowl), as are the gravies and coleslaw. We had an honest and hearty farmhouse beef stew for $3.25. Although the bread was pasty, it was compensated for at the other end of the meal by excellent cheesecake from the Christodlis family's cheesecake factory. They bake 25 varieties, including almond, peach, pear, pecan, raisin, peanut butter, rum, and coconut. Mrs. Christodlis won't charge you a cent for a short treatise on the Greek origin of cheesecake.

HOURS 24 hours, every day of the year.

DIRECTIONS Eastbound: From Exit 32 turn left at light. It's just past the next light, on left.

Westbound: From Exit 32 turn right at bottom of ramp. It's just past the second light, on left.

THE READING ROOM, *Exit 39, Farmington*

When he established Connecticut's first grist mill on the banks of the Farmington River in 1650, Deacon Stephen Hart could never have anticipated that 280 years later the old mill would serve as backdrop for D. W. Griffith's silent film classic *Way Down East,* with Lillian Gish bounding across ice floes, tottering ever closer to the perilous falls. Neither could he have known that the place would later become a small complex of boutiques and home to one of Connecticut's most captivating restaurants.

Absolutely pleasant in every respect, the Reading Room derives its charm from a kind of New England–style rustic elegance —simple but tasteful, comfortable but unpretentious. Perched over the water, the airy, carpeted room is amply appointed with bentwood chairs, brass kerosene (now electric) lamps, butcher-block tables set with stoneware and fresh flowers, and lovely views of the curving river. Decorating the walls are framed covers from old *Collier's* and *New York Times Book Reviews* (including one announcing Hemingway's latest, *For Whom the Bell Tolls*). It's just the kind of place where you would love to spend some time with a good meal and a good book. There is a fine little bookstore next door and, for those who fail to bring their own, a wooden rack holds reading material.

There's another kind of "bring your own," involving another rack, at the Reading Room. Because it has no liquor license, the restaurant allows regulars to label and stow their bottles. Of course, anyone is welcome to brown-bag a bottle of wine.

The menu, not surprisingly, looks like a book, with chapters for appetizers, entrées, and desserts. Fish comes fresh each day, and daily specials, like the restaurant itself, are refreshingly different. For lunch, you'll find Italian sausage turnovers, sole cooked with fresh apples in Calvados and cream, or seafood salad with shrimp, mussels, langostinos, pineapple, and walnuts, all in the $4.25–$5.95 range. Each day features a different sandwich; with garden salad, it goes for $4.50

Dinners too are different here: veal Madagascar, roast duckling in a light raspberry sauce, or filet of sole with spinach, mushroom, and tomato stuffing, for example. They run from $9.25 to $13.50. For dessert try the Reading Room's tollhouse cookie pie, a strange but delectable hybrid that looks like what its name suggests.

HOURS Mon.–Sat. 11:30 am–2:30 pm and 5:30–10 pm; Sun. 11 am–2 pm.

DIRECTIONS From Exit 39 (a left-lane exit for eastbound travelers), enter Route 4 West. Go straight through one light and bear right at blinking light 0.2 mile from the exit. Turn left at the second light after the blinker (Garden St.) and then right onto Mill Lane at the second stop sign. After 1 block, turn left into the parking lot of Helen Winter's Grist Mill.

BANDO RESTAURANT, *Exit 43, W. Hartford*

You won't have to crane for a peek at your neighbor's meal to decide what to order here. At Bando, the Korean, Japanese, and Chinese specialties, or at least fairly authentic plastic replicas thereof, are on display in a large glass case. Each item is labeled and colorfully painted. In Korea, where these models—as well as the cook—come from, such displays are commonplace.

On the basis of our plastic preview, we opted for fried mandoo, steamed soybean curd (tofu), and Norimaki sushi. The sushi, vinegared rice and diced Oriental vegetables stuffed in a wrapper of purple seaweed ($4.35), was artfully presented with pickled radishes, garlic, and ginger, which despite our hesitations, proved quite palatable, in a pickled sort of way. Steamed tofu (95 cents for a full pillow) came topped with sesame seeds, diced scallions, and shredded carrots; its mild flavor nicely cushioned the piquant sauce. Our favorite, though, was the mandoo ($2.10 as dinner appetizer/$3.45 as lunch entrée), which are fried dumplings enclosing ground pork, spring onions, and cabbage. They were a bit greasy but worth it for the rich, interesting flavor and pleasing aftertaste.

Mrs. Kyung Lee, who presides over Bando's woks, studied Japanese and Szechuan cooking as well as her native Korean before coming to this country five years ago. As a result, the menu includes tempura, sashimi (raw fish with fresh vegetables—Wednesday through Friday only), spicy chicken, and sweet-and-hot pork with tofu. Dinners are generally $4–$6. Szechuan seasoning can be requested in either searing or forgiving doses.

The reasonably priced lunch menu ($2.10–$4.50) is more limited, and mostly Chinese, but includes four Korean specialties.

The restaurant itself is plain and simple, decorated only with a few inexpensively mounted Oriental pictures that look as though they were cut out of a calendar. You can sit in a white wooden booth or at the counter, which offers a great view of the spectacular display case.

HOURS Lunch: Mon.–Fri. 11:30 am–2:30 pm; no lunch on weekends. Dinner: Every day 4:30–9:30 pm.

DIRECTIONS From Exit 43 turn right at the light onto Park Rd. It's on the left after 0.6 mile.

THE AETNA RESTAURANT, *Exit 46, Hartford*

The Aetna has got to be the swankiest, glitziest, most jazzed-up diner we've ever seen. An Art Deco eruption of chandeliers, glass bricks, oval windows, textured stainless-steel wall panels, etched glass, and plush furnishings, the Aetna could be mistaken for a Miami Beach bar mitzvah joint. But don't expect kreplach.

The food here is mostly Greek. If that suits you, and you're in a campy mood, you'll get a bang out of the Aetna.

There's something for everyone on the menu—pure Greek (lamb souvlaki, spanakopita), American (fisherman's platter or broiled pork chops with apple sauce), and in between (filet of flounder with feta cheese, broiled chicken à la Greque). These dinners run $5.50 to $8.75. Naturally, you can get a Greek salad, but it'll cost ($5.50); sandwiches aren't cheap either ($4–$5).

Top it all off with a cup of mud-thick Greek coffee—you may wish to thin the viscid stuff with a shot of ouzo.

HOURS Sun.–Thu. 11 am–10:30 pm; Fri. & Sat. 11 am–midnight.

DIRECTIONS From Exit 46 turn right at the light onto Sisson Ave. Right at the next light onto Farmington Ave. Go ½ mile. It's on your right. Don't worry, you'll see it.

MOZZICATO CAFFÈ
PIPPIE'S RESTAURANT
TRUC, *Exit 27, Hartford*

See descriptions on pp. 80–82 for two Italian restaurants, one quite inexpensive, and a moderately priced Vietnamese place.

DIRECTIONS From junction of I-84 and I-91 go south on I-91 to Exit 27. Then follow directions given.

Note: East of Hartford, I-84 continues as I-86 (see p. 29).

I-86

Connecticut, Massachusetts

Connecticut

REIN'S NEW YORK STYLE DELI AND RESTAURANT, ***Exit 96, Vernon***

With names like Weiner and Schwartz, we felt eminently well qualified to judge Rein's Deli. Perched on an embankment that practically hangs over the interstate, Rein's Deli looks more like a Roman bathhouse than a Brooklyn chow house, and from the sign on the window, "Come In and Re-Lox," we were prepared for more talk than action.

The restaurant itself is a large, square, well-lit room with orange tables and no embellishments save a few signs that try, a bit too hard perhaps, to get the point across: "FLUSHING" points the way to the rest rooms, which are labeled "MENHATTAN" and "QUEENS." With a strong suspicion that this deli was, as its name suggests, more New York *style* than New York, we got down to business with a bowl of chicken soup ($1.15). We were wrong; it was without a whiff of doubt, the real thing—no bouillon cubes or canned broth in this Jewish penicillin. Even the matzoh balls were done right—light and fluffy, just like Aunt Rita's at Seder. The stuffed cabbage ($2.50 as dinner appetizer/$4.95 as lunch entrée) was as good as Mom's, though the raisins in the sauce made it a tad sweeter.

Manager Les Kahn is a soft-spoken, smallish man who needed only one word and a gesture toward the deli counter to describe what the place has to offer: "Everything." He's right. It's a kosher orgy, starring knishes and kugel, blintzes, borscht and bagels, whitefish and lox, not to mention herring in cream sauce, pot cheese, and even Greek salad, Brooklyn-style (with matjes herring instead of feta). A bagel with Nova Scotia lox is $3.95, a bowl of thick mushroom and barley soup, $1.25. Sandwiches are made strictly from Hebrew National meats ("We wouldn't dare substitute"), and run from $2.50 to upwards of $5 for triple-deckers ("You won't go away hungry"). Entrées and salad plates are in the $4.50 to $7 range. And then, oh no, come the desserts ("What do you mean you don't have room for dessert?"). There are cheesecakes and sour cream cakes, cream cheese brownies and chocolate pecan pies, bread and noodle puddings, stewed prunes, cheese strudel, hand-dipped chocolates from Brooklyn, and rock candy. We tried the ruggelach—first one, then two, then ten of those spiral almond and raisin cookies that make life worth the trouble. We just don't know where they got Grandma Pearl's recipe.

If you pass up a stop in Vernon and find yourself lusting for gefilte fish at 3 am, you can find another Rein's deli, this one open 24 hours, downtown in the Hartford Civic Center.

HOURS Summer: Mon.–Wed. 7 am–9 pm; Thu. & Sun. 7 am–10 pm; Fri. & Sat. 7 am–11 pm. Winter: Same, but opens at 8 am every day.

DIRECTIONS Eastbound: Believe it or not, the easiest way is to take Exit 97, cross over the highway with three left turns, reenter I-86 westbound, and get off at Exit 96. Then, as below. (It's simple, really, and only a mile out of the way.)

Westbound: From Exit 96 turn right. It's in the first building, on right.

KENT PIZZA
TOLLAND PIZZA, *Exit 99, Tolland*

When we started this project, we were told that nothing but tacky Italian joints could be found along Interstates 84 and 86. We proved our informants wrong in many towns along those routes, but just in case there are hungry kids in the back seat, or you just happen to be in the mood for a pizza place, here are two to choose from, practically next door to each other. Both have pizza and grinders, fast service, plastic atmosphere, and low prices. Tolland Pizza is larger, with a dining area separated from the serving counter. Kent Pizza has hamburgers, hot dogs, and spinach pie, as well as the expected.

HOURS **Tolland Pizza:** Mon.–Thu. 11 am–11 pm; Fri. & Sat. 11 am–midnight; Sun. noon–10 pm.

Kent Pizza: Every day 11 am–9:30 pm (sometimes later).

DIRECTIONS From Exit 99 turn right if eastbound, left if westbound, and go ½ mile. Both places are on your left, in neighboring shopping plazas.

Massachusetts

THE DICKENS TAVERN, *Exit 4W, Sturbridge*

The Dickens Tavern looks as though it couldn't decide whether to be a country inn or a brick-plants-and-oak café, so it's got a little of each. Set in a Colonial building that has been through a few awkward growth spurts, the basement-level restaurant has barnboard and brick walls, heavy rustic-style furniture, old-fashioned (now light-bulbed) lanterns, and a menu that promises "Yankee Home Cooking."

A bit anomalous, perhaps, that the prized desserts of this "Yankee Home Cooking" should be carrot cake and California mud pie (mocha ice cream and chocolate syrup in an Oreo cookie crust), but that's the way it is here. At dinner, you can get old-style dishes like roast turkey, pork tenderloin, Boston scrod, or fish and chips (most $7–$8), but you can also get B.P.O. cuisine—fried potato skins, their own seafood pie ($7), and seafood or beef bourguignon crepes ($4.50). Lunch dishes run from $2.75 for a hamburger to $4.95 for a chef's salad or fried clams; there are omelettes, sandwiches, and crepes in between.

The most interesting thing about the Dickens Tavern is its wintertime soup bar. For $2.95, you can help yourself to rolls and a bottomless bowl of soup, with seven varieties to choose from. When we were there, they offered a chunky fish chowder, minestrone, cream of mushroom, potato leek, French onion, split pea, and chicken noodle. In summer, the soup gives way to a chef's salad bar.

HOURS Lunch: Mon.–Sat. 11:30 am–2:30 pm; Sun. (brunch) 10:30 am–2:30 pm. Dinner: Sun.–Thu. 5–9 pm. Sandwiches between mealtimes.

DIRECTIONS Exit 4W puts you on Route 20 West. Go about ½ mile, through one traffic light; it's on your right.

ROM'S, *Exit 4W, Sturbridge*

Make no mistake about it, Rom's is touristy, what with its seating capacity of 700, a staff of 225, and no fewer than three bars. But make no mistake about this either: it's still a genuine family operation, the food is good, and the prices are very reasonable. That's how it got so big, and you may find that its decor, which isn't authentic anything, is something of a relief in a town devoted to preserving every brick and nail.

Once Rom's was a tiny take-out dairy bar, serving soft ice cream and some Italian specialties. The dairy bar is still there, white and gleaming, and even though it's now glass-enclosed for winter operation, there is still a crazy-quilt of signs on the wall offering every sort of Italian dish, fruit drink, ice cream concoction, and Lord knows what else, "to go."

If you pass up this earthy splendor for the formal restaurant behind it, you'll find a very Middle American dining room with Windsor chairs, dark woodgrain Formica tables, and huge picture windows in every wall.

Here eight members of Romaldo Roscoli's family preside over their sprawling empire. The pasta is all homemade (except the spaghetti) and nothing is frozen (except the shrimp). The tomato sauce is stronger at home, they told us, but the milder version offered to the public was still very flavorful, and the stuffed green peppers were simply wonderful.

Rom is as proud of his prices as he is of his mother's recipes. An Italian combination plate (veal, sausage, mushrooms, peppers, meatballs and spaghetti) is just $6.95. A humble plate of spaghetti all by itself is but $2.95; with peppers, $3.65. There are also pizzas (from $4.25), sandwiches ($2.50 to $4), and a pretty complete American menu, comparably priced.

If you like the sound of all this but a 700-seat restaurant isn't your cup of tea, there's a solution. Just about everything is available "to go" at the dairy stand, and in summer there are picnic tables close at hand.

HOURS Summer: every day 11 am–10 pm. Winter: Sun.–Fri. 11 am–9 pm; Sat. 11 am–10 pm.

DIRECTIONS See **The Publick House,** below.

THE PUBLICK HOUSE, *Exit 4W, Sturbridge*

There's no missing this place if you're in Sturbridge. It's a large 18th century inn right in the middle of town, and it's quite an operation. While we confess to a predilection for old inns, the Publick House is a bit too much like Olde Newe Englande Disneylande for our taste.

The original dining room, which dates from 1771, is really very nice—low ceilings, exposed beams, old wood floor, and a huge fireplace on which an open-hearth breakfast is sometimes cooked. And the food, though expensive, is certainly good—traditional New England fare, well prepared and nicely presented. But there's no mistaking the fact that the Publick House is making big bucks from Old Sturbridge Village tourists who just hate to leave history behind. To prolong the experience they descend en masse upon the Publick House, and there they may not always find what they expect.

The restaurant has five dining rooms, and only the lucky will get the good one. You're just as likely to be seated in what was once a barn, and looks it, or in a large addition behind it which feels new and looks surprisingly tacky—not so bad for a medium-priced meal perhaps, but when dinners are mostly in the $12–$15 range (with a few at $7–$11), we expect more.

Lunches here run from $5 to $7.25. Two eggs all by themselves are a dollar each, while a full breakfast of juice or fruit, two eggs, toast, and coffee is $3.95.

The lunch menu, by the way, is printed on "yellowed" paper in an 18th century typeface, but they couldn't resist spicing it up with those lithographed advertisements from the 1880s.

See what we meane?

HOURS Every day 7:30–11 am and noon–8:30 pm.

DIRECTIONS Exit 4W leads you to Route 131. Take a left at the light, toward Sturbridge Center. In 0.6 mile, **The Publick House** is on the right; 1 mile farther, you'll see **Rom's,** also on the right.

I-89

New Hampshire, Vermont

New Hampshire

THE NATURAL SELECTION
B. MAE DENNY'S
THURSDAY'S RESTAURANT, ***Exit 1, Concord***

See descriptions on pp. 152–155.

DIRECTIONS To get to these restaurants from I-89, it's easiest to get on I-93 North at Exit 1. Then go about 2 miles to I-93, Exit 14, and follow directions given. The detour won't cost you more than five minutes.

WARNER VARIETY STORE AND RESTAURANT,
Exits 8 and 9, Warner

Almost everything is homemade here—not just the rich abundance of pies, cakes, muffins, and soups, but even the heavy tables and lacy calico curtains that adorn the lunchroom section of this tiny general store. But don't look for anything arty. It's run by and for the local people of this friendly town, and it's utterly without pretension.

If you can forget about quiche and spinach salad and be happy with soup, grinders, pizza, and simple sandwiches, this is the place for you. What will make you especially happy is the absolutely delicious corn chowder they cook up for just 65 cents a cup. And you won't be disappointed by the pastries. The pizza (65 cents a slice) and grinders ($2–$3) were decent, but nothing to write books about.

A few dinners are available, ranging from franks and beans for $2 to a high of $3.95 for fried haddock with potatoes, vegetables, and bread. Two eggs and toast are $1.10.

Warner, by the way, is a very pleasant little town, well worth a few minutes of poking around. You'll find a squat, solid library of brick with quite a bit of fancy ornamentation over its arched windows. It looks more like a bank, while the bank looks like—and is—an old white clapboard farmhouse.

HOURS Every day 6 am–10 pm.

DIRECTIONS Northbound: From Exit 8 turn left at end of ramp. Go 0.1 mile and bear right onto Route 103 West. Go 1 mile; on the right.

Southbound: From Exit 9 turn left at end of ramp. Go 1.3 miles on Route 103 West to center of town. On the left.

PETER CHRISTIAN'S TAVERN, *Exit 12, New London*

Here you can have absolutely delicious sandwiches and a wide variety of homemade soups in as pleasant an old tavern atmosphere as you're likely to find. Peter Christian's is in an 18th century inn that has been converted to apartments, and the restaurant, though furnished with recently rough-sawn booths and tables (hardly authentic), has all the warmth and lively good cheer this kind of place should have.

Peter Christian is serious about his sandwiches. He's gone so far as to develop a special sweet-and-sour mustard sauce that would make even package white bread taste good. But don't worry about putting it to the test. The bread is good—rye, pumpernickel, whole wheat, and fresh-baked rolls. On these you get simple deli sandwiches for $3, or more elaborate concoctions for a little more.

Beef stew is $2.75 a mug; onion and vegetable soups are available every day, and the soup du jour might be broccoli and mushroom, cream of celery with almonds, or Italian sausage with beans (about $1.75 for a generous mug). Half a sandwich for half the price can be had with soup or one of the three salads.

In summer there's a beer garden here. Monday night is homemade pasta night, and Tuesday features Mexican specials.

HOURS Mon.–Sat. 11:30 am–12:30 am; Sun. noon–11:30 pm.

DIRECTIONS From Exit 12 turn right if northbound, left if southbound, following signs for New London. It's about 3 miles to Peter Christian's, on the left.

LANDER'S, *Exit 18, Lebanon*

Here's a real oddity. On the outskirts of this northern New England town is a modern brick fortress of a building, belted by a row of gilded metal awnings that look like enormous automobile pistons sliced on the diagonal. The sign out by the road, with lettering in Ho-Jo's orange and blue, would be at home in front of a Polynesian nightclub in a suburban strip.

Surprising architecture for New Hampshire, and a surprising cuisine within. Or maybe not. This is Lebanon, after all, so why shouldn't the cooking be Lebanese? Along with standard American items, the enormous dining room serves up the likes of grape leaves, stuffed cabbage, and baked kibbie ($5.45 each), shish kabob ($6–$11), and string beans with meat and onions in tomato sauce ($4.95). We found the grape leaves to have a subtle bite that grew on us with each forkful. The fresh Syrian bread that accompanies each dish was quite good, and the hummus, though mild, was tasty. The portions were generous; our side order of grape leaves was more than enough for a light lunch and cost only $3.50.

For xenophobic travelers there are the usual American sandwiches at moderate prices.

On your way out of Lander's you might want to catch the four paintings of belly dancers that adorn the bar. It had been a while since we'd seen that sort of thing.

HOURS Tue.–Sat. 11 am–10 pm; Sun. 11 am–9 pm; Closed Mon.

DIRECTIONS From Exit 18 turn right if northbound, left if southbound, onto Route 120 North, following signs for Hanover. Go 0.7 mile and you'll find **Lander's** on the left. Can't miss it.

THE OWL'S NEST, *Exit 19, Lebanon*

Whenever an idea catches on, it's inevitable in America that someone will try to do it in the biggest possible way. Stained glass caught on as restaurant decor, and the Owl's Nest set out to be second to none. In fact, the subtitle of the place reads: "Restaurant and Stained-Glass Museum."

And that it is. No fewer than 210 Tiffany-type lamps hang from every square foot of ceiling space, and if you still want more, there are 73 stained-glass panels in the windows, on the walls, and even in the phone booth. Only three are genuine Tiffany, but all are old and have been brought here from every corner of the country.

All right, it's gimmicky. There's no arguing the point, especially when you add into the picture the bar with its inlay of 1028 silver dollars, the bookshelves stuffed with cast-off *Reader's Digest Condensed Books* (suitably aged), and the old barn beams imported to enhance the atmosphere. All the same, the Owl's Nest is a warm and comfortable place that makes relaxing easy—especially if you sip a drink on the couch before the roaring fireplace. And all that colorful glasswork is impressive, gimmicky or not.

The food is good, if not gourmet—mostly steaks and seafood for dinner ($7.50–$11.95); sandwiches, both plain (about $2.50) and fancy ($3.25) for lunch, along with soups from scratch (50 cents a cup) and entrées like grilled hamsteak, fried scrod, clams, scallops, and sirloin tip from $3.95 to $6.95. A special treat is the sensuously colorful salad bar, just brimming over with fresh fruits and crisp vegetables of every sort.

Much of the Owl's Nest's local fame rests on its seafood smorgasbord, available every Friday and Saturday night. It's $15, but you get all you can eat from an enormous variety of seafood, including oysters on the half-shell, steamed shrimp, crab legs, and even gefilte fish. Desserts include all the immoral favorites.

HOURS Mon.–Fri. 11:30 am–10 pm; Sat. 11:30 am–11 pm; Sun. noon–11 pm.

DIRECTIONS From Exit 19 turn left if northbound, right if southbound, onto Route 4 East for about ½ mile. It's on the right.

Vermont

THE COOLIDGE HOTEL
THAN WHEELER'S, *I-91 Interchange, White River Junction*

See p. 113 and p. 114 for descriptions of these two excellent choices.

DIRECTIONS From I-89 turn north onto I-91 and follow directions given.

BROOKSIE'S DRIVE-IN, *Exit 2, Sharon*

From the outside this place looks as pedestrian as a dairy bar. You'd never guess that its kitchen is home to a chef who graduated from the Culinary Institute of America (and who once quit a prestigious country inn in a dispute over the subtleties of nouvelle French cuisine).

Yes, you can get standard highway fare here, including the Bar-B-Que that gave Brooksie's its original claim to local fame. All that's been well preserved. But since Mark Anthony Radicioni and his family took over, this restaurant has been changing. "I want to raise the culinary consciousness of the area," says this well-trained chef whose creative enthusiasm just can't wait for an excuse to dream up a new concoction.

So far, he's invented a subtle, not-too-sweet maple butter, and a stuffed mushroom appetizer composed of cream cheese, crabmeat, sherry, spices, and a topping of Parmesan. To the American standbys on the menu he has added such continental dishes as coquille St. Jacques and seafood fettucini. But Mark really waxes eloquent over what he's named the "Paris Breast." It's a 16-inch doughnut, filled with whipped cream, bananas, and fresh strawberries, and topped off with more of the same.

Prices here aren't bad at all, considering the cuisine. Half a dozen mushroom caps are $1.75. Coquille St. Jacques tops the fancy dinners at $9.95; others are a few dollars less. And the Bar-B-Que is the same bargain it always was at $2.95.

HOURS Sun.–Thu. 7 am–9 pm; Fri. & Sat. 7 am–10 pm; closed Tuesdays, and all of December and January.

DIRECTIONS From Exit 2 follow signs ¼ mile to Sharon. **Brooksie's** is on the right.

BLACK FOREST CAFÉ, *Exit 3, Bethel*

A stop at the Black Forest Café feels like stepping into the kitchen of an old friend. Perhaps it's the warm and smiling hostess, Heidi Nikolaidis, who loves to chat with her customers from the open kitchen area. Or maybe it's the informal at-home ambiance, with its blue and white checked tablecloths, blue floral wallpaper, wood floors, and bay windows. Whatever it is that makes this place so genuine, we were charmed the moment we walked in.

And in no way is the cooking subordinate to the atmosphere. Before Heidi and her husband Nick came to Vermont eight years ago, they ran a catering business in New York City. Among their patrons were ambassadors, cabinet members, Hollywood celebrities, and a few astronauts. The fine cuisine that won Heidi and Nick so many distinguished admirers is what they now serve to anyone who walks in the door.

Nick is Greek and Heidi, Bavarian. It's no surprise, then, that they feature Greek and German specials at lunch and dinner (breakfasts are quite American). It would not be unusual to find, as lunch specials, avgolemono soup (a Greek egg-lemon broth with rice), sauerbraten with spaetzle (German noodles), and spanakopita (spinach pie) with tossed salad. Such lunch entrées, along with others that sound closer to home (tuna club on sourdough bread, mushroom omelette with bean salad), generally run $3–$4.

A quarter-pound "Black Forest burger" with Russian dressing on English muffin is $2.35.

Although entrées are a joint effort between husband and wife, desserts are entirely Heidi's domain. And what a royal domain it is! We aren't the first to proclaim its goodness: her Doboz and Black Forest cherry tortes have been featured in *Bon Appétit,* "Good Housekeeping's" *Country Living,* and *Restaurant Business* magazines. We tried the cherry torte and loved it—rich in rum and locally grown cherries that Heidi had canned herself.

The Black Forest Café is open for dinner only two nights a week, but the Thursday night buffet (5–8 pm) is worth waiting for. No country potluck supper, this: it's a gourmet buffet starring the likes of stewed lamb, fried squid, spinach and potato ring, stuffed grape leaves, and fish pilaf "à la Kyvely." Unlimited portions for just $6.95!

HOURS Mon.–Wed. 7 am–3 pm; Thu. & Fri. 7 am–8 pm; Sat. 7 am–3 pm; closed Sun.

DIRECTIONS From Exit 3 turn right onto Route 107 West. In 1 mile, you merge with Bethel's Main St. It's about ¼ mile farther, on the left.

THE AUGUST LION, *Exit 4, Randolph*

Father, mother, and son are all Leos in this restaurateur's family, and the place opened in the month of August. Thus . . . "The August Lion." There must be lots of Leo lovers, because no sooner had Steve Vargo opened his doors than patrons began bringing him lion after lion. Stuffed lions, plaster lions, glass, clay, and wooden lions, even macramé lions, along with batiks, paintings, drawings, needlepoint, and hooked-rug lions!

These proud but warm-hearted felines are now scattered by the dozen throughout the decor, which can only be described as a Vermont-style combination of rustic Early American and Victorian. A copper-colored tin ceiling (in lion pattern, of course) covers most of the floor space, and a wood stove keeps guests warm in winter.

The Lion has a terrific reputation that focuses on seafood, the salad bar, and especially desserts. A friend of ours goes into ecstasy describing the chocolate silk pie. The lengths to which the owner goes over cheesecake is a story in itself: the Amaretto and chocolate versions come from Rowinski's in Boston; the plain, from Mother's and Baby Watson in New York City; for the rest he drives to Cambridge, New York, to buy it from the nuns of New Skete Monastery.

The seafood is all fresh, and it includes such standbys as scrod ($6), scallops, scampi ($8.50), and lobster. There are pork and beef as well, along with nightly specials such as Veal Oscar and Shrimp Napoleon, and an all-you-can-eat salad bar for $3.75.

Lunches feature deli sandwiches and a variety of omelettes and burgers that run from $2 to $4.25. Much of the lunch menu can be had in the lounge all evening.

HOURS Mon. & Wed.–Fri. 11:30 am–2 pm and 5–9 pm; Sat. 5–10 pm; Sun. noon–8:30 pm; Bar menu, 2–9 pm; closed Tue.

DIRECTIONS See **Rainbow Restaurant,** below.

THE RAINBOW RESTAURANT, *Exit 4, Randolph*

Randolph is at the geographical center of Vermont, and the Rainbow Restaurant is the center of Randolph. It is a window on small-town Vermont life. Just about everybody who's anybody (or nobody) will soon pass by if he isn't inside the Rainbow already. Nurses and doctors from the hospital, teachers from the high school, the owner of the funky old movie theater, employees of Vermont Castings—the foundry that makes woodstoves with gritty names like Defiant and Resolute—all sip coffee and gossip at the Rainbow. Elegant it ain't, but it's clean and neat; for a friendly, homey personality, the Rainbow can't be beat.

The menu is just about what you'd expect from a short-order breakfast and lunch place, but it is a bit surprising to find that owner Bob Jones cooks his own sandwich meats. The roast beef clubs ($3.25 with French fries) and hot roast beef sandwiches ($3.20 with home or French fries) come highly recommended. Sandwiches of the BLT/egg salad/grilled cheese variety are lower —in the $1–$2 range. Breakfasts are hefty—a plain omelette with toast and a big stack of home fries goes for $1.25.

HOURS Mon.–Fri. 6 am–4 pm; Sat. 7 am–2:30 pm; closed Sun.

DIRECTIONS From Exit 4 take Route 66 West to Randolph (not Randolph Center). After 2.6 miles, Route 66 ends at a traffic light. Continue straight, now on Route 12 South. Turn left with Route 12 South, and you'll see **The August Lion** on your right, just over a bridge. For **The Rainbow Restaurant,** continue 0.2 mile to Depot Square. It's on the left, just before the railroad tracks.

RUNWAY RENDEZVOUS RESTAURANT, *Exit 7, Barre*

The local people say they come here for the club sandwiches and homemade soups, but we know their real weakness: Piper Cubs and long views. This is the place to gaze out on textured landscapes and watch the planes taxi right by your table. But don't expect the Barre-Montpelier Airport to have JFK action. All of six commercial flights a day take off here and five land. Try not to blink or you may miss the exodus of passengers. On clear weekends, private planes add their putter to this awesome din.

The planes may be small, but the steaks are hefty at the airport's Runway Rendezvous Restaurant—its kitchen specializes in large Delmonicos and T-bones. With six booths that nose right up to the large windows, the restaurant is a pleasant spot for airplane gazing, and the waitresses give you plenty of time in which to do it.

HOURS Mon. 7:30 am–2 pm; Tue.–Sat. 7:30 am–9 pm; Sun. 7:30 am–7 pm.

DIRECTIONS From Exit 7 take Route 62 East, following signs to airport. Turn right after 1.2 miles. Another 1.2 miles takes you to the terminal. Restaurant is inside.

HORN OF THE MOON CAFÉ, *Exit 8, Montpelier*

This may be Vermont's only all-vegetarian restaurant, but what really distinguishes it from other natural foods places is the flavor. Ginny Callan, the owner, is especially proud of the way she handles spices—she's determined that her food taste as good as it is good for you. If what we tried was typical, she's succeeding in spades, and a straight-laced townsman admitted, though a bit grudgingly, that Horn of the Moon has the best coffee around.

The atmosphere is rustic and unembellished. High ceilings, white walls, and large windows give a sense of space, light, and cleanliness, while color comes from the frequently changing display of local art. There's no shortage of anti-nuke, political, and nutritional manifestos scattered about the large window seat.

The Horn of the Moon is a three-meals-a-day restaurant. Breakfast goes from the usual two-eggs-any-style (75 cents) through omelettes, bagels, granola, and daily pancake specials ($2.10), to sautéed tofu, mushrooms, and onions with tahini ($1.50). There's a real bargain for lunch made only with Vermont products: a bowl of soup du jour (from scratch, of course), a glass of cider, a small loaf of sourdough bread, butter, and alfalfa sprouts for $2.50. Three kinds of salad, five dressings, and four breads including chapati and pita, along with various sandwiches and a lunch special, make up the rest of the menu. Dinner continues the lunch menu, and adds a daily special such as spanakopita or whole wheat pizza ($4.50), or quiche, salad and bread for $4.25.

And don't forget dessert: the poppy seed pastry alone will make the trip memorable.

HOURS Mon. & Tue. 7 am–3 pm; Wed.–Sat. 7 am–8:30 pm; closed Sun.

DIRECTIONS Exit 8 puts you on Route 2 East. After 1.1 miles, turn left onto Route 12 North (Main St.). Take Main St. ¼ mile to Langdon. Left on Langdon. Restaurant is on your right, just before the bridge.

THE WAYSIDE RESTAURANT, *Exit 8, Montpelier*

Here's a diner-style restaurant jazzed up with Formica and a not-too-thick veneer of Early American cum Olde English. It may not be authentic anything, but it's cozy enough in its own way, unpretentious and clean. Best of all, the local people—businessmen to barflies, bureaucrats to just plain folks—seem to love it dearly. On the Wednesday night that we visited, the place was mobbed.

The homemade breads, pies, and soups seem to be the foundation for its local reputation. The split pea soup we tried was good enough. So too the hamburger that comes charbroiled if you ask for it that way. Most reassuring was the first-rate kosher pickle.

If it's good straight food you're after, the Wayside is a pretty fair bet. Prices are moderate and the menu is ample.

HOURS Mon.–Sat. 6:30 am–9:30 pm; closed Sun.

DIRECTIONS From Exit 8 follow Route 2 East for 3 miles to Route 302. Bear right on Route 302 for 0.8 mile to the restaurant, on your right.

STICKY FINGERS DAIRY BAR, *Exit 9, Middlesex*

To be frank about it, the only really exciting thing at this exit is the bridge over the Winooski River. It gives a great view of the gorge below. An island that looks like it's glued to a stem of solid rock stands high above the water, exposing fifteen feet of multicolored strata.

Bring your own picnic lunch. But for dessert you might try the ice cream at Sticky Fingers.

HOURS The river is open 24 hours. The dairy bar is open from mid-May to mid-October, 11 am–7 pm.

DIRECTIONS We'll leave it to you this time. The town (population less than 100) is only ½ mile from the exit. We doubt you'll get lost.

SOUP'S ON, *Exit 10, Waterbury*

Almost no one knows that tired little Waterbury hides what may be one of the area's best restaurants. It's run by an ex-teacher and an ex-social worker who are determined to serve first-rate food where you'd least expect it. The ambiance here is a bit on the homemade side, with wooden folding chairs and plain pine tables, but it's well conceived, and everyone's very friendly. And don't be put off by the unimpressive building. Taste first, then decide.

There's a special dinner every night during the week, and on Saturday owners Ken and Trish Feld offer ethnic cooking—Mexican, Indian, Italian, Spanish, Polish, Russian, etc. It was French Night when we visited, and the beef Bourguignon was full-flavored and wonderfully pungent. So was the vichyssoise that accompanied it. With bread baked on the premises (four kinds) and spinach salad made from the Felds' own garden, how can you go wrong, especially in the $5 range?

Soup's On also serves bagels and continental breakfasts. For lunch they offer sandwiches on bagels, kaiser rolls, pita, or their own bread (80 cents to $2.50). Soups from scratch are their signature, and they offer three kinds of salad with three homemade dressings. Lunch specials include such treats as an avocado and shrimp crepe ($1.65) and mushroom quiche ($1.80). For dessert, you can have Ben and Jerry's ice cream (see p. 55), cheesecake, or other favorites of the eighties.

This restaurant really deserves your support. The owners know their food is good, so they make it a no-risk adventure for you. Satisfaction is guaranteed—if you're not happy with your meal, tear up the check and walk out!

But we doubt you will.

HOURS Mon.–Thu. 8:30 am–8:30 pm; Fri. 8:30 am–midnight; Sat. 11:30 am–3:30 pm and 6 pm–9 pm; closed Sun.

DIRECTIONS Take Exit 10 toward Waterbury and Route 2. At the stop sign turn left. This is Main St., which you should take just past the tiny town center to Foundry St. Left on Foundry for 1 block and then left again. Half a block brings you to **Soup's On.** Total distance to restaurant is only 1 mile.

DAILY BREAD BAKERY, *Exit 11, Richmond*

You can't sit down to eat at the Daily Bread Bakery, but don't pass it up if you don't mind munching in the car, on the bakery steps, or along the banks of the Winooski River (see p. 45).

The building was originally a shirt factory and later a bead parlor. As the story goes, a steady stream of people saw the word BEADS splashed across the window, added an imaginary "R," and came inside to request bread. In 1979, Betsy Bott fulfilled their Freudian slips by starting a bakery.

The Daily Bread Bakery is her one-woman operation. It is the brightest spot in this well-weathered town, and it's got the people of Richmond hooked on breads, cakes, pies, cookies, and croissants. We sampled some almond sweet rolls that were as good as any we've had anywhere. Betsy also sells coffee, milk, and mint tea (brewed right in your cup in a bamboo strainer).

The Daily Bread has a rotating schedule of lunch items. Tuesday is quiche day; Wednesday, cheese pie; Thursday, Sicilian pizza; Friday, calzone (pizza dough turnovers with cheese filling); and Saturday is the day for leftovers at half the already reasonable price.

HOURS Tue.–Thu. & Sat. 6:30 am–3 pm; Fri. 6:30 am–6 pm; closed Sun. and Mon.

DIRECTIONS From Exit 11 follow Route 2 East for about 1½ miles to the town of Richmond. Turn right on Bridge St. (signs point to Huntington) and left into a parking lot. Bakery is at back of the large white building facing you.

ABOUT BURLINGTON

No longer is Burlington merely the state's largest city, home to the University of Vermont, and a tranquil spot from which to view Lake Champlain and the Adirondack Mountains beyond the far shore. Now it is famous for its socialist mayor and recognition as "The People's Republic of Burlington" in the "Doonesbury" comic strip. Politics aside, Burlington is a very civilized and livable little city, replete with all the amenities that give life its charm, and especially rich in restaurants.

You'll find a good many of them on Church Street, now closed to vehicles and landscaped with trees and sculptures—as inviting an outdoor mall as we've ever seen. Though Burlington lacks any sizable ethnic populations, the city offers fine examples of Mexican, Chinese, French, and Jewish cuisine. You'll also find vegetarian dishes served cafeteria-style, a sandwich restaurant with a prodigious menu, and very good, very fresh ice cream at two places that make their own. If you prefer not to grapple with downtown traffic, though it's relatively light here, there is a fine old diner, the Parkway, in South Burlington.

Of all Burlington's restaurants, we had two favorites: Leunig's, a small, sophisticated café with Old World charm, and the Déjà Vu, certainly among the most stunningly beautiful restaurants to be found anywhere. It is also the one in which we had an unforgettable potage Neufchâtel, our very best bowl of soup in all New England.

PARKWAY DINER, *Exit 14E, South Burlington*

If you'd rather avoid downtown traffic, try the Parkway Diner, a genuine Worcester lunch car—but with a difference. Instead of the usual Gothic lettering, the Parkway has a candy-striped exterior. Another surprise is the number of Greek dishes on the menu. Finally, there's draft beer, a rare item in the world of diners.

George Hatgen, purveyor of the Parkway's American and Greek cuisine, prides himself on family recipes that are likely to pique your curiosity. But don't even bother asking how he makes his lovely lemon soup or orange-flavored tea cookies. He'll just tell you, with a sheepish smile and a full accent, "That one's a secret from the old country."

Hamburgers are $1.05 at the Parkway; sandwiches run $1.35 to $2.25, and dinners $3.50 to $5, including French fries and coleslaw. A bowl of soup costs only 90 cents. Especially reasonable—and tasty—are the Greek specialties like spinach pie (65 cents a slice) and baklava (95 cents).

Inside, the Parkway demonstrates how pretty the old lunch cars can be. It has nice tilework on walls and counter, real wooden booths, and a restful cream-and-brown color scheme throughout.

HOURS Mon.–Sat. 6 am–9 pm; closed Sun.

DIRECTIONS Exit 14E puts you on Route 2 East toward South Burlington. The **Parkway** is 1½ miles down, on the left.

DÉJÀ VU CAFÉ, *Exit 14W, Burlington*

Déjà Vu is without a doubt one of the most gorgeous restaurants you'll ever come across. When you consider that the food is excellent French cooking and the prices no higher than at a neighborhood eatery, it's a place not to be missed if you've got the time to savor its splendors.

Brian Fox worked for more than three years to renovate this old building, driving the town of Burlington crazy with curiosity all the while. When this young perfectionist finally opened his doors, what people found was a stunningly sculptured environment of high ceilings, staircases, and multilevel nooks and crannies. Dark, sensuously smooth, polished rock maple sets the tone everywhere: in the tables, chairs, railings, moldings, and the bar, all of them crafted by Fox and his co-workers with painstaking attention to detail. We hesitate to say that brass, brick, leather, and fine stained glass provide the accents, for fear that the clichéd versions of this sort of decor will come to mind. Let's just say that Déjà Vu is in a class by itself.

The restaurant's excellence is more than architectural. Here we sampled potage Neufchâtel, a slightly smoky, full-flavored, absolutely wonderful soup made from cream cheese, leeks, ham, and spinach. It was as good as any soup we've tasted anywhere, including some of the posher Manhattan spots. We also tried the cassoulet, a white-bean casserole with chicken, sausage, and lamb, which was very good, though not quite so memorable as the soup. But at $5.75 for an enormous portion, who's going to quibble over the fine points?

The lunch and dinner menus at Déjà Vu are nearly identical, except that the more expensive entrées (like tournedos forestière,

$12.95; chicken breast stuffed with oysters, spinach, and a whiff of fennel, $7.95; and sweetbreads with mushrooms in Madeira sauce, $10.95) are left out at midday. Common to both menus are five soups, eight tempting appetizers (including a chilled, marinated salad with chicken, toasted almonds, and brown rice, $2.65), four other salads ($1.75–$3.35), several crepes, omelettes, and quiche ($3.50), and about five relatively inexpensive entrées from $4.25 to $6.95. Wonderfully caloric desserts are offered in abundance, but our hearts went out to the humbler whole poached pear stuffed with chocolate mousse.

If you venture the few blocks of city traffic it takes to get to Déjà Vu, we promise you this: despite the name, it is not likely to be anything you've seen before.

HOURS Lunch: Mon.–Sat. 11:30 am–2:30 pm; Dinner: Sun.–Thu. 5–9:30 pm; Fri. & Sat. 5–10:30 pm; Late dining: Sun.–Thu. 9:30–midnight; Fri. & Sat. 10:30 pm–1 am.

DIRECTIONS See end of Burlington entries, p. 57.

LEUNIG'S OLD WORLD CAFÉ, *Exit 14W, Burlington*

Even from the outside we found something engaging about Leunig's. Perhaps it was the classical music played softly through an outdoor speaker, or the comfortable, sophisticated ambiance we could see through the large windows. Inside, we found everything we had hoped for: a wonderful aroma emanating from an enormous brass coffee machine, wine, hors d'oeuvres, thoughtfully prepared light meals, daily newspapers for the reading, and pleasant-looking customers obviously enjoying their surroundings. We also found, presiding over all this Old Worldliness, Dennis Morriseau, whose personal story is as interesting as his restaurant.

Born a local farmboy, Dennis enrolled in law school in Washington, D.C., hated it, quit, and returned to Vermont to enter politics as an anti-war candidate for Congress in 1970. Fed up with the Democrats, he helped found a new party, the Liberty Union, which still exists on the fringes of Vermont politics. After the war and two more unsuccessful bids for Congress, Morriseau turned to carpentry, dabbled in solar construction, and eventually moved into real estate—which was how he fell upon an old storefront at the corner of Church and College streets. While he was contemplating converting it to a restaurant, he became smitten with the work of an Australian cartoonist, Michael Leunig. Persistent attempts to purchase the American rights to Leunig's best-selling book were fruitless until, as a final gesture, Morriseau named his new café for the Australian. From then on, things moved very quickly. Not only did Morriseau bring out the book, but he also received a visit from the cartoonist and threw a bash in his honor at the café.

Knowing the café's story certainly added a dimension to our visit, heightening our enjoyment of Leunig's fine food. We had an excellent breakfast here—the challah French toast with pure maple syrup ($2.50) was thick and luscious, gently flavored with something we couldn't quite identify (vanilla?). A simple breakfast of two eggs with homemade whole wheat toast goes for $1.50, and corned beef hash with eggs is $2.95. There are also pastries (two croissants with warm Brie, $2.50), bagels, fresh-squeezed orange juice, and homemade sausage patties.

Later in the day, you might enjoy a broiled pita roll with mushrooms, avocado, cheddar, and bacon ($2.95), a pocket sandwich of tarragon shrimp and cucumber ($3.65), or other sandwiches, both exotic and conventional. There are also quiche ($3.95, with salad and bread), a giant antipasto ($4.50), soup, salad, fruit plates, and after 3 pm, some interesting hors d'oeuvres—prosciutto and pears, bacon-wrapped water chestnuts, or small potato knishes, for example. Any time of day can be tea time at Leunig's, with crumpets, scones, and the house coffee cake brought out for the occasion.

Whatever strikes your fancy, you can enjoy it at the marble counter, where you can chat with Dennis, or at a small wooden table by the window, where you can watch the world walk by on Burlington's new Church Street mall.

HOURS Mon.–Fri. 8 am–11 pm; Sat. 9:30 am–11 pm; Sun. 10:30 am–11 pm.

DIRECTIONS See end of Burlington entries, p. 57.

FRESH GROUND COFFEEHOUSE, ***Exit 14W, Burlington***

The Fresh Ground boasts of its big portions, small prices, and healthy homemade food. Folks we know in Burlington swore it was so, and after a visit we had to concur.

This is the only natural foods cafeteria we've come across. From the street, you descend a short flight of stairs, walk past the inevitable bulletin board, and enter a lively, somewhat funky room. You quickly see that the thing to do is to pick up a tray and slide it past the large blackboard menu. No cellophane-wrapped salads here. You can watch the workers dip right into vats of salad and steaming cauldrons of soup to fill your order. Once served, pick a table downstairs or, tray in hand, negotiate the steep staircase leading to the upstairs dining area, a somewhat spiffier room than the one below.

Most entrées (spinach lasagne, eggplant parmigiana, stuffed peppers) cost between $3 and $5. A big bowl of the day's stew—ratatouille, for example—is only $2.25 or so. Homespun soups like "Cream O'Mostly Potato" are 75 cents a cup/$1.45 a bowl, and most sandwiches—hot turkey and Swiss on grilled bagel, for instance—are around $2.50. While we stood in line we were able to see quite a few healthy helpings go by; all of them looked highly appetizing and amply portioned.

Glancing around over good fresh coffee and an enormous hunk of pineapple-carrot cake (just 95 cents), we observed a crowd that was more collegiate than spiritual and more convivial than political—not the norm for restaurants of this genre. Whether it is the influence of nearby UVM or the Fresh Ground's own vibrations, we don't know. But we were happy to be there and, as far as we could tell, so was everyone else.

HOURS Mon.–Thu. 7:30 am–9 pm; Fri. & Sat. 7:30 am–1 am; Sun. 10 am–2 pm (classical music brunch) and 4–8 pm (Beggar's Banquet).

DIRECTIONS See end of Burlington entries, p. 57.

THE ORIGINAL GOTHAM CITY DELICATESSEN, *Exit 14W, Burlington*

This is probably the closest thing to a true Jewish deli north of Hartford and south of Montreal. The owners have gone to real pains to import the authentic stuff from New York, and they've wrapped it up in good modern design based on light colors, mirrors, and a store-length skyline mural.

And the service is fast. You order at the counter, pay, and carry your meal to a table or one of the park-bench–style booths. Careful! Don't spill the chicken soup.

Whenever possible, Gotham City's meats are the real thing. The owners have somehow secured a steady supply of Hebrew National corned beef, salami, and franks, but the pastrami situation is "iffy." Those of you who are hooked on Hebrew National pastrami had best ask what the day's brand is.

No matter what brand of meat, you'll always be able to get it with mustard on rye, but the counter man won't laugh too hard if you prefer mayonnaise on white. The rye is from Albany, and it's good, but the deli is searching for a supply from the Big Apple.

Standard deli sandwiches with pickle and chips will run you about $2.50–$3. You can also buy chopped liver, pickled herring, all-beef franks, and some things to satisfy kosher vegetarians. Strawberry cheesecake is $1.75; bagel and cream cheese, 65 cents; Dr. Brown's Cel-ray soda, 75 cents. The only side order the Gotham City Deli can't provide is Yankee games on the radio.

HOURS Mon.–Thu. 11 am–9 pm; Fri. & Sat. 11 am–midnight; closed Sun.

DIRECTIONS See end of Burlington entries, p. 57.

LA PATISSERIE, *Exit 14W, Burlington*

Voilà! This downtown Burlington bakery comes about as close to achieving the character implied by its name as you are likely to find in Vermont. "Not much competition," you say? True, but give La Patisserie a try. You'll find Napoleons, palmiers, croissants, bouchées, French and American breads (including Jewish rye), and a veritable flower garden of gorgeous cookies. There are also four varieties of quiche, sold by the slice ($1.75) or whole ($6).

Pay for the goods and run, or sip coffee at one of four small tables and linger.

HOURS Mon. & Wed. 8 am–5 pm; Tues. 8:30 am–5:30 pm; Thurs. & Fri. 8 am–5:30 pm; Sat. 8:30 am–5 pm; closed Sun.

DIRECTIONS See end of Burlington entries, p. 57.

CARBUR'S, *Exit 14W, Burlington*

Carbur's is different. You sense it as soon as you walk in. Filtered light, casual decoration, and rough wood give the place an almost Western feel. But the decor isn't all that's different about Carbur's. Check out the menu.

Here, in 9 chapters and 25 pages, complete with a table of contents and an appendix, is a compendium of 127 different sandwiches, all uniquely Carbur's, right down to the mayonnaise. We provide a sampler:

The Ausable Spasm is the biggest seller. (The Ausable Chasm is a 20-mile-long gorge in nearby New York State.) The menu calls it "what happens if you overgorge yourself," and it consists of roast beef grilled with Swiss cheese, tomato, and Carbur's garlic mayonnaise ($3.21). The Burger Man of Alcatraz also cops a good proportion of the lunchtime sales. It's an English muffin that encases a ¼-pound charbroiled hamburger with bacon, melted sharp cheese and, again, the garlic mayo ($3.17, or $4.07 for a ½-pounder). If Carbur's menu sounds like fun, read on.

The Sanitary Landfill may dispose of you forever: grilled knockwurst, coleslaw, tomato, raw onion, melted American cheese, and sauce à la Russe ($3.22). Lady Chatterley's Liver comes in three versions—unabridged and unadulterated, abridged and adulterated, and condensed. The adulterated ($3.68) consists of roast beef, chopped chicken liver, lettuce, tomato, and horseradish mayo. The Bellows Falls, which you are asked not to mispronounce lest you embarrass the waitress, is "slices from the erogenous zone of turkey, corned beef, provolone cheese, lettuce, tomato, and chili mayo" in a club sandwich.

Can you bear one more? The Carburator ("What do you call someone who ate at Carbur's?") is a club sandwich of crabmeat salad, turkey, tomato, and lettuce with tarragon mayonnaise. We'll spare you further Carburisms, but we should add that the menu includes chapters on soups, salads, beverages, and vegetarian sandwiches.

If you don't have time to wade through this tome of a menu, you can order a Noontime Quickie from a separate document that is an edited version of the monster menu. Noontime Quickies are guaranteed to reach your table within 15 minutes of ordering, or your money back.

Around the corner at 115 College Street is Carbur's Rib-it Room, a full-fare steak house with the unmistakable Carbur's touch: "Ah, what foods these morsels be . . ."

HOURS Mon.–Thu. 11:30 am–10 pm; Fri. & Sat. 11:30 am–midnight; Sun. noon–10 pm.

DIRECTIONS See end of Burlington entries, p. 57.

UVM DAIRY BAR
BEN AND JERRY'S HOMEMADE, *Exit 14W, Burlington*

Here are two ice creameries, each unique in its own way.

"UVM" is local lingo for the University of Vermont, and UVM's dairy science building houses a dairy bar that is locally adored. The products it sells come from the miniature milk packaging and ice cream manufacturing plant located in the very same building. The dairy bar exists only for the benefit of students and others in the know. Decor is nonexistent, and there is no sign, no advertising at all. In fact, the university would probably prefer that we not pass on this discovery, so don't mention our names!

But there's something wonderful about buying in one room the ice cream you watched come into being in the next, and we thought you'd like to hear about it. If you're not too rushed, give a look.

You'll see the dairy bar first, but go on down the hall through the doors. You might act as if you belong, but no one seems to mind in any case. Behind the large windows to your right are the milk storage tanks and Rube Goldberg machinery that rhythmically clinks and clanks as it folds, fills, and seals milk cartons. On the other side of the hall is the ice cream works, where an operator sits before what looks like a large stainless-steel washing machine that discharges half-gallon after half-gallon of the stuff. Ask questions—everyone we met was friendly, and for no particular reason they gave us a complete tour of the place, happy to indulge our every request.

Then go back to the dairy bar and sample what you saw. You can have your ice cream in cones, shakes, or sundaes, all remarkably inexpensive. Yogurt and cheese from commercial dairies are available too.

To tell the truth, the ice cream here doesn't taste much better than good commercial varieties, but you'll know it's fresh—the milk was in the cow that very morning.

Ben and Jerry's doesn't show you how they do it, but the ice cream they come up with surpasses the dairy bar's in quality and variety of flavors. Now a Burlington institution, Ben and Jerry's had its moment of glory when mentioned in a *Time* magazine cover story on the quest for the world's best ice cream.

The renowned stuff is sold all over Vermont in little pint containers like those of Häagen-Dazs, which it rivals in taste (and price), but at the shop you can get it by the cone or dish with all the appropriate toppings. Ben and Jerry's Homemade is farther from the interstate than UVM's Dairy Bar, but it is open longer hours. Take your pick—for different reasons, both places are delightful.

HOURS **UVM Dairy Bar:** Mon.–Sat. 10 am–5 pm; closed Sun.

Ben and Jerry's: Mon.–Thu. 11:30 am–11 pm; Fri. & Sat. 11:30 am–midnight; Sun. noon–11 pm.

DIRECTIONS FOR BURLINGTON RESTAURANTS From Exit 14W it's about 1½ miles along Route 2 West to downtown Burlington. Before you get there, after just 0.7 mile, you'll find the **UVM Dairy Bar.** Look for signs on your right: "Campus Ticket Sales" and "Carrigan Dairy Science." Pull into the parking lot and enter the nearest building through a side door.

For downtown restaurants, take Route 2 West (Main St.) from Exit 14W directly into town. The first major cross-street is Winooski, 1½ miles from the exit. If you turn right onto Winooski, you will find **Ben and Jerry's** on your left at the fourth light (Cherry St.); continuing to the fifth light and turning left onto Pearl will put you in front of **Déjà Vu,** on your left.

Back on Main St., instead of turning as above onto Winooski, you can continue into town, passing on your right **Gotham City Deli** and **La Patisserie** before arriving at the next cross-street, Church. Turn left on Church for **Fresh Ground Coffeehouse,** half a block down on the right; or, turn right from Main onto Church, go one block, and you'll see **Leunig's Old World Café** on your left at the corner of Church and College.

Back on Main St. again, continuing into town without turning, after Church you'll come to a square, and then St. Paul's St. Turn right onto St. Paul's and look left for **Carbur's.**

Too complicated? All these restaurants are very close to one another. Simply drive downtown, park, and consult your friendly, passing Burlingtonian.

THE BLACK ROSE, *Exit 15, Winooski*

This friendly restaurant and bar has a reputation for delicious and unusual foods. Its formula for success lies in the flexible menu, which adjusts to the season and—more important—to the cook. Guest chefs are not unusual at the Black Rose, and the offering of the day is what the cook does best.

The lunch menu offers good sandwiches, three kinds of salads with four dressings, a cheese board ($2), hummus platter ($2.75), pâté maison ($2.85), and a strudel of filo pastry with a different filling each day ($3.75).

Nightly dinner specials are more tempting still. Typical is a main course of curried beef in pastry with yogurt-mint sauce; it comes with mint pea soup and a Romaine-based salad topped with peanut vinaigrette. All this is just over $5, and if you want to skip the soup, it's $1.10 less.

The feel of the place is light, modern, and informal. An old tin ceiling presides over white walls. Natural oak is in evidence, but not overwhelming; lace curtains and white tablecloths add a nice touch, unusual in this sort of decor. Antique vending machines decorate the bar, including one right out of a filling-station men's room. Scratched into the paint is the offer of recaps at half price.

There's live music at the Black Rose on Wednesday, Friday, and Saturday nights, and the music fits the musicians as the food fits the chef.

HOURS Every day, 11 am–midnight.

DIRECTIONS From Exit 15 take Route 15 West toward Winooski. Go 0.6 mile; it's on the right at 17 E. Allen St.

CINDY'S DINER, *Exit 19, St. Alban's*

When we produced our first *Interstate Gourmet*, a slim volume covering only the corridor between New Haven and Burlington, readers from St. Albans wrote to us, vexed that we had stopped just short of their town and Cindy's Diner. With this book, we apologize and address the problem.

On the definition of diners, purists insist that if you can't move it, it's not a diner. They may be right, in which case Cindy's is not properly named. But we aren't really purists, and no matter what you call it, you won't argue that Cindy's is an authentic village lunchroom with local color, good home cooking, and low prices.

Here, a bowl of chunky soup is only 80 cents. Equally low priced are the breads, pies, and muffins, all homemade. Sandwiches run from just 80 cents for egg salad to $2 for a clam roll. Burgers are $1.15 to $2 with the works and a side of fries. For dinner, expect the likes of baby beef liver with onions, fried shrimp (or scallops), or thin-sliced roast beef. For $4–$5 you will get the main course, soup, potato, and vegetable or cottage cheese.

HOURS Mon.–Thu. 5 am–7 pm; Fri. 5 am–9 pm; Sat. 5 am–2 pm; Sun. 6 am–noon.

DIRECTIONS Exit 19 puts you directly on the road to St. Albans. In 1 mile turn right at the T and drive 0.6 mile to **Cindy's** on left. Another 0.2 mile puts you in front of **The Blue Lion** on your right.

THE BLUE LION, *Exit 19, St. Alban's*

Here's one of those all-but-extinct old village restaurants that dates to the days when oak paneling was just the way things were done, not something tacked up beside stained glass and potted plants to produce a "with it" atmosphere. At the Blue Lion the wood is varnished, not fashionably natural, which somehow gives it all the more charm. With its enormous wagon-wheel chandeliers, its cozy booths, its total lack of pretensions, the place is comfortably warm and worn, like a good old pair of shoes.

The Blue Lion is a three-meals-a-day restaurant with decent, honest food at moderate prices. Two eggs with potatoes and toast are $1.55. Homemade soup du jour is 75 cents a cup/$1.35 a bowl, and a hamburger goes for $1.95. Sandwiches are around $2.35, and you'll find lunchtime specials like baked chicken for about $3.50.

You can order sandwiches at dinnertime, but if you're hungrier than that there are typical American entrées at $6–$12 and some Italian dishes at $4–$5.50, not to mention an all-you-can-eat antipasto deal on Wednesday night.

The fish is fresh, and the vegetables aren't, but one especially nice feature here is the salad bar. It includes steamed shrimp! Not the best steamed shrimp the world has ever seen, mind you, but steamed shrimp all the same. It's a good place for a better than average highway meal, and we can almost guarantee you'll like the ambiance.

HOURS Mon., Tue., & Thu. 9 am–9 pm; Wed. & Sun. 9 am–9:30 pm; Fri. & Sat. 9 am–10 pm.

DIRECTIONS See **Cindy's Diner,** above.

COLUMBE'S BAKERY, *Exit 21, Swanton*

One of the brighter points in Swanton is Columbe's Bakery, whose beauty shines in its display case, not its decor. There are assorted strudels (the apple was quite good), blueberry nut cakes, apple squares with cream cheese, fruit boats, and hot cross buns. Mexican tea cakes, made from the Cookie of the Year recipe in *Baker's* magazine, were a bit of a surprise here in the northwest corner of Vermont.

If it's just a short break and a light snack you're after, Columbe's Bakery may hit the spot. Take your pastry and coffee to the orange Formica counter that faces out through two large windows. You'll have a chance to view small-town Vermont as you may never have seen it before—Swanton is home to Vermont's only Indian tribe, the Abnaki.

HOURS Mon.–Sat. 6 am–6 pm; Sun. 6 am–1 pm.

DIRECTIONS From Exit 21 turn left if northbound, right if southbound. Drive 0.9 mile and you'll see it on the left, just before the square.

I-90

Massachusetts

THE ORIENT EXPRESS, ***Exit 1, West Stockbridge***

West Stockbridge is a snazzy town with a restaurant to suit your every whim, or nearly so. If it's the exotic you crave, try the Orient Express, a Vietnamese place that takes its name from the famed Paris–Istanbul train. It's right by a railroad station in a cluster of renovated buildings that form a sort of arty shopping center.

Both decor and food here are delicate. Old beams peek through the renovation work here and there, but the overall feel is quiet, light, and very, very pleasant. Colorfully set wicker tables, with flowers, fill several small rooms. The walls are white, the floors terra-cotta, and one perfectly placed large orange tree provides the final touch.

The food was milder than we expected for Vietnamese cooking. Ga Xao Nam—chicken breast with straw mushrooms, vegetables, and rice—came in a delightfully delicate sauce, and the vegetables were perfectly cooked—crisp without a hint of toughness. The asparagus and crab soup, however, was disappointingly bland.

There are about 20 entrées on the menu, running from $3.75 to $5.25 for lunch. Dinner will cost about $2 more.

HOURS Mon.–Thu. 11 am–9:30 pm; Sat. 11 am–10:30 pm; Sun. 2–9:30 pm.

DIRECTIONS Westbound: From Exit 1 go right at the end of the ramp, one block to a stop sign. Turn left at sign onto Route 102 West. Go

0.3 mile to village center and turn left into a small street just after Masiero Variety Store on left. Restaurant will appear on left.

Note: You cannot reenter I-90 West at this exit. Take Route 102 West out of town. This will lead you to the next entrance to I-90, about 5 miles away, in New York.

Eastbound: You cannot exit from I-90 East in West Stockbridge. You must take the last exit in New York, B3, onto Route 22 North. Immediately turn onto Route 102 West, which will take you straight to West Stockbridge in about 5 miles. In the village center make a right turn just before Masiero Variety Store, on the right. You'll see the restaurant on the left.

You can reenter I-90 East at Exit 1, just ½ mile from town.

BERKSHIRE AUTO/TRUCK PLAZA,
Exit 1, West Stockbridge

The local people come here when they're feeling campy or just plain looking for a bargain. ("They give you the same steak there for $5 that costs $10 at a fancy place.") But it doesn't feel like a truck stop. The low building houses a large, airy restaurant done up in relaxing tones of brown and yellow. Counter area and game room are well separated from the dining area, which, though plasticky, has a fair quantity of real greenery and jungle-scene wallpaper.

But plants alone don't make a brick-plants-and-oak café. No quiche here—just a truckers' menu with solid stuff like steak-and-egg breakfasts ($4.89), Butt steak ($6.95), meatloaf ($4.95) and ¼-pound hamburgers ($1.99). A breakfast for mere mortals, two eggs, toast, and juice, goes for $1.69. The eggs were fresh, the coffee decent, and the pancakes heavy—trucker-style, we guess.

HOURS 24 hours every day of the year.

DIRECTIONS Westbound: Follow directions for **The Orient Express,** above, but continue on through the village (don't turn left) for 2.3 miles from the exit ramp. On the right.

Eastbound: You must exit I-90 at Exit B3 onto Route 22 in New York. Follow directions for **The Orient Express,** above. The restaurant will be on the left, 2 miles before town.

SHAKER MILL TAVERN, *Exit 1, West Stockbridge*

This place has been a tavern for as long as anyone can remember, but in 1980 it was redone in the fashionable wood, stained-glass, and plants decor, with a new menu to match. Half the building is a restaurant, featuring good charbroiled hamburgers ($3.50), quiche ($3.50), steamed mussels ($2.95 for a small order), three kinds of vegetarian sandwiches, soups from scratch, and even a caviar-and-sour-cream omelette ($5.50). There are Romaine-based salads for $2–$3 and a special version with almonds, mushrooms, and cheese for $3.95.

The other half of the Shaker Mill is the tavern itself. Though done up in lots of dark wood, many large windows with stained-glass borders give things a light feel with colorful accents. And here we saw the biggest Tiffany lamp we've turned up yet—nearly a yard across. Even without the piano this would be a comfortable place to hang out, especially with its exotic selection of wines and beers.

There are six full dinners offered here, running from $8 for baked chicken with sauce du jour to $11 for a sirloin. And don't forget dessert—they're all homemade.

HOURS Apr.–Dec.: every day 11:30 am–1 am; Jan.–Feb.: Tue.–Sun. 4 pm–1 am; closed Mon.; closed in March.

DIRECTIONS Westbound: Follow directions for **The Orient Express,** p. 61, but go 0.6 mile on Route 102 to the other side of the village. It's on the left.

Eastbound: Follow directions for **The Orient Express,** p. 62, but go only about 4½ miles on Route 102. It's on the right, just before the village.

LE PETIT POIS (Westbridge Inn), *Exit 1, West Stockbridge*

If your palate and your pocketbook are up to it, you might try true gourmet dining at this small country inn. The Westbridge boasts ten homey rooms, all of them done up in Colonial wallpaper, chenille bedspreads, antiques, and pine floors. Downstairs there's a very handsome lounge, and just off to one side is Le Petit Pois, the love's labor of a New York chef who brought his talents to the Berkshires. The dining room is a mixture of city niceties (pink tablecloths) with country style (exposed beams and rough pine floors).

The menu is country French, varying with the seasons. In winter it features lamb stew and cassoulet, a casserole of white beans, lamb, duck, and sausage. There are also game dishes, when available, and 11 hors d'oeuvres, from Hawaiian oysters to fresh goose liver. In summer you'll sometimes find outdoor cooking over an open grapevine fire.

The prices are steep: $16.50 for the cassoulet and $19.95 for a veal chop bedecked with three kinds of mushrooms. Lunches are $8–$18. Rooms at the inn are $30–$40 in winter, $40–$65 in summer.

HOURS Thu.–Tue. noon to 2:30 pm and 6:30–9 pm; closed Wed.

DIRECTIONS Follow directions for **The Orient Express,** pp. 61–62. The **Westbridge** is just across Main St. (Route 102) from the Masiero Variety Store.

JOE'S DINER, *Exit 2, Lee*

* *Color, not cuisine*

According to our local informants, Joe's is the hub of life for plain folks in this straightforward town. There's a new façade of brick and redwood on the place, but Joe is not trying to fool anyone. Inside are the old linoleum floor, the three Formica tables, and the twelve tattered stools that have been there for years. And if you sit yourself down on one of them for an hour, you'll probably know everything that's going on in town. It's that kind of place. Decent food and no decor, but lots of roots sunk deep into local life.

Hamburgers here go for all of 75 cents, and a two-egg breakfast is just a buck. Two dollars will get you an Italian sausage sandwich. If you want to spend more than that, you might as well go to the Morgan House. Read on.

HOURS Joe opens at 6 am on Monday and doesn't close again until 6:30 pm on Saturday. (Nothing happens in town on Sunday.)

DIRECTIONS From the end of the ramp at Exit 2 follow Route 20 for 1.3 miles, through the town center, to a T. Turn left at the T, and you'll see it immediately on your right in a small block of buildings.

THE MORGAN HOUSE, *Exit 2, Lee*

The Morgan House has been an inn since 1853, and it hosted so disparate a collection of notables as Buffalo Bill, Ulysses S. Grant, and George Bernard Shaw long before its current owners bought it from Mrs. Nat King Cole. Fortunately it's still much as it was, with a friendly, cozy atmosphere and solid New England cooking.

Especially charming is a small dining room with only four tables. The low ceiling, exposed beams, stenciled walls, and glowing fireplace aren't a decorating scheme. That's just the way it's always been.

For lunch the Morgan House offers burgers, Reubens, and the like, all on homemade bread ($2.50–$3.75). Homemade soup comes by the cup ($1), bowl ($1.50), or crock ($1.95). There are seven full luncheons, from calves liver with onions and bacon ($4.95) to broiled scallops in parsley and lemon butter ($6.50). The dinner specialty is duckling with cheese and Dijon mustard sauce.

If a night in the area suits your plans, consider one of the Morgan's eleven rooms. They match the mood of the restaurant and are only $25 on off-season week nights. Perhaps you'll sleep in Grant's own bed—a fitting end for a day's odyssey.

HOURS Lunch: Mon.–Sat. 11:30 am–2:30 pm; Dinner: Mon.–Thu. 5–9 pm; Fri. & Sat. 5–10 pm; Sun. noon–9 pm.

DIRECTIONS From Exit 2 follow signs for U.S. 20 West. Go 0.8 mile. On the left, just as you reach the center of town.

THE FOSTER HOUSE, *Exit 3, Westfield*

If you ask the man in the toll booth for a good local restaurant, he's likely to send you here, probably because this is where he himself eats. The Foster House has been a restaurant of some sort since 1849, when the Mennonites sold what had been their church to an enterprising innkeeper. But don't come looking for 19th century charm. It's a plain-folks place, without pretensions. "We're not top-notch," says John Mavromatis, the gentle owner. "But what we do we do well."

We had a fine roast beef sandwich, and that's the sort of thing to ask for here. The menu is straight American and the prices modest. A Reuben is $2.50; full lunches, $2.25–$4.50. The roast beef on rye with a cup of soup and coffee is only $2.25. Dinners are $4.95 to $9.50.

Oh, and don't look for a 19th century building either. This is one of those places with a street-level façade wrapped around the original exterior. Windowless, it makes the place look more like a bar, which it half is, than a restaurant. Inside it's plasticky, but in a warm sort of way, and almost cozy.

Westfield, by the way, is known as Whip City, and local boosters claim it to be the whip capital of the world. We're not sure about that questionable honor, but you'll find the old brick factory of the Advance Whip and Novelty Company not far from the Foster House. You'll also find nearby several vacant, aging brick behemoths, former railroad hotels from the days when Westfield was a major junction on the New Haven line. No one has yet converted them to arty shopping centers. It's not that kind of town.

HOURS Tue.–Thu. 11 am–2:30 pm and 4–9 pm; Fri. & Sat. 11 am–2:30 pm and 4–10 pm; Sun. 11:45 am–9 pm; closed Mon.

DIRECTIONS Turn right at the end of Exit 3 onto Route 202 South, toward Westfield. Restaurant is on right, 0.9 mile from exit.

THE GOOD TABLE, *Exit 3, Westfield*

Downtown Westfield is the kind of area that tends to be swept aside by the inexorable march of shopping centers. But the Good Table gives you a chance to experience a small downtown that's still alive and kicking. What's especially nice is that someone cared enough to make this village lunchroom into something a bit more cheerful than just another sandwich place. It's pleasant, light, and airy (festive, almost), brightened by red tablecloths and fancy chandeliers.

For the most part the food is good but simple—we suspect that no one here was trained in Paris. Standard sandwiches and homemade cakes, pies, and puddings are very modestly priced. If you're looking for breakfast (always available), you'll find the usual egg, toast, and coffee for 99 cents, but a little more as well: eggs Benedict and eggs Bavarian with toast and coffee, $2.40 each. Maybe someone did spend some time abroad.

HOURS Mon.–Fri. 5:30 am–3 pm; Sat. 5:30 am–2 pm; Sun. 5:30 am–1 pm.

DIRECTIONS Follow **The Foster House** directions above, but continue south on Route 202 over the bridge and into downtown. Turn right on School St., the fourth light from the bridge (1.8 miles from highway). Restaurant is ½ block up, on left.

THE GALLEY, *Exit 4, West Springfield*

The Galley is a little Lionel train station of a building in white clapboard with black shutters and a tiny cupola. Classic New England almost, but for the 1940s-ish looking neon sign that hangs above the door, humbly displaying a painted cup of coffee and the simple boast "Good Home Cooking." Such modesty appeals to us.

It's true that a diner would have better fit the sign, but the fact is that this is a seafood cafeteria. You can tell from the interior decorating—fishnets dangling from the ceiling divide the serving area from the tables.

Well, the place is clean and plain, despite this feeble gesture at a theme. And you won't go broke. They run a breakfast special of juice, toast, eggs, and coffee for all of 59 cents. Hamburgers are $1.20, and fried chicken, shrimp, or scallops, $3.75.

HOURS Mon.–Fri. 6 am–7 pm; Sat. 6 am–3 pm; Sun. 7 am–noon.

DIRECTIONS From Exit 4 bear right at ramp and follow signs for Riverdale St., West Springfield, Route 5. Go 0.8 mile. It's on the right.

FITZSNUGGY'S, *Exit 4, West Springfield*

See description on p. 87.

DIRECTIONS Follow directions for **The Galley,** above, but continue on U.S. 5 past the Galley and under the overpass. It's about a mile to the first light after the overpass. Go a bit farther, and it's on the right.

DR. DEEGAN'S MARKET DELI RESTAURANT w/spirits, *Exit 6, Chicopee*

You might guess from the name that this is a place with an identity crisis. Well, it is, but deliberately so.

Square in front of the door stand the glass display cases typical of delis, stuffed with salami, pastrami, corned beef, and all the other good things you'd expect. The lighting is bright, and off to one side are bentwood chairs and mock-butcher-block tables adorned with bowls of half-sour pickles.

But if you walk through the deli and into the next room, you'll find yourself in a dark and very handsome lounge with new-but-real oak paneling and a handmade oak door that is the pride and joy of owner George Dakis.

Go through the lounge and you'll be in a dining area, the feel of which is about halfway between the other two.

The explanation is simple. George wanted to be different, and he wanted both a plain deli and a comfortable bar. At the same time, being thought of as operating a drinking place bothered him. Hence the diminutive "w/spirits" in the name.

And food *is* the real business here, so much so that George cooks his own corned beef, which is served up on rye for only $2.25. The potato salad was blessed with a tang that made it the best we've tasted in a deli, and a side order is just 60 cents.

All the other standard deli dishes are available at comparable prices, and if we rated restaurants as *Consumer Reports* rates stereos, we'd have no trouble declaring this one a "Best Buy Establishment." And you can pick the room to suit your mood.

HOURS Every day 10 am–2 am.

DIRECTIONS Take a right at the end of the Exit 6 ramp onto Burnet Rd. Go 0.3 mile. It's on the left.

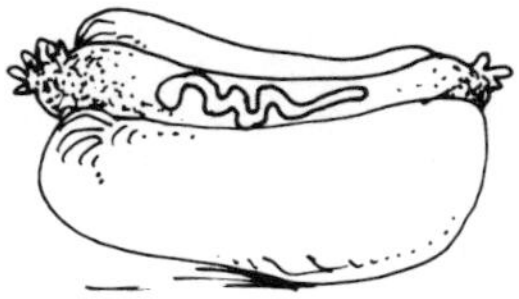

MILLER'S DAIRY BAR, *Exit 7, Ludlow*

There's almost nothing at this exit, but we did come across a little dairy bar that used to be part of the ice cream factory right next door. Alas, now it gets its waistline expanders elsewhere, and the food, served up in a bright, harsh environment, is only Woolworth quality.

But the prices are very modest, and the people, including the customers, were friendly local folks. You could do worse.

HOURS Every day 7 am–10 pm. Till 7:30 in winter.

DIRECTIONS From Exit 7 turn left at end of the ramp onto Route 21 South. Go 0.4 mile; it's on the right.

PALMER RESTAURANT, *Exit 8, Palmer*

Palmer is an utterly unretouched, unfixed-up, unpreserved little town whose chief claim to distinction is precisely that. In fact, the most fixed-up thing we saw here was the Palmer Restaurant, and it's not really putting on the dog. It's got a new suit of clothes, but only because of a fire a few years back.

Nice clothes, too. Or at least different. From the outside it's a little stucco building in Mediterranean white, with oval windows that suggest a kitschy seafood joint. But no, you step inside and see very pleasant walls and booths of honey-colored pine. Everything's clean and very up to date, so you change your mind and guess it will be a sort of small-town quicheateria.

But still, something doesn't fit. In the wall at each little booth is an inverted U of translucent glass block. That's hard to classify. And then you notice the black-felt diner menus up above the counter, looking delightfully out of place against the trendy natural wood.

Well, diner food it was; the service was lightning fast, and although the pancakes were heavy, the sausage and eggs were very good ($1.75). Hamburgers are all of 90 cents, and $1.25 will get you a BLT.

We liked it, and more power to whoever insisted on that glass block!

HOURS Mon.–Sat. 5 am–5 pm; Sun. 7 am–noon.

DIRECTIONS Turn right at the end of the Exit 8 ramp, following sings for Route 181. Go 0.8 mile to second light and turn left. It's on the right, 1½ blocks up.

DAY AND NIGHT DINER, *Exit 8, Palmer*

Like many of these unspoiled Worcester Car diners, the Day and Night has become something of an *objet d'art*. Or at least it was painted by artist John Baeder and ended up on a greeting card. There's no mistaking why he chose this one. It's a beauty, in red and yellow enamel, pink arched ceiling, tile floor, and red-checked curtains on the oak-trimmed windows, unchanged since 1941.

The clientele are mostly local, and from all walks of life. Almost anyone can appreciate owner Tom Weatherbee's goal of goodly portions at decent prices. And he goes to some lengths to make them tasty. The dinner specials, the spaghetti sauce, the stews, and some of the desserts are homemade, and the mashed potatoes don't come out of a box.

A roast beef dinner with those real potatoes will cost only $3.10. Stews are around $2.50, and American chop suey, $2.10. A hamburger is 95 cents; two eggs, toast, and coffee, $1.25 (breakfast is served all day). A bottomless cup of surprisingly good coffee costs 40 cents.

HOURS Mon.–Fri. 6 am–7 pm; Sat. 6 am–2 pm; Sun. 7 am–noon.

DIRECTIONS Same as for **Palmer Restaurant,** above, but turn right instead of left at the second light. It's on the left, a short 2 blocks from the turn.

ROM'S
THE PUBLICK HOUSE, *Exit 9, Sturbridge*

See descriptions on pp. 32–34. These are the only places hereabouts in which you won't feel silly in a necktie, and Rom's is a very good bargain.

DIRECTIONS Exit 9 will put you on I-86 South. Go just a bit on I-86 and then take Exit 4W to Routes 131 and 20 (Sturbridge and Brimfield). From there follow directions under I-86 entries.

CAMPANALE'S GRAFTON HOUSE RESTAURANT, *Exit 11, Grafton*

Pretty good food at a pretty good price in a comfortable but undistinguished environment is what you'll find at this neighborhood Italian restaurant.

The low building looks like a cross between a train station and a barn. Within, there's a bright coffee shop, a more subdued dining room in black leatherette cum barnboard, and a local pub.

Italian is the specialty, with substantial sauces that are pungent and full of good tomato flavor. There's nothing frozen, and the soups, including gazpacho and onion, are all made from scratch.

Italian dinners are in the $4.50 range, and American standards cost from $4.25 to $8.95. A buffet for two includes antipasto, lasagne, ziti, meatballs, sausage, eggplant parmigiana, fried green peppers, and garlic bread. That's an awful lot of good eating for $14.95.

There's a large selection of modestly priced sandwiches and grinders at lunchtime. The breakfast menu is more than reasonable, with two eggs, toast, and coffee for $1.09. A two-egg omelette with ham or bacon is $1.49. Children's menu.

HOURS Coffee shop: Mon.–Fri. 6 am–2 pm; Sat. & Sun. 6 am–noon. Dining room: Mon. 11 am–5 pm; Tue.–Thu. 11 am–9 pm; Fri. & Sat. 11 am–10 pm; Sun. noon–8 pm.

DIRECTIONS From Exit 11 turn right and follow road into Grafton. **Campanale's** is 1 mile, on the right.

LONGFELLOW'S WAYSIDE INN, *Exit 12, South Sudbury*

* *Far, but unique*

This is no place for a convenient stop, but if you've got the time for a country drive, a palate for fine food and a penchant for history, don't pass up the Wayside Inn.

Its chief claim to fame is that it was the setting for Longfellow's *Tales of a Wayside Inn:*

One Autumn night, in Sudbury town,
Across the meadows bare and brown,
The windows of the wayside inn
Gleamed red with firelight through the leaves
Of woodbine, hanging from the eaves,
Their crimson curtains rent and thin.

The place was already old when the poem was published in 1863.

As ancient is this hostelery
As any in the land may be,
Built in the old Colonial Day,
When men lived in a grander way.

In fact it was in the late 1600s that the inn was first licensed. But what makes it so wonderful now is not so much the authenticity of its dark-paneled, low-ceilinged, unprettied-up dining and drinking rooms. They *are* superb, roaring fireplaces and all, and we know of no place else that has this simple warmth and true ancient feel. What is even more unusual, however, is the way the inn bustles with good feeling. Waitresses carry loaded trays down narrow halls to the various dining rooms, mixing with and bumping into guests who are just wandering around from room to room, drinks in hand, peering into endless nook after cranny. Some of the dining rooms are so small that when you stumble in you feel you've walked into a private house. But no one seems to mind, and the whole place feels like a big party in someone's wonderful old house.

The main dining room is unfortunately not so cozy as the many small ones, but the food is uniformly excellent. Solid Yankee cooking, with dinners priced from $9 for baked scrod in cheese sauce to $17.50 for a 1½-pound lobster. Roast goose with apple stuffing and tangerine sauce is a rare treat at $12.50. Full luncheons run $4.75–$6. The rolls and muffins here are made from flour that's been stone-ground on the premises.

There really are rooms in the inn, but you'll have to make reservations well in advance. Do it if you can. It's an experience.

HOURS Mon.–Sat. 11:30 am–3:30 pm and 5–9 pm; Sun. noon–8 pm.

DIRECTIONS Don't be alarmed. It's not as bad as it sounds. But it isn't simple either. The easy way is from I-495 or I-95. These cross I-90 not far from Exit 12. You can take either of them north to U.S. 20 and then follow 20 to Sudbury. But if you like back roads, read on:

From Exit 12 take Route 9 East for 2.1 miles to exit for Edgell Road/Main Street/Framingham. Go to end of ramp and make a left at the light.

Go over highway, straight through the next light, and straight on for 2 blocks to Vernon St. at the end of the commons. Left onto Vernon, and then first right onto Grove St. Go 3.1 miles on Grove to a T. Then make a left onto Edmonds, followed by an immediate right onto Wayside Inn Rd. Go 2.1 miles to light, and then straight another 1.1 miles to the inn, on the left.

Don't forget—it's an adventure.

ORIGINAL COPPER KETTLE, *Exit 12, Framingham*

You're in the suburbs here—species: upper middle class. Wall-to-wall condos nearby, and if you're driving an Alpha Romeo that needs a quick repair, you'll find a dealer just up the road. But this is no place for eating.

Right at the exit is the Original Copper Kettle, housed in a structure that looks like (and was) a chain restaurant. Standard highway stuff at modest prices, beneath a silly, spiraling roof. But it does have the virtue of being open 24 hours a day.

AEGEAN RESTAURANT, *Exit 13, Framingham*

Tucked away in a pocket of suburbia, all but blotted out by gargantuan shopping centers, and well hidden behind a Kentucky Fried Chicken joint, is a little Greek restaurant that would probably feel more at home in some downtown neighborhood. If it were downtown, the Aegean probably would not have put together an interior that matches its actual surroundings. It's clean and bright, with white walls, vinyl seating and Formica tables. Not ugly, but not warm and inviting either. A few lonely travel posters featuring

Apollo and Poseidon constitute the only visible evidence of an ethnic restaurant.

But your taste will discern what the eyes miss. The moussaka was surprisingly good for the $3.50 price tag, a trifle heavy but very flavorful, and we kept looking forward to the next bite. And certainly it was ambrosia in comparison to anything else you're likely to stumble on hereabouts.

For $3.75 you can get spinach pie with salad, or souvlaki. Five dollars buys a special platter that ought to hold you for a while: stuffed grape leaves, Greek sausage, meatballs, spinach pie, tomatoes, boiled eggs, olives, and feta cheese.

The Aegean also serves sandwiches, omelettes (with feta, $2.50), American dinners ($5–$7), and breakfast till 11 (one egg with meat, $1.50).

HOURS Mon. & Tue. 8 am–8:30 pm; Wed. 8 am–9 pm; Thu.–Sat. 8 am–10 pm; Sun. 8 am–8:30 pm.

DIRECTIONS From Exit 13 follow signs for Route 30 West/Framingham. Follow 30 for 1.2 miles, through three lights, and look for a Kentucky Fried Chicken place on left. The **Aegean** is just beyond and behind it.

BEETLE'S LUNCH, *Exits 18 & 20, Allston*

At Beetle's Lunch we had the very best breakfast of our entire six-state eating campaign. Two large, bright yellow eggs were scrambled with sautéed fresh scallions and handsomely presented between slices of whole wheat toast astride a generous portion of peppery, unpeeled home fries and onions, topped by a dollop of sour cream. And on the side, a glass of delicious, pulpy fresh orange juice—we saw it being squeezed. All that cost not a penny more than $1.65.

It was two years ago that four young women who had worked in a variety of local restaurants concluded that they could do better for less. They rented a small but clean hole-in-the-wall on Allston's Harvard Avenue, not far from Boston University, furnished it with bare-bones minimum, and began to cook up the healthiest, freshest, homiest food they possibly could: fresh-squeezed fruit juices and imaginative fruit frappes, crisp garden salads, blintzes with sour cream and blueberry sauce, omelettes, stews, hefty sandwiches, homemade bread, challah French toast, and much, much more. None of their entrées are over $4; some are under $3. A frappe costs $1.25, and the high-octane version—with protein powder, nutritional yeast, bran, wheat germ, and a raw egg—is $2. It'll put a tiger in your tank.

Deservedly, Beetle's Lunch caught on, and a crowd of appreciative young working people from the neighborhood began to collect here for breakfast and lunch. Many, it seems, were in rock bands, and they brought tapes to play for their friends. The band we heard over the loudspeakers was, shall we say, not as palatable as the food. When we aired our feelings about the volume, the waitress graciously explained the situation and offered to turn it down.

We suggest that if your musical taste—or distaste—agrees with ours, bring your own tapes to Beetle's Lunch. They'll play whatever comes along. Or let your reactions to the amplitude be known. We promise you'll find the food much more agreeable than the music.

HOURS Tue.–Fri. 6:30 am–5 pm; Sat. 9 am–4 pm; Sun. 10 am–4 pm; closed Mon.

DIRECTIONS If eastbound, take Exit 18 (Allston-Cambridge); if westbound, take Exit 20 (Allston-Cambridge). Otherwise, directions are identical: On the exit ramp, follow signs for Allston-Brighton, which put you onto Cambridge St. Go 0.6 mile and turn left at fourth traffic light. (It's Harvard Ave., no matter what the sign says—look for antique shops on the corner.) Go two blocks on Harvard, cross Brighton Ave., and you'll see it on the left—120 Harvard Ave.

I-91

Connecticut, Massachusetts, Vermont

Connecticut

BASEL'S, *Exits 4 & 5, New Haven*

"This isn't just a restaurant, it's a party," announces Lou Basel at 9 o'clock every Thursday, Friday, and Saturday night. And so it seems, as 70 or so guests rise from their meals to circle a central core of tables. They dance hand-in-hand to the gay rhythms of live Greek music (American style) as Lou leads them through the steps. What makes it especially nice is the easygoing friendliness, the mixture of ages and nationalities, and the fact that no one seems to mind if you can't quite get it right. Everyone's smiling, and almost everyone's dancing.

But it most emphatically *is* a restaurant. The cuisine is authentic Greek, featuring such entrées as moussaka, kota yiahini (chicken baked in a tomato-onion-wine sauce), dolmathes (grape leaves stuffed with beef and rice), souvlaki, and arni tou fournou (lamb in tomato sauce). It's as good as any Greek food we've ever tasted. If you're really hungry you can start off with spanakopita as an appetizer. A steal at $2.50, it is a large multilayer pastry crust encasing cheese and spinach. Lunches are $2.75 to $4.75, and dinners range from about $7 to $10.

HOURS Mon. 11:30 am–2 pm; Tue. & Wed. 11:30 am–2 pm and 5–9 pm; Thu. 11:30 am–2 pm and 5 pm–1 am; Fri. 11:30 am–2 pm and 5 pm–2 am; Sat. 5 pm–2 am; closed Sun.

DIRECTIONS See **Annie's Firehouse Soup Kitchen,** below.

ANNIE'S FIREHOUSE SOUP KITCHEN, INC., *Exits 4 & 5, New Haven*

Annie's is a favorite with the university/young professional crowd. The soups are all carefully homemade from fresh ingredients, and the bread is baked on the premises. On a given day you might have your choice of gazpacho, pollo Jerez, onion soup, or fish chowder, along with salads, quiches, and—in winter—a stew or two.

Beyond the basic soup and salad ($4.65 at lunch and $5.65 at dinnertime), there's a nightly full-dinner special at $7.95. For Sunday brunch, Annie has gone for some unusual variations of the normal breakfast fare: she offers apple-raisin pancakes, sweet-potato waffles, Jamaican French toast, and eggs with Hollandaise—any of them with ham or bacon at $5.95.

The ambiance is a very pleasant version of the natural oak, plants, and antiques decor. There is lots of white wall space, and quite a bit of sandblasted brick too, since this really was a firehouse. Located in one of New Haven's older neighborhoods, it was renovated about five years ago. They added windows to brighten things up, and built the tables on old sewing machine stands. Condiments are available from a Victorian ticket booth/gazebo that watches over this comfortable little place. An outdoor patio was under construction when we visited.

HOURS Mon.–Thu. 11:30 am–3 pm and 5:30–9 pm; Fri. & Sat. 11:30 am–3 pm and 5:30–9:30 pm; Sun. 11:30 am–3 pm and 5–8 pm.

DIRECTIONS Northbound: From Exit 5 (Ferry St.) take a sharp left and go 0.3 mile to second light. **Basel's** is on your left (933 State St.). From here turn right onto Edwards St. for **Annie's,** on your right (19 Edwards).

Southbound: From Exit 4 (State St.) bear right and then at light turn right again onto State St. Go 0.2 mile to **Basel's,** on your right (933 State St.). From here turn left onto Edwards St. for **Annie's,** on your right (19 Edwards).

THE RED BULL DINER RESTAURANT, *Exit 12, North Haven*

This is what happened to the '30s-style diner when it hit the '60s. Because railroading was on the wane, it no longer made sense to manufacture diners that reflected the prestige and luxury of railroad dining cars. Thus began the Greco-Mediterranean era of diner construction. The new diners were done up in stucco and ersatz brick, and their interiors (rest rooms included) modernized with all kinds of plastic and tilework. Archways of imitation stone suddenly appeared like plastic flamingos in a front yard.

But the menus are usually large, and the Red Bull's is no exception. It features Italian main dishes, soft-shell crabs, and much, much more. There are also lots of omelettes, blintzes, and deli sandwiches, most priced between $1.65 and $2.75 (more for still fancier creations). Dinners are $4–$6.

You'll find the food more digestible than the decor.

HOURS 24 hours, every day of the year.

DIRECTIONS From Exit 12 turn right onto Route 5. Go ½ mile; you'll see it on the right.

ROUTE 72 DINER, *Exit 21, Berlin*

It's the genuine article, even if its food isn't gourmet, not even by diner standards. Small on the outside, the Route 72 looks almost as if it belongs to an electric train set. But the inside is light and spacious enough, done up in light blue and stainless steel, with mosaic floor tile, and so on. The menu features more salad plates than most such places, and the prices are better than reasonable. Hamburgers are 95 cents; two eggs, etc., are $1.15.

HOURS Mon.–Sat. 5:30 am–4:30 pm; closed Sun.

DIRECTIONS Take Exit 21, turning right at the end of the ramp. Go 1.3 miles west on Route 72. Look right.

MOZZICATO CAFFÈ, *Exit 27, Hartford*

We discovered that as I-91 passes through Hartford's South End, it brushes the edge of an Italian neighborhood complete with all the restaurants, caffès, bakeries, and pastry shops you'd expect from a Little Italy. We couldn't try them all, but two caught our eye. (See also **Pippie's** below.)

The Mozzicato Caffè offers an unusual and authentic combination of Italian specialties: coffees, light lunch items, pastries, and ice cream. All this is enticingly displayed along a 25-foot counter. In fact, the whole place is laid out with clean, modern lines that reflect the best sort of modern Italian design. The large windows and yellow-brown color tones make for a pleasant, sunny effect, and there is even a small bar.

For lunch, we sampled the arancini, a breaded pyramid of rice, mozzarella, and meat in tomato sauce. It costs only a dollar and is a tasty meal in itself. Also available are spinach pizza, and a wonderful-looking folded pastry shell stuffed with spinach and sausage. This beauty goes for $2, and it'll feed two. And no fewer than 36 flavors of soft Italian ice cream (gelato) are made on the premises, with about eight available at any one time. Fragole is the local favorite.

There's a piano in the back that bears a sign: "If you can play . . . PLAY." Who knows? If you're really good, you may be able to play for your pasta.

Actually, the caffè is an adjunct to a bakery, also run by Gino Mozzicato. If you like your meal, you can go next door and take home anything from a four-foot wedding cake to dozens of delicious-looking pastries or fresh-baked Italian bread.

HOURS Mon.–Thu. 9 am–11 pm; Fri. & Sat. 9 am–1 am; closed Sun.

DIRECTIONS Northbound: From Exit 27 turn left at stop sign, then left again at light onto Airport Rd. ■ The fourth light on Airport Rd. is Franklin Ave. Right on Franklin for 3 blocks to Bushnell. It's on the corner, on your left.

Southbound: Exit 27 feeds you directly onto Airport Rd. Then, as above from ■.

PIPPIE'S RESTAURANT, *Exit 27, Hartford*

At Pippie's you can get your meal almost for free if you plan your travel right. During Happy Hour, this Italian/American restaurant sets out a tempting display of pizza, salad, and a mild sausage dish. It's in the bar, and you must imbibe to partake, but there's no charge for the buffet.

Don't limit yourself to the freebies. This is one of Hartford's more popular Italian places. Pippie Scotia, owner and cook, makes his own pasta for the lasagne, manicotti, and ravioli. He also brings in fresh veal daily. The ample menu is augmented by pizza that is said to be the best in town. We couldn't judge all the competition, but what we sampled at Pippie's was certainly very good.

Dinners here will run you from just over $5 for spaghetti in tomato sauce to $12.90 for steak pizzaiola or shrimp scampi. Chicken cacciatore is in between at $8.85. Small plain pizzas are $4.10; large, $8. A lunchtime sandwich special on hard roll with soup and salad or potato goes for $3.95.

HOURS Mon.–Thu. noon–10:30 pm; Fri.–Sun. noon–midnight; Happy Hour: Mon.–Fri. 4–7 pm; Sat. 1–4 pm.

DIRECTIONS See **Truc,** below.

TRUC, *Exit 27, Hartford*

We knew that Hartford's South End is predominantly Italian, but we also knew that a restaurant called "Truc" couldn't be of that genre. Further investigation revealed what we suspected—it's a Vietnamese name, pronounced "True," and the restaurant has the same owners as the Orient Express in West Stockbridge, Massachusetts, p. 61. As befits their respective neighborhoods, Truc is lower-toned than its well-dressed sister in the Berkshires, but it's got the same good Vietnamese food with slightly lower prices (lunch $3–$5, dinner $5–$7).

HOURS Lunch: Tue.–Sat. 11–2 pm; Dinner: Tue.–Sun. 5–9:30 pm; closed Mon.

DIRECTIONS Northbound: From Exit 27 turn left at stop sign, then left again at light onto Airport Rd. ■ The third light on Airport Rd. is Wethersfield Ave. Turn left here for **Pippie's** (on the corner) and, about ½ mile down, **Truc,** on the right at 735 Wethersfield Ave.

Southbound: Exit 27 feeds you directly onto Airport Rd. Then, as above from ■.

AETNA RESTAURANT

BANDO, *I-84 West Interchange, Hartford*

See p. 27 for good Greek food in a campy atmosphere; p. 26 for excellent, inexpensive Korean specialties.

DIRECTIONS Turn onto I-84 West in Hartford, and then follow directions given. But bear in mind that you will have to return to I-91 North (not South) through some city traffic.

WINDSOR HOUSE, *Exit 37, Windsor*

Side by side on the tranquil Windsor village green are a pair of restaurants as different in character as could be. One, the Windsor House, is pure New England, while the other (see **Anthony's** below) could be found at any small-town crossroads in America.

The Windsor House has been a stately hotel-restaurant since the 1830s. The spacious main dining room has an Early American feel, and the tables are attractively set with small print napkins. The pub room has Tudor-style stucco walls and a copper-topped bar. In contrast, a smaller, glassed-in dining room is done up in the late–20th-century look—natural oak with lots of plants.

Dinners run from about $6 for manicotti to $22 for Chateaubriand for two. There are a dozen seafood dishes from $7.50 to $11 and a solid selection of meat dishes including veal Marsala, all at comparable prices. Luncheon specials are $4 to $5, and sandwiches with French fries or coleslaw are available for just under $3.

Anthony's-on-the-Green serves a quick breakfast and lunch daily. It's right next door.

HOURS Mon.–Fri. 11:30 am–2:30 pm and 5–9:30 pm; Sat. 5–10 pm; Sun. 11:30 am–6:15 pm. Closed July and August.

DIRECTIONS From Exit 37 go 1 mile east on Route 305, bearing right at fork onto Route 159 South. One block takes you to the village green. You can't miss it from there.

STELLA'S LOUNGE and CHARLES TEN RESTAURANT, *Exit 42, Windsor Locks*

Here's a real discovery.

Stella almost gave us the bum's rush when we introduced ourselves. She soon warmed up but it wouldn't have mattered. We just couldn't resist including a restaurant with a well-deserved reputation for delicious Polish cooking and all the local color you could ask for.

To begin with, the building was built "brick by brick" by Stella's husband, Charles Tenerowicz, back in the '30s. It sits just across the road from the canal that gives this town its name. Inside the small pub, every available inch of wall space is covered with some sort of memorabilia—clock, plaque, bottle, advertisement, or picture. With the old wooden bar and booths, and the local clientele, it adds up to a comfortable and genuinely charming atmosphere in which to relax from the drive.

And what food! The service is slow, says Stella proudly, and she's equally proud of the cast-iron pots in which she cooks the hearty Polish standbys: kielbasa, pierogi (stuffed dumplings), gołabki, and a wonderful cabbage soup that seems to have a delicate hint of lemon. (Stella wouldn't tell.) Everything is made to order. The dinners are about \$3.50–\$4.50, and a big bowl of soup can be had for \$2.25. There are also grinders, pizza, steamers, and sandwiches. You can eat in the small barroom or in the attached dining area.

HOURS Mon.–Fri. noon–midnight; Sun. noon–11 pm; closed Sat.

DIRECTIONS From Exit 42 turn left onto Route 159 toward Windsor Locks. Go ¼ mile; it's on the left.

Massachusetts

FILLIN' STATION TOO, *Exits 4 & 5, Springfield*

Here's a diner in new clothes, with some nice finishing touches on the menu. Practically beneath the interstate as it passes over Springfield, this little brick building is guarded by two fuel pumps from the days when gasoline was called ethyl and muscles did the pumping. Inside, the antique-car motif is carried further by photos, advertisements ("Time for a new Ford—only $525"), and an Art Deco mural of a Model T. Situated in an older urban neighborhood and open 24 hours, Fillin' Station Too has, as one waitress puts it, "a lot of character and a lot of characters."

Known locally for its big breakfasts (buttermilk pancakes with two eggs and ham will certainly fill 'er up for a mere $2.65), the restaurant is cultivating a dinner crowd by offering nightly homemade specials. Seven ounces of baked or fried scrod, fresh zucchini, and French fries go for only $2.70. Other dinners are in the $3–$4 range. A crock of fine onion soup is a house specialty, served with melted cheese and croutons ($1.20). And you can top off your tank with a piña colada milk shake for $1.10.

HOURS 24 hours, every day of the year.

DIRECTIONS Northbound: From Exit 4 turn left at the light to cross under the highway. One-half block past the next light is the restaurant on your right, at 84 W. Broad St. Park in rear.

Southbound: From Exit 5 turn right at light. Restaurant is on your right, half a block up at 84 W. Broad St. Park in rear.

ICHABOD'S
MR. C. MAGOO'S, *Exits 6 & 7, Springfield*

Side by side, within sight of the interstate in downtown Springfield, these two restaurants compete for honors in the brick-plants-and-oak category.

At **Ichabod's,** the appetizers are tempters—scallops wrapped in bacon and broiled ($4.25) or stuffed mushroom caps ($2.85), for example. Sandwiches are served on light or dark rye, hard roll, or Syrian bread, priced from $2.50 to $3.50. Dinners run from $3.25 for quiche or Hungarian goulash to upward of $7 for breaded scallops or a New York steak. In the mid-range are shrimp scampi ($5.95) and shish kabob ($3.95).

At **Magoo's,** the meals are lighter. Chili, cream of broccoli soup, chicken salad almondine, sandwiches and burgers of six varieties are all in the $2–$3 range. Although Magoo's menus are printed on paper bags, we doubt they'll be used to take home uneaten seafood crepes. Made from scallops and swordfish simmered in white wine and topped with Mornay sauce, they are just too good for the dog.

HOURS **Ichabod's:** Sat.–Tue. 11 am–1 am; Wed.–Fri. 11 am–2 am.

Mr. Magoo's: every day 11:30 am–11 pm.

DIRECTIONS See **The Student Prince and Fort Restaurant,** below.

THE STUDENT PRINCE and FORT RESTAURANT, *Exits 6 & 7, Springfield*

This German restaurant is a Springfield institution with all the "gemütlichkeit" you could ask for. It's the sort of place that celebrities get taken to when they are in the area. Old wood and an Old World feel of warmth and comfort are everywhere.

In the Student Prince lounge, the walls are a collage of Germanica: antique cuckoo clocks, swords, glassware, plates, and beer steins. Twelve hundred beer steins, in fact. Some of these decorate the dining area too, but the atmosphere there is more subdued.

From the kitchen come almost 100 German dishes served year-round. Geschnettzle—veal sautéed with shallots in Rhine wine and cream—is the chef's special delight. In spring, there's shad and shad roe, and in summer, poached Gaspé salmon in Hollandaise. And, of course, you can always find sauerbraten, wiener schnitzel, knockwurst, and hasenpfeffer.

If you want still more Germanica, you might like to know that the restaurant's calendar is splashed with seasonal celebrations. During Oktoberfest, waitresses wear peasant dresses and a singing Fräulein strolls among the tables, while guests feast on specialties like Münchener brathendl (chicken, Munich style) and zarte kalbshaxen (tender veal shanks). At the February Game Fest, it is possible to order venison stew, broiled bear steaks, haunch of hare, or roast pheasant. For the May Wine Festival, the Student Prince and Fort Restaurant again change costumes, donning garlands of flowers and erecting a gaily striped maypole in the center of the main dining area. Waitresses ladle woodruff-scented May wine and floating strawberries into glasses that seem to empty as quickly as they fill.

Dinner prices at the Student Prince and Fort are $7–$9 à la carte, while complete luncheons go from $2.35 to $3.15. Practically everything—from sausages to pastries—is made on the premises.

Guten Appetit!

HOURS Mon.–Sat. 11 am–11 pm; Sun. noon–11 pm.

DIRECTIONS Northbound: From Exit 6 (Springfield Center) you are fed into East Columbus Ave. Swing around slightly to the right (don't reenter highway) to merge with traffic. Follow Columbus Ave. through several curves for 0.3 mile to Worthington St. on your right (shortly after the Bay State West complex). ■ **Ichabod's** is clearly visible from the corner; next door is **Mr. Magoo's.** For **The Student Prince,** park here and walk to Fort St. through the brick passageway next to Ichabod's. It's across the street.

Southbound: From Exit 7 move into the far left lane; it puts you through a U-turn under the highway and then feeds you into East Columbus Ave. Go 0.1 mile to Worthington St., on your right. Then, as above from ■.

FITZSNUGGY'S, *Exits 13B & 13S, West Springfield*

Since Fitzsnuggy's opened in 1979, its customers have walked away with 35,000 copies of the 10-page accordion fold-out menu, compliments of owner Naif Makol. If punning is your style, it is as entertaining as menus come.

Here's a guided tour that should help you steer your way through the bill of fare:

Appetizers and light meals, which Fitzsnuggy's calls "Tantalizing Titillators," greet you first. They include "Spudnick" (an "out of this world baked potato" with crumbled bacon and melted cheese for $1.95), "High Steaks" (steak teriyaki with baked potato and onion rings for $3.10), "Lord of the Rings" (a "hobbit-forming" pile of fried onions), and "Quiche Me Quick" (the day's quiche).

After soups and salads—including, for example, "You Tuna Me On" ($2.95)—the menu moves on to burgers and sandwiches. The "Clark Gobble" is turkey, of course ($3.25), while Fitzsnuggy's grilled-cheese club is called "The Lunchpack of Notre Dame."

After wading through 67 items like those, you will have navigated the first side of the Fitzsnuggy's road-map menu. Sound like pun? On to the flip side.

Oven-baked omelettes include the "Eggsistential," with fresh spinach, mushrooms, and Swiss ($2.90), and the "Eggstravaganza," a compendium of bacon, sausage, mushrooms, onion, cheese, and pepper ($3.25).

But enough of this. We'll just tell it straight. There are also full dinners at Fitzsnuggy's. Cheesy Chicken Broccoli is the favorite. Born as a humble chicken pie, it evolved into hunks of chicken and broccoli on egg noodles in cheese sauce ($4.40).

The atmosphere here is jazzy, like the menu. A veritable botanical garden hangs from the ceiling. There's lots of glass and stainless steel, a 15-foot fish tank, and youthful waitresses who sally forth in designer jeans—each cut for a nice, snug fitzy.

HOURS Mon.–Thu. 11 am–3 am; Fri. 11 am–4 am; Sat. 7 am–4 am; Sun. 7 am–3 am.

DIRECTIONS If northbound, take Exit 13S; if southbound, take Exit 13B. Either way, you will be fed onto Route 5 South (Riverdale St.). **Fitzsnuggy's** is just past the first light, at 918 Riverdale.

ABOUT NORTHAMPTON

Northampton is the home of Smith College, which shares the Pioneer Valley with Amherst, Mount Holyoke, Hampshire, and the University of Massachusetts. That'a prestigious group, and so as you might expect, this is a cosmopolitan little town, filled with boutiques, galleries, theaters, and bookstores. Even if things sometimes shade a bit toward the precious, all this certainly makes for great eating.

There's one of everything here: very good French, Szechuan, Italian, and natural foods restaurants; classic diners, a brick-plants-and-oak café, a wonderful patisserie, an excellent ice cream parlor, a cheap, but good, soup kitchen, and even a quality all-American seafood restaurant. Far too much, really, for us to be fair to all, so we've featured a few and mentioned some others. There are still more, so don't be afraid to explore.

PAUL AND ELIZABETH'S, *Exits 18 & 20, Northampton*

A great favorite in town is Paul and Elizabeth's, located in Thorne's Market, which is a Main Street mall with dozens of craft shops and trendy establishments of every sort. Paul and Elizabeth's offers natural foods with a difference: a touch of class instead of funk. Co-owner Paul Sustick is proud of that. He wants to prove that healthy eating need be neither dull nor on the fringe. His real goal is educational, he says. "I'm not in this to make money. There are easier ways to make a living."

Just glancing around at the modern, slightly severe surroundings, you wouldn't guess you were in a health food restaurant. The only hint is the abundance of natural wood (hardwood, varnished and shiny—not rough-sawn pine). From the high, patterned-tin ceiling hang large paper lanterns. The walls are white with big windows, and the only dark color comes from a few tall orange trees.

"What you eat is part of you," declares Paul, revealing his culinary bent. What you'll eat here is lightly battered vegetable tempura ($3.75), broiled fish with salad, rice, and tea ($3.95), or black bean soup accompanied by a whole wheat roll, salad, rice, and tea ($2.95). For sandwiches you can get fish, hummus, egg salad, or other meatless spreads on pita or whole wheat, with coleslaw, for around $2.75. Omelettes are $3.25, soup about $1.50, and seven salads, including watercress and tabouli, run $1.25 to $3.75.

Dinner is not expensive here, with scallop tempura tops at $7.50. More typically priced are pan-fried noodles with sautéed vegetables in tamari sauce ($4.95) or marinated and broiled tofu with vegetables, on a skewer, served with brown rice and salad ($5.95). Soups and salads from the lunch menu are still available at dinner, but they are joined by appetizers like Antipasto Paul and Elizabeth—marinated fresh fish and vegetables on lettuce, topped with garnishes and Vermont cheddar.

HOURS Mon.–Sat. noon–10 pm; closed Sun.

DIRECTIONS See end of Northampton entries, p. 94.

BEARDSLEY'S CAFÉ-RESTAURANT, *Exits 19 & 20, Northampton*

Beardsley's is the undisputed focal point of haute cuisine in this part of New England.

If you're up for a really fine dinner you might try Pintadeau au Martinique—Cornish game hen marinated in vermouth, lime juice, shallots, and herbs, and then roasted to order. Or perhaps entrecôte au Roquefort would please you—it's pan-sautéed prime sirloin garnished with Roquefort butter. These and other entrées come with a salad made from Bibb, Boston, and Romaine lettuce, and run from $9.50 to $16.95.

Appetizers include a pâté of veal, pork, and chicken seasoned with hazelnuts, spices, and Cognac ($3.50); a chicken-liver mousse ($2.95); half a smoked trout with a cream sauce of horse-radish and shallots ($5.25); and ratatouille ($3.50). Of course, there's a wine list of 80 selections to match this sort of cookery.

Beardsley's lunch menu is more familiar. A bowl of soup with French bread is only $1.95. Salads come three ways: garden, Greek, and spinach. There are also crepes, omelettes, and sandwiches with a French accent (including "le hamburgeur"). These run from $2.50 to $5. A daily luncheon special ($5–$6) offers more unusual dishes.

The decor here is a marvelously tasteful blend of modern and Victorian. There's a feeling of light and space amidst the old wood and antique fixtures, but most important is the restrained understatement.

HOURS Mon.–Sat. 11:30 am–2:30 pm and 5:30–10 pm; Sun. 10:30 am–2:30 pm and 5:30–9 pm; Café menu: Mon.–Sat. 2:30–4:30 pm.

DIRECTIONS See end of Northampton entries, p. 94.

THE SOUP KITCHEN, *Exits 18 & 20, Northampton*

A name as simple as "The Soup Kitchen" captures the unencumbered atmosphere of this narrow, brick-walled restaurant on Northampton's Main Street. The sophistication of its cuisine, however, could support a much fancier title.

Each month, over 75 different soups—both vegetarian and meat—are made from scratch and served on butcher-block tables adorned with fresh flowers in Coke bottles. The variety available on any given day is sufficient to satisfy even the most narrow palate. For example, on one spring evening we found Portuguese vegetable soup (a sort of minestrone with a noticeable but not overpowering tang), cream of celery, seafood bisque (richly embellished with sizable chunks of shrimp and other shellfish), and the pleasantly spiced chili con carne that is available every day.

The Soup Kitchen's salad options are equally diverse. In addition to a Romaine-based garden salad, there is a spinach salad, a Greek salad, a Caesar salad with mushrooms, cabbage, bacon (optional); and a house specialty known as Salad Fetoushe, consisting of cukes, tomato, and lettuce, all marinated in an oil-and-vinegar base.

Quiche, cheese blintzes, and special entrées such as eggplant moussaka also appear on the slateboard menu. Like the soups, they come with fresh bread from the bakery right next door. "It's the best loaf north of New York," insist the college kids who are Soup Kitchen regulars. There's also an eye-catching display of desserts.

If reaching the Soup Kitchen through a few blocks of downtown Northampton traffic costs you three or four minutes, the quick service—five minutes, tops—will repay you. Beer and wine (as well as herb teas) are served, and prices are reasonable.

HOURS Mon.–Sat. 11:30 am–9 pm; closed Sun.

DIRECTIONS See end of Northampton entries, p. 94.

JACK AUGUST'S HOUSE OF SEAFOOD, *Exits 18 & 20, Northampton*

No, it's not a chain. This is the original Jack August's, with no connection to anything else of a similar name. It's been in the August family for fifty years now, and people in the area know it's special.

Not only is 90 percent of the fish fresh (the waitress will tell you what's frozen), but Jack August's is also a fish store with the day's catch displayed on ice.

The exterior is ordinary, but when you step inside, you'll see that the Augusts have managed to create the feel of a shore-side chowder house. The booths and wall paneling are of plain wood painted nautical gray. Overhead dangle a few fishnets, while the walls are decorated with starfish and model ships. Red and white checked tablecloths enliven the whole scheme. It's really not too gimmicky; it's just plain nice.

The menu has nearly all the down-home fish dishes you can think of—baked, broiled, fried, stewed, or chowdered. And you'll find that the fried isn't too greasy here—just juicy and tender. But if you're dieting, they'll be glad to do a special preparation for you.

The local favorite is the mixed plate of fried clams, scallops, shrimp, swordfish, haddock, and halibut that costs $7.50. Baked trout is $6.25, and haddock steak is $5.95. A bowl of clam or oyster stew can be had for $3.50, six oysters on the half-shell for $3.75, or a fried-fish sandwich for $2.50. Children's portions are half price.

HOURS Tue.–Thu. 11 am–7:30 pm; Fri. & Sat. 11 am–8 pm; Sun. 11 am–8 pm; closed Mon.

DIRECTIONS See end of Northampton entries, p. 94.

SUSANNE NAEGELE'S BAKERY, *Exits 18 & 20, Northampton*

Without a doubt Naegele's is the best bakery in this area, and there are even stories of its having been declared the best in New England. We haven't come across better French bread anywhere, not to mention the sourdough, which comes in white, whole wheat, and rye, and the marvelous soft pretzels. Wonderful French pastry too—delicate and rich, but never too sweet. You can choose from Linzer tortes, Sacher tortes, Napoleons, and much, much more, all beautifully displayed.

By any standards these are excellent products made with Old World care on machinery actually imported from France and England just for the purpose. Take these delights with you, or eat there with any of five coffees and many teas. There's a lovely dining area at the rear of the store.

Don't miss it.

HOURS Mon.–Sat. 9 am–6 pm; closed Sun.

DIRECTIONS See end of Northampton entries, p. 94.

SZE'S, *Exits 18 & 20, Northampton*

A very good Chinese restaurant, featuring Szechuan cooking. You'll have to go to New York to do much better. The environment is modern, tasteful, and very pleasant. Lunches are mostly around $3; dinners, $4.95–$7.50. Yu-Hsiang eggplant (with pork and hot sauce) is a great favorite ($5.25). Often a wait at dinnertime.

HOURS 11:30 am–9:15 pm (till 10:45 Fri. & Sat.).

DIRECTIONS See end of Northampton entries, p. 94.

ANDIAMO, *Exits 18 & 20, Northampton*

Fine Northern Italian cooking in an impressive all-white dining room. The pasta is homemade, and if you like it, you can buy some to take home. Dinner only, in the $5–$10 range.

HOURS Mon.–Thu. 5–9:30 pm; Fri. & Sat. 5–10 pm; Sun. 11 am–9:30 pm.

DIRECTIONS See end of Northampton entries, p. 94.

BART'S ICE CREAM CORNER, *Exits 18 & 20, Northampton*

For luscious ice cream, you couldn't do much better than Bart's. They even offer their seductive flavors in three different butterfat contents. Nice home-baked goodies, too, and a pleasant enough seating area. Eat here, diet at home.

HOURS Mon.–Thu. 7:30 am–11:30 pm; Fri. 7:30 am–midnight; Sat. 8 am–midnight; Sun. 9 am–11:30 pm.

DIRECTIONS See end of Northampton entries, p. 94.

FITZWILLY'S, *Exits 18 & 20, Northampton*

A prototype of the brick-plants-and-oak café, Fitzwilly's has been around since before most of us ever heard of sand-blasted brick in restaurants. Stained glass, skylights, copper lamps, tin ceiling, quiche, Reubens, spinach salads, fried potato skins, cute names for the sandwiches: Fitzwilly's has it all. Two bars and two dining rooms, with a conversation area in between. Very collegiate and frequently very, very busy. Boozy coffees are big sellers.

HOURS Mon.–Sat. 11:30 am–11:45 pm; Sun. 10 am–11:45 pm.

DIRECTIONS See end of Northampton entries, below.

BLUE BONNET DINER, *Exit 20, Northampton*

Not nearly so special as the Miss Florence, but only 0.4 mile along Route 5 from Exit 20 (a southbound exit only), on the right, beneath a Coke bottle almost as big as the diner itself. No surprises.

HOURS Every day 5:30 am–midnight (till 1 am on Fri. & Sat.).

DIRECTIONS FOR NORTHAMPTON RESTAURANTS Northbound: From Exit 18 turn left onto Route 5 North, which becomes Pleasant St. Go straight, not left, at the fork. It's about 1 mile to a light at Main St. in the center of town. ■ From here you can turn right to find first **Sze's,** on the right, then **Fitzwilly's,** on the left, and finally **Jack August's,** on the right, just past the railroad bridge.

Or, starting again at the light ■, you can turn left to find, on the left and all within a block, **Beardsley's, Naegele's Bakery,** and Thorne's Market (containing **Paul and Elizabeth's**). **The Soup Kitchen** is across the street from Thorne's. **Bart's Ice Cream** is a bit farther up Main St. on right. Continue along Main, bearing left onto a small side street as Main curves right, and you'll see **Andiamo** on the left, at 12 Crafts Ave.

Southbound: Take Exit 20. The ramp leads you onto Route 5 South, which in 1.4 miles brings you to a light at Main St. This is the same light as at ■ above, but you've approached it from the opposite direction. So just reverse the above directions. Left for **Sze's,** etc., and right for **Beardsley's,** etc.

MISS FLORENCE DINER, *Exits 19 & 20, Florence*

Miss Flo, as she is locally known, is the Duesenberg of diners, a classic in every detail, and utterly unchanged since she was born in 1940. She's got it all, from arched ceiling with fans, old wood paneling, floor tile, stainless-steel walls, and thin counter seats inside, to awnings and antique lettering on the outside. Here, the counter men wear T-shirts, and waitresses have been known to

shout food orders back to the cooks, just like it's s'posed to be. Miss Flo has been written up in *The New York Times* and *Diners of the Northeast,* and she's revered by the nearby Smithies. A local institution, to be sure.

Tom Alexander, the owner, gets a bit annoyed if you get too caught up in the ambiance. He's most proud of the home cooking, which at these prices can't be beat.

The menu is enormous—literally something for everybody. You'll find chow mein ($3.75) next to chicken cacciatore ($4.45) next to mushroom caps and bacon ($3.45) next to roast stuffed duckling ($6.95). If that's not enough diversity, you'll find lox and bagels (three kinds of bagels), fried tripe, and lobster en casserole. Of course, there's also a tremendous selection of sandwiches, all at reasonable prices. The humble hamburger goes for 85 cents.

HOURS Sun.–Thu. 4:30 am (early enough?)–10:30 pm; Fri. & Sat. 4:30 am–11 pm.

DIRECTIONS Located in the town of Florence, Mass., Miss Flo's a bit harder to reach than other places, but worth it.

Northbound: Take Exit 19. At bottom of ramp go straight across Route 9 onto Damon Rd. Go 0.8 mile on Damon to light. Go straight. The road name here changes to Bridge St. Follow directions below from Bridge St. to diner.

Southbound: From Exit 20, turn right at the first light, which puts you on Bridge St. Go 1.6 miles to Chestnut St. on left (florist is at right). Take Chestnut to first light, which is Main St. Right on Main, for 0.2 mile to **Miss Flo** on right.

FILLIN' STATION ONE, *Exit 25, Whately*

This restaurant rises from a sea of asphalt like a 1950s vision of the space age. It's a diner in stainless steel and floor-to-ceiling windows. Widening a good three feet in every direction as it goes from ground level to roofline, the building looks as if it's about to take off. It was moved here from nearby Chicopee, apparently to the annoyance of Whately, whose zoning laws forbade any sort of sign that would be visible from the interstate. In order to draw attention his way, the owner somehow got a nearby house painted pink with enormous purple polka dots. The polka dots—indeed, the entire house—are gone now, and the Fillin' Station has sunk back into invisibility to all but those who know. But it's right there at the interchange, accessible as any McDonald's.

It's a fun stop, featuring diner fare (we recommend the blueberry muffins), and what manager Jean Better calls "the fastest cup of coffee in New England." Try to chat with Jean while you're there. She's got a lot of charm, and she'll tell you the God's honest truth about what's good on the menu or anything else about the place.

HOURS 24 hours, every day but Christmas.

DIRECTIONS Take Exit 24 (Whately). Turn onto Route 5 South toward Whately. It's a stone's throw, on the left, by the BP station.

SERETTA'S, *Exit 26, Greenfield*

In both food and decor, Seretta's seems to have a dual personality. With highly glossed wooden booths, old-timey magazine ads on the walls, and tiny glass creamers on the tables, the restaurant has one leg in the '30s. But the jukeboxes have yielded to delicately painted porcelain tiles that give Seretta's a touch of contemporary flair.

At lunchtime, plates and glasses clink as waitresses bustle about, serving Greenfielders for whom this is the midday meeting place. The lunch menu includes diet specials like tomato stuffed with tuna, seafood fresh from Boston, and the usual assortment of sandwiches ($.85 to $1.40).

In the evening, the lighting is dimmed and Seretta's is transformed into what you might expect from its name: an Italian restaurant serving pizza, some interesting appetizers (potato skins stuffed with bacon or cheddar cheese, for example), and pasta dishes in the $3–$5 range.

HOURS Mon.–Thu. 5:30 am–9 pm; Sat. & Sun. 5:30 am–10 pm; Sun. 5:30–11 am.

DIRECTIONS Exit 26 puts you into a traffic circle from which you can take Route 2A East into Greenfield. Go 0.9 mile; **Seretta's** is on the right, between the police station and Beneficial, at 265 Main St.

FIVE 'N' TEN PUB
FOUR LEAF CLOVER RESTAURANT, *Exits 28 & 28B, Bernardston*

Bernardston (say "BER-nuds-tin" if you want to sound like a native) has two restaurants that match the character of the town itself—modest but inviting.

Although its prices are slightly higher than five and ten cents, the **Five 'n' Ten Pub** is pubby indeed—lots of dark wood paneling, small wooden tables, and a bar. It offers an interesting selection of breakfast items, light sandwiches, and salads, along with house specialties like pocket bread loaded with homemade chili, lettuce, tomato, and melted cheese, or an open-faced burger on black bread with grilled onions and melted Swiss (both are $2.50). At breakfast time, two eggs, juice, toast, and coffee are only 99 cents, while kielbasa links with eggs and home fries go for $2. Like many of the traditional English pubs that John and Debbie Tustin are trying to emulate, this one is situated in an old inn; it is undergoing a gradual renovation for future operation.

Full meals as well as sandwiches can be had just around the corner at the **Four Leaf Clover.** This family restaurant prides itself on fresh seafood brought in daily from Boston and cooked in any manner requested. Since 1949, owner Charles Skiathitis has had his hands in every aspect of fish cookery from scaling to saucing. Piping-hot clam chowder comes out of his kitchen in bowls imprinted with a Chinese design—a touch of the exotic in an establishment that otherwise feels very American. Prices are reasonable—dinners average $5.50, while a hamburger with onion rings is a giveaway at $1.15.

HOURS **Five 'n' Ten Pub:** Tue.–Sat. 6–10 am and 11 am–9 pm; Sun. 8 am–midnight; closed Mon.

Four Leaf Clover: Mon.–Thu. 10 am–9 pm; Fri. 10 am–9:30 pm; Sat. 9 am–9:30 pm; Sun. 9 am–9 pm.

DIRECTIONS If northbound, take Exit 28B; if southbound, take Exit 28. Either way, turn right onto Route 10 South and go 0.6 mile to the **Five 'n' Ten Pub,** on right. For the **Four Leaf Clover,** turn left here onto South St. and go 0.1 mile; it's on the right.

Vermont

AUTUMN WINDS, *Exit 2, Brattleboro*

Intimate and tasteful, with excellent food in a continental vein, Autumn Winds is hidden away at the rear of the Main Street Gallery, a former dime store that is now home to some of Brattleboro's artier businesses. Its sequestered location makes it a challenge to locate for those who don't know the town, but it also gives the restaurant a lovely view of the Connecticut River and Mount Wantastiquet beyond. The glassed-in deck, pine-paneled and perched high above the water, takes full advantage of the scenery, and provides as lovely a lunch spot as is to be found.

"We do everything the hard way—no microwaves, no portion control, our own soup stocks, everything. I left New York to get out of the nine-to-five rat race, but now it's nine to midnight," says co-owner Bob Artig with a smile of manifest pride. Before opening, he and Marsha Heller, the chef, planned Autumn Winds for three years, designed it, and even wielded the hammers that built it.

With great results. Not only is the atmosphere warm and elegantly relaxed—soft salmon and brown colors, wallpaper, plants, and natural wood—but the food is good enough to have attracted the attention of *Gourmet* magazine. The magazine featured Autumn Winds' scampi recipe, and we suggest that *Gourmet*'s epicurean editors also take a look at the beef and mushroom crepe with its rich, full flavor and smooth sauce. Or the wonderful chocolate mocha cake.

There are about eight dinners, from $7.50 (for a vegetarian quiche) to $15.95 (for lamb chops with mint vinaigrette). Veal piccata goes for $11.95; chicken breast stuffed with Virginia ham, spinach, and Vermont cheddar is $8.95. If you'd be happy with lighter fare, and you're willing to forgo a table on the popular greenhouse deck, a light—and low-priced—menu that includes Mexican specialties is available on weekday evenings.

Lunchtime can be fancy or just sandwiches (around $3.50), soup/salad/bread ($3.75), or prosciutto and fruit ($3.50). Be it beef Bourguignon or a burger, at Autumn Winds it'll be special.

HOURS Mon.–Thu. 11:30 am–9 pm; Fri. & Sat. 11:30 am–10 pm; closed Sun.

DIRECTIONS From Exit 2 turn left onto Route 9 East to traffic light (Main St.). Look directly across the street and slightly to your left and you'll see Main Street Gallery. It's in there.

THE COMMON GROUND, *Exit 2, Brattleboro*

This worker-owned natural foods eatery started nursing today's bean sprout generation before anyone else had heard of tofu or tamari, but it now pulls in a crowd as diverse as its international fare. In two spare and unpretentious rooms, you are as likely to plunk down your self-served soup bowl next to a lawyer as to an artist in paint-smeared overalls.

Here, crackers and hummus (chickpeas mashed with lemon, garlic, and sesame seeds) are a popular appetizer, while for main courses whole grains and fresh vegetables are the order of the day. So are honey and maple syrup as dessert sweeteners, herb teas (15 of 'em to choose from—but freshly ground coffee too), and a serve-yourself counter with a big pot of vegetarian soup and a salad. In addition to the wok and grill specialties on the menu, there is a rotating schedule of international dishes—mushroom moussaka, tamale pie, and eggplant parmigiana, for example. Lunch prices are all very reasonable—$2.50 to $3.50; most dinners run between $5 and $7, but there's always brown rice, tofu, and stir-fried vegetables at $3.30. The food, by the way, is not strictly vegetarian, although the tone certainly is. Beer and wine are served, and a pass-the-hat musician adds garnish to the ambiance on weekend evenings.

If you decide that this wholesome Vermont living is too good to leave behind, you can peruse the extensive bulletin board for a local farmstead.

HOURS Mon., Wed.–Sat. 11:30 am–9 pm; Tues. 11:30 am–4 pm; Sun. 10:30 am–1:30 pm and 5:30–9 pm.

DIRECTIONS From Exit 2 turn left onto Route 9 East to traffic light. Turn right (Main St.) for one block. Turn right again (Elliot St.). **The Common Ground** is one block down, on the right, just before the parking lot. Up one flight of stairs.

THE TAVERN, *Exit 3, Brattleboro*

This place is done up in the best sort of '80s taste: exposed wooden beams, hanging plants, floor-to-ceiling windows, earth tones, and natural light. Get the picture? In winter, add a glowing fire.

The food seconds the decor—it's the new American cuisine of spinach salad ($2.45 and $3.45), crepes and quiche ($2.75 to $5.50), and four kinds of fondue. The selection of sandwiches would please anyone who likes to experiment with what's put between two slices of bread. Grilled meatloaf and cranberries with melted cheddar; sourdough roll with avocado, tomato, sprouts, and melted cheese; and turkey on date-nut bread with currant sauce (all $3.25) are but one-sixth of the innovative collection.

With a storefront of its own behind the restaurant, the **Great Expectations Pastry Shoppe** serves up some pretty snazzy items that find their way into the dining room: pumpkin cheesecake, carrot cake, pecan pie, English trifle, and more.

All in all, the Tavern is a very pleasant place for a meal, a snack, or a late-night drink. Its atmosphere isn't hurt by the personable young waitresses who dart about in long skirts and leotard tops.

HOURS Every day 11:30 am–midnight.

DIRECTIONS From Exit 3 turn right at the light and go 0.7 mile south on Route 5. **The Tavern** is on the left, its charm belied by the Colonial Motel's "Welcome Tom and Amy Keller"–type sign.

THE GOLD NUGGET, *Exit 3, Brattleboro*

It's heartening to know that there's one place, at least, where local ownership won out over conglomerate cooking. Here, in a former A&W stand, five members of the Hodgdon family (all women) run a breakfast and lunch place with a big local following.

You can tell from the road that it's no ordinary lunch stand. A large, hand-painted picture of a bear fishing below a cascading waterfall curves over the roof and pours down the front window. (It seems the father of this family worked on the Alaska pipeline.) The old A&W menu that towered over the parking area has been converted to a deep-sea mural complete with diver, lobster, anchor, and octopus. (He's in the seafood business, too.)

Grace Hodgdon is the head cook here, and it was she who invented the Nugget's chowder-from-scratch recipe. Check it out for $1 a bowl. Her sister-in-law Anna does the baking at home, bringing in such treats as doughnuts and wild-rice muffins fresh each morning. Grace's daughter Vicky is manager, night cook, and food preparer, while another daughter, Pat, is the big brain behind the operation, concentrating on bookwork and ordering. Grace's niece Loreli is a waitress. There's only one key personality who isn't a Hodgdon—the local lady who bakes the whole wheat bread after stone-grinding the flour herself!

Two eggs, toast, and fries are $1.10 at the Gold Nugget, with coffee and bacon, $2.25. Special sandwiches, including a vegetable concoction, are $1.95; more common varieties about $1.50. Add 40 cents for homemade bread. There's yogurt with raisins, honey, and nuts for $1.75.

HOURS Mon.–Sat. 5 am–4 pm. (If you're there at 5 you can help the truckers take the chairs off the tables.) Closed Sun.

DIRECTIONS From Exit 3 turn right at the light onto Route 5 South. In 1 mile it's on the left, slightly hidden—look for its colorful sign.

CONDELLO RESTAURANT AND PIZZERIA, *Exit 3, Brattleboro*

Whether you choose the pleasant little restaurant in the front or the strictly functional pizzeria around the back, you'll find first-rate Italian cooking prepared by a chef with 17 years' experience in the old country.

Maria and Giuseppe Condello are up at six each morning to start the sauces simmering and the breads rising. They do everything themselves, absolutely from scratch, and it shows. The pizza, for example, comes on a marvelously light crust with a full-flavored sauce that just had to have cooked a long time ($3.50 and up). The sausage topping, a delicate, sweet Italian version, is made right here. Spaghetti is served with a dozen different well-executed sauces including garlic and oil, chicken liver, shrimp, and clam ($4.50 to $7.50). For vegetarian epicures, Giuseppe makes a lovely asparagus parmigiana ($4.95)—fresh asparagus in summer.

It's hard to point to the most popular dish at Condello's—with confidence, regulars often ask Giuseppe to order for them—but tortellini Alfredo must rank high. Tortellini are small, doughnut-shaped pasta creations, stuffed with ground veal and cheese. At Condello's they're cooked al dente, flavored with basil and nutmeg, and then garnished with a rich cream sauce. It is reasonably priced at $6.50, but meatless fettucini Alfredo comes in at the same price. Yes, Condello's pricing does seem a bit inconsistent and sometimes a bit high. Bean soup, for instance, is revered by his devotees, but at $3.25 a bowl, most of us would just as soon get on with the main course.

There's another kind of price you'll have to pay if you want pizza. Unfortunately, it's available only in the back room, which is dominated by a monstrous jukebox that at any given moment has about a 50 percent chance of being played. There's no place in the tiny room that offers refuge, but if you plead with Maria, she'll turn the volume down to mere fortissimo.

Still, not even loud music can drown out the flavors of Condello's carefully prepared, homemade food. And don't walk out the door without trying one of Giuseppe's own cannoli. If you've tasted better, please tell us where.

HOURS **Pizzeria:** Mon. & Wed.–Sat. 11 am–10 pm; Sun. 3–10 pm. **Restaurant:** Mon. & Wed.–Sun. 4–10 pm. Both closed Tuesdays and much of May.

DIRECTIONS From Exit 3 turn left at the light. Go ¼ mile. It's on the left, just after Susse Chalet.

CURTIS'S BAR-B-Q, *Exit 4, Putney*

Although it has been here only a few years, Curtis's Bar-B-Q has become a Putney institution. Some of Curtis's customers—who had heard about him as far away as Texas and Florida—are used to outdoor pit barbecues, but here in the north country there isn't anything else like it.

It's a little toolshed of a building that Curtis built himself out of two-by-fours, locust posts, tin, and screening. Smack in the middle of the dirt floor is the 4-by-4-foot cement-block pit that holds the coals (all from hardwood he cut and stacked himself).

Architecturally, that's all there is to it, but socially there's a whole lot more. On summer afternoons and evenings, Curtis's is hopping like a sideshow at Ringling Brothers (which the large Day-Glow sign is painted to resemble). The small parking area is crowded with every kind of vehicle, from motorcycles to Mercedes. If he's not behind the serving window, Curtis is circulating among the picnic tables, swapping tales with old friends and making new ones.

It's not hard to befriend the likable Floridian, especially after you've tasted his food. Ribs, chicken, and a few side dishes—

that's all there is, but that's all there need be. Curtis drives 75 miles to get the ribs from a meat packer in Springfield, Mass., because, as he says, "they just don't come like this anywhere else." You can watch them slowly roasting in arm's-length slabs, each swollen with juicy meat. For $3.50 you get three or four delectable ribs, slightly charred on the surface, tender and juicy inside. Half a good-sized chicken goes for $3. In the last five minutes of cooking, Curtis bathes the meat with his special sauce—the recipe's been a family secret for over 60 years, so don't expect to get it out of him.

Soft drinks and his own baked beans round out the menu. If you want anything else, you'll have to bring it yourself. Beer maybe, but a bottle of Château Mouton-Rothschild might seem out of place.

HOURS Open "as soon as the snow melts" (April sometime) until "end of hunting season" (Thanksgiving weekend).
Thu.–Sun. 11:30 am–9 pm; closed Mon.–Wed.

DIRECTIONS Northbound: From Exit 4 turn left (signs for Putney Village). Cross over highway and look to your right. He's adjacent to the Mobil station, just before Route 5.

Southbound: From Exit 4 turn right onto Route 5 North. Drive about ¼ mile and look right. He's adjacent to the Mobil station.

VILLAGE ROOM, *Exit 4, Putney*

With more and more urbanites transplanting themselves to Vermont soil, a new kind of melting pot is brewing. On the same small-town streets, "flatlanders," who go in for cross-country skiing and backpacking, mingle with "real Vermonters," who tend to prefer snowmobiles and deer hunting. It's happening all over the state, but in Putney it's a long-standing tradition.

Here, in the very building that housed America's first commune a century ago, is a little lunchroom that reflects Putney's eclecticism. The Village Room has a regular clientele of local working people, but it also accommodates a steady flow of "alternative types." The menu satisfies both camps.

Accompanying the traditional luncheonette menu (French toast with real maple syrup for $1.50; a BLT for $1.75) are such items as vegetable sandwiches on whole wheat bread ($1.95) and yogurt with fresh fruit, nuts, and a splash of honey ($1.95). The honey comes from owner Louise Stinson's own beehives, and you can put it in a mug of Celestial Seasonings herb tea. Louise uses her honey with buttermilk in cornbread; it's prepared according to an old frontier recipe that she dug up. All her soups are homemade, and seafood chowder with shrimp, lobster, and clams is her pride.

And if you want to celebrate because you just made it onto the U.S. Cross-Country Ski Team (you won't be the first from Putney), or because you just got a new Ford pickup, you can do it right here in the Village Room—Louise keeps champagne on hand for just such occasions.

HOURS 6 am–4 pm, daily; closed Sundays in June.

DIRECTIONS Northbound: From Exit 4 turn left. Bear right onto Route 5 North (signs to Putney Village). Restaurant is on the right after ½ mile.

Southbound: From Exit 4 turn right on Route 5 North for 0.7 mile. Restaurant is on your right.

WESTMINSTER MOTOR INN RESTAURANT, *Exit 5, Westminster*

The local people come here from Putney and Westminster West, from Bellows Falls and Saxtons River, from Walpole and Alstead, New Hampshire, across the Connecticut River. The daily attraction: the Westminster's buffet luncheon. From Tuesday through Saturday, 11 am until 2:30, it's all you can eat for $3. Three entrées—for example, Swedish meat balls, ham and cheese, and Italian sausage in spaghetti sauce—adorn the steam table, while lettuce, cottage cheese, baked beans, tomatoes, sliced onions, and mushrooms vinaigrette make up the salad bar. (Salad bar alone is available for $2.50.)

The restaurant interior is Ethan Allen style, neat and clean, with dark-stained wooden walls, red tablecloths, and white napkins perched like little tepees astride the plates. Oil paintings of the Covered-Bridge-With-Effervescent-Colors School line a shelf that rims the large dining room.

In addition to the buffet, there are other luncheon options (seafood Newburg or fried chicken, for instance, in the $3.50–$5.25 range). On some dishes, senior citizens get a discount of 10 percent.

Dinners are steak house fare: New York sirloin with mushrooms, tenderloin with Bordelaise sauce, broiled haddock, and lobster chunks ($6.50–$10). Baked stuffed shrimp dressed with a breadcrumb-herbs-and-Chablis stuffing is the house specialty at $8.50. And on Friday nights, an all-you-can-eat buffet with nine entrées and salad bar will send you tottering out the door only $6.50 poorer.

HOURS Tue.–Sat. 11 am–9 pm; Sun. 11 am–3 pm; closed Mon.

DIRECTIONS From Exit 5 follow signs for Route 5. Turn right on Route 5 South for 2½ miles. Motor inn and restaurant are on the left.

MISS BELLOWS FALLS DINER, *Exits 5 & 6, Bellows Falls*

* *Color, not cuisine*

If the Miss Flo (p. 94) is the Duesenberg of diners, then the "Miss Bell" is an old Ford pickup that's been hard at work for a long, long time. She's still running, but the dents, rust, and grease make you wonder how much farther she'll go.

This tiny diner boasts a marble counter, an oak refrigerator and paneling, an intricate three-color mosaic tile floor, some stained glass, railroad-type windows (thumb-latched in the corners), overhead fans, and a glass-brick entryway. If that's not enough, the booths are all wood, and the exterior is the classic enamel-covered metal. But believe us, you won't for a second suspect that anything here was preserved deliberately. The Miss Bellows Falls didn't get in on the craze for old things; she just aged ungracefully. Despite her classic lines, she remains a workingman's eatery, as befits this working town.

Most of the menu is on bespattered, 8-by-11-inch homemade

drawings that hang from a wire along the length of the counter. A smiling fish bathing in a frying pan advertises haddock for $2.35. Some happy Humpty Dumpty eggs offer one of their own with toast, juice, and coffee for 95 cents. Two chickens intent on their croquet mallets tempt you with you-can-guess-what at $2.20.

If it is character, authenticity, and economy that you want, the Miss Bellows Falls is the place to go. Bring the Bromo.

HOURS Mon.–Thu. 5:30 am–7 pm; Fri. & Sat. 5:30 am–9 pm; Sun. 6 am–9 pm.

DIRECTIONS See **The Yellow Rose Restaurant,** below.

THE YELLOW ROSE RESTAURANT, *Exits 5 & 6, Bellows Falls*

The Yellow Rose is a village restaurant with some differences. The decor is light and pleasant, simple but inviting. During the week the clientele are the ordinary people of Bellows Falls—storekeepers, clerks, shoppers—who breakfast on pancakes ($1.95), lunch on sandwiches (about $2.25), and dine on ham steak ($5.95). It's always been that way and it probably always will be.

But you'll see that there are also quiche and salad, bagels, and nightly dinner specials. Chinese food is featured on Wednesday, and Italian (with homemade pasta) on Thursday. At dinnertime the fluorescent lights go out, and candles and tablecloths soften the lunchroom feeling.

On Friday night things change. Local people still eat at the Yellow Rose, but they are joined by out-of-towners weekending at the **Andrews Inn** next door. Owned and operated in tandem with the Yellow Rose, the Andrews Inn is the only gay hotel in rural New England. As you might expect, the weekend clientele bring a style not often found in this blue-collar town—until recently the townspeople thought "gay" meant "merry." By now, their vocabulary, if not their consciousness, has been expanded.

On Saturday evening, the hotel lobby is converted to a gourmet restaurant serving treats like tournedos of beef ($15.50), salmon with Hollandaise sauce ($12.50), and mushroom-stuffed chicken breasts ($9.95). As leftovers, these delicacies appear in the Yellow Rose (at village restaurant prices) on Monday and Tuesday.

It was 1975 when this old brick railroad hotel, solid as a bank vault, was converted to its present use. There was some friction with the townspeople when the new owner took over, but by now tensions seem to have dissolved into a state of amicable coexistence.

Anyone is welcome at either establishment, but if you choose to try the gourmet dinner you'll be informed of the nature of things. It's all pretty candid here, without hostility. The feeling is matter-of-fact, friendly, and more straightforward than at many a "straight" establishment.

HOURS Winter: Mon.–Thu. 7 am–3 pm; Fri. 7 am–9 pm; Sat 8 am–5 pm; Sun. 8 am–3 pm; Gourmet dinner: Sat. 6:30–8:30 pm.
Summer: Mon.–Thu. 7 am–8 pm. Other days same as winter.

DIRECTIONS **Note:** Bellows Falls is between Exits 5 and 6. You can rejoin highway by continuing along Route 5 to next exit without retracing your steps.

Northbound: From Exit 5 bear right, following signs for Route 5 North. On Route 5, go 2.6 miles to the fork and bear right toward business district. **The Yellow Rose** is on your right, at the village square. Continue through town for ½ mile to **Miss Bellows Falls,** on left.

Southbound: From Exit 6 take Route 5 South for 3.6 miles. **Miss Bellows Falls** is on the right. Continue ½ mile to the village square; **The Yellow Rose** is on the left.

THE PADDOCK, *Exit 7, Springfield*

The back side of the Paddock's menu lists mileages to major cities all over the U.S. and the world (1670 to New Orleans; 10,772 to Melbourne). Restaurant manager Libby Lausier doesn't claim to have served guests from every one of these ports, but the Paddock's reputation is far-flung indeed. "I'm sure that someone, somewhere, doesn't like the food here, but he hasn't spoken up," she declares, proudly and honestly.

Restaurants that look like barns aren't altogether rare in Vermont, but the Paddock is true to its name: it's a barn that now looks like a restaurant. Centuries-old hand-hewn beams hold up the structure, while the walls and tables are of plain wood and the floor is unflossed. "It's genuine rustic, no monkey business," says Libby with upbeat confidence as she walks past dining booths built into what were once cow stalls. To make the point, she pushes open a little window next to a table. The window is just the right size for a horse's head. "This is how they fed the stock in those days," she adds.

Because an unaltered barn would be too dark for family dining, an entire wall of the Paddock has been replaced with glass. The expansive window lets in not only light, but also a lovely view of lush woods, manicured grounds, terraced stonework, a goldfish pond, and a nearby river.

The food, as you might expect, is American as apple pie (or lemon meringue, or coconut cream, or any of a dozen others served here). Some entrées: roast turkey with sage dressing, pork chops with apple jelly, fried shrimp butterfly style, pan-fried brook trout, and Alaska king crab (the chef's specialty).

Everything—absolutely everything—is made from scratch on the premises, and nothing—absolutely nothing—is frozen. A full-time pastry chef prepares 20–25 desserts to choose from, twice that number on holidays.

Prices ($7.95 to $12.95) are for complete dinners: cheese and crackers, entrée, potato, vegetable, salad, rolls, beverage, and dessert. You can get a second helping for an extra dollar. A low-priced children's menu is available.

The Paddock takes no reservations. "If they can't seat you in the dining room, they'll seat you in the living room," says a frequent guest. We're not sure it's true, but she certainly caught the spirit of the place.

HOURS Tue.–Fri. 5–9 pm; Sat. 5–10 pm; Sun. noon–3 pm and 5–8 pm; closed Mondays and all of January.

DIRECTIONS From Exit 7 follow signs for Springfield (Routes 11 West and 106 North). Go about ½ mile to Paddock Rd., on the right. Restaurant is 0.4 mile up Paddock Rd.

HAPPY FAMILY CHINESE RESTAURANT, *Exit 7, Springfield*

Curious about such things, we stopped to see what future was in store for an old Springfield diner that had just been painted bright blue and orange. Our enthusiasm quickened when we found it under renovation by an Oriental construction crew. Could it be . . . ?

Yes! Under construction was a Chinese diner, perhaps the first in Vermont, maybe in all New England. And no chop suey, we were told. Only Szechuan, Hunan, and other authentic Chinese cuisines.

It's to be called the Happy Family (all of whom were busy at work with picks and saws). We wish them well. Hard work and good food make great success for happy family.

DIRECTIONS From Exit 7 follow signs for Springfield. Restaurant is on your left, 3.1 miles from the highway, just beyond the Jones and Lamson factory complex.

WINDSOR STATION, *Exits 8 & 9, Windsor*

In the '60s and '70s, new restaurants tried to appear old by adopting historical motifs; railroading became one of the popular themes to dine by. By now, the age of golden spikes and iron men might be a hackneyed design for a restaurant, but this one manages to avoid clichés.

For one thing—and it's a big plus—the building is an actual passenger depot that dates back to 1900. Trains still roar by (although they no longer stop here), and for two minutes after their passing the owners knock 50 cents off the price of drinks. The depot's yellow pine ceiling, once covered with grime and cobwebs, is as intricate as a fancy floor. All the memorabilia on the walls come from the original building—no zealous restaurateur combed antique shops from Maine to Oregon in search of railroading mementos to clutter every corner. Pictures depicting the depot's active youth were donated by local folks during the building's reconstruction; they were grateful to see something good come of the neglected station that had served them well. Some had even worked in the round Station Master's Room, now a secluded dining area.

On one side of the entrance to current-day Windsor Station is a lounge famous for its lampshade made of 400 Coke bottles. Light meals at moderate prices ($3.50 average) are served here. For example, the "Olde English Cheese Delight": tomatoes and bacon on toast, covered with melted cheese, and served with coleslaw and French fries for $2.90.

The main dining area serves continental cuisine and a few old-fashioned New England dishes like "salmon pea wiggle," fish and peas in white sauce. Luncheon entrées are in the $2.50–$5 range. The dinner menu ($7–$11) has a strong emphasis on veal and seafood (swordfish in light mustard sauce is a specialty). Owners Rudy and Pat Alghieri have a hard time being modest about their French onion soup; they enthusiastically recall the time it was sampled by a chef from "up valley" who "went absolutely crazy."

HOURS Mon.–Thu. 11:30 am–2:30 pm and 5:30–9 pm; Fri. & Sat. 5:30–10 pm; closed Sun.

DIRECTIONS **Note:** Windsor is between Exits 8 and 9 on I-91. Rejoin highway by continuing on Route 5 instead of retracing your route.

Northbound: From Exit 8 bear right at end of ramp, following signs to Windsor. Go 0.3 mile and turn left on Route 5 North. Go 5½ miles into town center and turn right on Depot Rd. Restaurant is facing you at end of road.

Southbound: From Exit 9 turn left, following signs for Windsor. Go 3.8 miles into town on Route 5 South. Turn left on Depot Rd. Restaurant is at end of road.

SKUNK HOLLOW TAVERN, *Exit 9, Hartland*

Hartland Four Corners may have one more corner than Hartland Three Corners down the road, but it's got one fewer general store. In fact, the Skunk Hollow Tavern is the only commercial establishment of any kind in Hartland Four Corners, and if the Tavern didn't charge for its services, you might think you were in someone's living room.

Upstairs is the dining area. Intimate and elegant, it is as close to a living room as a restaurant could possibly be—probably because it once was. Covered with paisley tablecloths that match the curtains, nine small square tables stand around one of Vermont's own Defiant wood stoves (removed in summer). The low ceiling, clean white walls, blond hardwood floor, and bay-window alcove reinforce the feeling of unaffected simplicity.

The cuisine matches the decor—the menu is small but the food is very well prepared. There are six appetizers, six entrées, and six desserts to choose from, including escalopes of veal ($9.25), chicken curry ($8.75), and pan-fried fresh fish of the day ($9.60). Despite its price tag ($13.25), the bouillabaisse—fresh fish stew seasoned with saffron—keeps Skunk Hollow's small but faithful dining-room clientele returning time after time. And for good reason: it's simply superb.

Downstairs, Skunk Hollow Tavern is a different animal. Here too, the owners did little to embellish the original room; it is an undisguised basement taproom. The earthy feeling of an 18th century pub comes right out of the masonry walls and exposed woodwork, both of which belong to the original structure. On cold days, a crackling fire in the old brick fireplace completes the picture.

Meals downstairs are pub-style, but with an American accent. Fish and chips, pizza, breaded veal, vegetable quiche, and steamed mussels are in the $2.50–$4.25 range. Spicy spaghetti

Sicilienne ($3.50) is a favorite with the downstairs crowd. All in all, it's a very hospitable place to have a meal, a drink, or a round of darts.

HOURS Wed.–Sun. 6 pm–10 pm; closed Mon. & Tue.

DIRECTIONS From Exit 9 take Route 5 North to Hartland. Turn left at intersection of Route 5 and Route 12. Go 1.3 miles and turn left at the tiny post office. **Skunk Hollow Tavern** is the third building on your right.

LANDER'S
THE OWL'S NEST, *Exit 10, White River Junction*

See pp. 37–38 for descriptions of a Lebanese restaurant (in Lebanon, N.H.) and a place with hundreds of Tiffany-style lamps.

DIRECTIONS At Exit 10, I-91, get on I-89 East and go to Exit 18 or 19. Then follow directions given.

THE COOLIDGE HOTEL, *Exit 11, White River Junction*

It's well worth the five-minute drive into White River Junction just to look at this fine old railroad hotel and peek into its elegant dining room.

White River is a hard-working, dirty-brick town that has seen better days, and so had the Coolidge until it was renovated in 1970. Now it's the local showplace. The lobby is a light, comfortable, high-ceilinged room decorated in an unaffected modern style with several inviting couches and a fireplace. In the dining room, gracefully fluted white columns contrast quietly with blue floral wallpaper and eight chandeliers that, according to the maitre d', are in the Venetian style of Archduke Franz Joseph. The tables are beautifully set with bright white linen.

The Coolidge's food equals its decor in quality. The menu is mostly continental, drawn from France, Italy, Switzerland, and Austria; it features five veal dishes along with beef and fish. Veal in wine and cream sauce with mushrooms is a delicious house specialty, and the fresh zucchini that comes with it showed us what gastronomic heights that humble vegetable could achieve. The dinner includes appetizer, soup, salad, green vegetable, potato or rice, bread, and coffee—all for $10.95. Not bad, really, for a total experience.

You can lunch in this same environment for equally modest prices. Chowder, a steak sandwich, and coffee are only $2.95; a full lunch of beef Stroganoff is only $4. There's even a roast beef sandwich for $1.95!

HOURS Mon.–Fri. 11:30 am–2 pm and 6–10 pm; Sat. 6–10 pm; closed Sun.

DIRECTIONS Take Exit 11 and follow signs for Route 5 North and White River Junction. At 0.9 mile, Route 5 goes off to the left. Keep going straight for about ½ mile into town. At the stop sign, go around the block with a right followed by two lefts. It's ½ block from your final left to the hotel (on your left).

THAN WHEELER'S, *Exit 11, White River Junction*

The front of the menu says "Than Wheeler's with Muriel," and Muriel's presence is felt everywhere. After years of world travel, during which she visited—and cooked—on every continent, Muriel Barclay-de Tolly (she's French Canadian) decided in 1978 to settle in the old railroad town of White River Junction. It was her intention to open a restaurant and tavern that would serve as a warm, sincere place, full of cozy, quaint corners like a French cabaret—a place where people would feel comfortable meeting each other without the pace and pressure of a singles bar.

From the looks of things, she has succeeded. We were there in midafternoon, not ordinarily a bustling time of day for rathskellers like this, but there was an amiable group of people talking, eating, reading newspapers, and playing cribbage. Muriel's welcoming smile was so genuine that we were almost ready to move in. And her food certainly didn't change our minds.

Muriel is known around town for her soups. Local people often buy them just to take home. French pea is on the menu every day, and her soups du jour include the likes of cream of asparagus, cream of broccoli, and fish chowder.

The blackboard that greets visitors announces all kinds of specials. Ham steak with pineapple chunks and cheddar cheese, for example, is $3.25. It includes rolls and a salad with Muriel's mildly cheesy dressing that we found altogether delightful. Chicken almondine is her special favorite. Although chicken, raisins, almonds, bananas, and mild curry sauce may seem an incongruous potpourri of flavors, Muriel has a way of bringing them into an absolutely delicious meld. It is served on a bed of rice for $4.75, or in a crepe for $3.25. Muriel also offers some fancy sandwiches like open steak with pepper and onions on rye, pumpernickel, or bulky roll ($3.50, with salad).

The restaurant, by the way, is named for a famous White River personage, Nathaniel ("Than") Wheeler, who in the '20s was a railroad man, philanthropist, and colorful character about town. Once you meet her, you'll see why Muriel named the restaurant for him.

HOURS Mon.–Sat. 11:30 am–midnight; closed Sun.

DIRECTIONS Next door to the **Coolidge Hotel** (above), under a red canopy.

PETER CHRISTIAN'S TAVERN, *Exit 13, Hanover*

Peter Christian's is a pubby sort of place lodged in a cellar that opens onto Hanover's impeccable Main Street. Dartmouth students and local people all seem to agree on the quality of its food, and we have to concur. There are excellent soups, sandwiches, and salads, plus a sweet-and-sour mustard sauce that turns a sandwich into a memorable event.

You go down a few steps and through a small arched door into a dark but very pleasant room. Although the tables and booths are made of heavy walnut-stained pine, and matched by imported barn beams, there's nothing oppressive about the place. The plates and mugs are all hand-thrown pottery, and there are even fresh flowers on the tables. Local art work enlivens the walls, and the likes of Simon and Garfunkel play quietly in the background.

Standard meat and cheese sandwiches are made with Peter's famous sauce on rye, pumpernickel, whole wheat, or roll (about $2.75). Reubens, turkey and Boursin (garlic cheese), and other fancy combinations are $3.25–$3.75. Half a sandwich is half the price; it's available with salad or soup. There are spinach and garden salads (sans iceberg), along with beef stew ($2.75 for a generous mug) and three soups from scratch.

At night, there's one dinner special somewhere between $4 and $6. It could be shrimp creole or chicken breast with almonds, but on Sunday it'll be Mexican.

If you arrive at the height of mealtime, be prepared for a 15-minute wait in a line that flows up the stairs and onto Main Street. But rumor has it that the wait can be fun—people seem to be in a good mood when they're coming here.

For dessert, if you are of the ice cream persuasion, you might check out the **Ice Cream Machine** at 27 Lebanon Street. Like half a dozen places in every state, it's said to have the best ice cream in the world.

HOURS Mon.–Sat. 11:30 am–12:30 am; Sun. 5–11:30 pm.

DIRECTIONS From Exit 13 turn left if southbound, right if northbound, onto Route 10A East. Go 0.8 mile, over Connecticut River, and into New Hampshire to first light. Right at the light, about two blocks. It's downstairs, on the right, just before the town offices, which are set well back from the street. The sign is small.

CARPENTER STREET AT THE 1820 HOUSE, *Exit 13, Norwich*

Here's as elegant and intimate a little restaurant as you're likely to find anywhere—and perfect for a highway break, with excellent cooking and light meals served at all hours.

Two sisters run Carpenter Street and describe its cooking as eclectic gourmet with a health food accent. Though discernible, the accent is light (and while some natural foods show their healthy faces, sheer pleasure is never sacrificed). Which, we guess, is just the way Connie and Christine Filbin want it to be—health at no cost to the discriminating hedonist.

Philosophical speculations aside, the sautéed veal, baked with prosciutto, white asparagus, Parmesan, and bread crumbs, was simply excellent ($11.95), as was the delicate chicken in champagne sauce with mushrooms and leeks ($9.25), and everything else we tried. A house specialty is linguini with broccoli, cauliflower, mushrooms, and cheeses ($7.50). There are also several wonderful-sounding fish and steak dishes.

Lighter food consists of a pâté served with French bread and gherkins ($2.75); baked Brie, rolled in sliced almonds ($6, but a large portion); chili ($2.50); pistou, a French vegetable soup with pasta ($1.75 cup/$2.25 bowl); three salads; and a variety of sandwiches from $3.50 up.

Carpenter Street is located in a renovated house that dates from 1820. It's done up in the very best modern taste—a goodly dose of natural wood, but an overall feel that is colorful and gay, with red tablecloths, sparkling glassware, and wallpaper in a William Morris pattern.

In summer, meals are served outside in the flower garden café. At any time of the year the restaurant is charming, especially in the parlor, now a small, sweet dining room.

HOURS Tue.–Sat. noon–2 pm and 6–10 pm (light meals, noon–12:30 am). Sun. 6–10 pm for dinner and 4 pm–midnight for light meals. Closed Mon.

DIRECTIONS At end of ramp from Exit 13 turn right if southbound, left if northbound, onto 10A West. Go 0.6 mile; it's on the right.

THE NORWICH INN, *Exit 13, Norwich*

The Norwich Inn is a great favorite among Dartmouth alumni and locals alike. It's a hard place to describe, with a flavor quite its own. The building dates from 1797, but don't come looking for classic lines. It's been added to and altered so many times that the result is . . . well, a big, white clapboard building.

Inside, the feel is half Colonial formal and half country funk. Some of the staff even wear blue jeans, although there's a lobby/living room that's highly decorated with formal drapes, Oriental rug, Colonial wallpaper, and furniture to match. But the rest of the place doesn't seem to be trying to be anything special at all. Another part of the lobby is sheathed in very ordinary wall paneling, and in the dining room the chairs are upholstered in green vinyl, while pink tablecloths peek out at the corners from under white ones.

That's its charm: a little of this, a little of that, and a lot of friendly people.

Many of the clientele we saw were older people who had come to enjoy nicely prepared stuffed filet of sole ($9.95), tournedos Rossini ($13.95), and veal Kottwiz ($11.25). There's an eight-inch rack of lamb (enough for two) at $14.95, and when they're in season you'll find such exotics as pheasant and shad roe.

Lunchtime offers a good variety of sandwiches ($3–$4). Entrées are $3.50–$6.95, and soup du jour plus salad bar is $3.50. You can get breakfast here too—around $3.50 for the works; $1.50 for two eggs and toast.

HOURS Breakfast: every day 7:30–9:30 am; Lunch: Mon.–Sat. noon–2 pm; Dinner: Mon.–Thu. 6–9 pm; Fri. & Sat. 6–10 pm; Sun. brunch: noon–2 pm; Sun. 6–8 pm.

DIRECTIONS See directions for **Carpenter Street,** above. **The Norwich Inn** is right across the street.

FAIRLEE DINER, *Exit 15, Fairlee*

We weren't the first to develop an abiding affection for this wonderful, unpretentious place. It's not even a classic diner—just a squat little clapboard building plunked alongside the Vermont Central railroad tracks. But still, its fame has spread, and people come quite a distance to see what the fuss is all about—much to the amusement of the local populace, no doubt, since nothing could change the fact that this is their restaurant, pure and simple.

What the fuss is about is splendid home cooking at very modest prices served by friendly waitresses who josh with their customers and love the place they work in. It's utterly undecorated—linoleum floors, six booths, a counter made from varnished plywood, and walls painted an unrelenting shade of yellow. But the Fairlee doesn't need decor. The warmth is in the people. "It's like family," one waitress told us. Half the local appeal seems to consist of kibbitzing, New England style. "Did Eunice take her ugly pills today?" asks one laconic fellow in flannel shirt and mud-caked boots. Some customers order by grunt, but it hardly seems to matter—either the waitress knows exactly what they want, or they're happy with whatever they get.

Homemade stews and soups are excellent here. Baked beans, from a family recipe, really *are* made in large crocks used only for that purpose. There are ten kinds of homemade muffins and almost as many doughnuts, along with a great variety of fresh-baked pies, puddings, and custards. Twenty-two full dinners come out of the Fairlee's kitchen, most costing around $3.50, with veal steak as low as $2.75 and porterhouse on top at $12.25. A large bowl of oyster stew is $2.30, baked beans $1.75, and a sandwich with fries costs under $2. Two eggs, juice, toast, and coffee are $1.50.

The Fairlee has been in the family of owner Maurice Roberts for three generations. We found him in the kitchen, hard at work converting a huge tray of roast beef drippings into pan gravy. "We can't compete with McDonald's," he says, with nary a trace of regret, "so we try to stick to home cooking and home recipes." In fact, the Roberts family did open a similar restaurant in nearby East Thetford, but that's as far as their expansion will go. "We thought of getting bigger and bigger, like the chains, but we don't believe that's the route to take. We'd rather work on quality and carve out a niche for ourselves that way."

Need we say more?

HOURS Mon.–Sat. 6 am–8 pm; closed on Sunday, but the Roberts' **Country Cooking** in East Thetford's Pioneer Plaza (Exit 14) is open Sunday, 8:30 am–6:30 pm.

DIRECTIONS From Exit 15 turn right if northbound, left if southbound. Go one block to a T and turn left onto Route 5 North. Then 0.6 mile to the diner, on the right. Look for the Coke sign.

COLATINA EXIT, *Exit 16, Bradford*

* *Untried, but likely*

Hot on the trail of a possible pun, we desperately wanted to learn the story behind this restaurant's name. But it was closed when we got there, and although we did get a tour of the place from a fellow who was getting ready for the night's work, we never did get the story. Alas, we didn't even get to taste the pizza.

But what we *can* tell you is this: for miles around we kept hearing that a place in Bradford called "Colatina Exit" had the best pizza in Vermont. All we know for sure, however, is that the pizza is thrown by hand, and that the dining room is sort of Vermont-Italian, a pleasant blend of barnboard, beams, macramé, tin ceiling, homemade Tiffanyesque lampshades, red-checked tablecloths, and candles in Chianti bottles with suitable quantities of colorful dripped wax.

Besides pizza, there are standard Italian dinners for $5–$6 and sandwiches around $2.50. The 16-inch pizza goes undecorated for $5, and another 50 cents will raise the diameter to half a yard. Complete bar.

HOURS Apr.–Oct.: Sun.–Thu. 5–10 pm; Fri. & Sat. 5–11 pm; November to March they close an hour earlier.

DIRECTIONS At end of Exit 16 ramp turn onto Route 25 East and go 0.4 mile to the light. Then left onto Route 5 North, which you follow for a mile to the center of Bradford. It's on the right.

MISS LYNDONVILLE DINER, *Exit 23, Lyndonville*

A true Yankee, Robert Frost once said, is a person who eats pie for breakfast. If you wish to verify his definition, stop at the Miss Lyndonville Diner between five and nine in the morning, when it is mobbed with a happy collection of college kids, construction workers, truckers, skiers, traveling salesmen, and just about anyone else who lives in or passes through Lyndonville. Among them, you'll find a healthy share of dyed-in-the-wool Yankees starting off their day with pie—most likely Miss Lyndonville's famous strawberry pie. Even in the coldest depths of north-country winter, Janet and Ashley Gray, the industrious owners, go to great lengths to obtain fresh strawberries, which they bake into deep, succulent pies that have been the subject of articles in more than one statewide publication.

Of course, pie is not the only item on the breakfast menu. Homemade bread and fresh jumbo eggs are standards here, and they are often combined to make French toast. For $1.95, you get three thick, deep-fried slices with real maple syrup. Two eggs, toast, and home fries are only $1.35. The soups are all homemade, a super bargain at 60 cents a bowl. Miss Lyndonville also offers steaks, chops, and fish dinners at around $4.50, along with modestly priced plain sandwiches and a variety of hamburgers, all available on homemade bread for a few cents more.

Most likely, the façade of Miss Lyndonville would not have moved the pen of Vermont's poet laureate. It's more Colorado than Vermont—a small, flat rectangle of a building with a wooden porch rail (or is it a fence?) running the length of the roof. Inside, there's evidence of the original diner, but things have been done over in so down-home a way that classification is impossible. Even if Miss L. doesn't win any design awards, it bubbles with a clean, light sense of cheerfulness from the moment you walk in the door.

HOURS Mon.–Thu. 5 am–2 pm; Fri. & Sat. 5 am–9 pm; Sun. 8 am–1 pm (breakfast only).

DIRECTIONS From Exit 23 turn onto Route 5 North and go 0.9 mile. It's on the right.

WILLY'S RESTAURANT, *Exits 23 & 24, East Burke*

* *Far, but excellent*

Willy's is a good ten minutes from the highway, but worth the detour if you've a taste for pungent, robust, German-style cooking.

George Willy III comes by it naturally. For almost eighty years his family ran a restaurant in New York City, and he started working for his grandfather when he was three. In 1979 George moved the whole operation to Vermont and, in good Vermont fashion, spent two years renovating an 1839 church to house it.

New York's loss is Vermont's gain. You can get an excellent sauerbraten here for $8.75, or sweet-cured, smoked pork, roasted with maple syrup and garlic (Willy's specialty), for $8.25. Both were terrific, no ifs, ands, or buts.

There are also many non-German entrées, from $7.75 for the absolutely fresh fish of the day to $24 for a Chateaubriand for two. But if you're looking for something really special, try the roast suckling pig, boned and stuffed with oysters, chestnuts, apples, celery, onions, and brown rice and basted with beer and garlic. That's surely worth the $15/person price tag. There's one slight problem with the roast pig: George needs a week's notice. Oh, another hitch: You'll need a party of fifteen.

Sandwiches and other light foods are available at the bar for around $3.50. Deliciously seasoned, enormous French fries come as freebies.

The high church ceiling, white walls, and plain wood furniture make for an atmosphere that is pleasant but a bit severe. Nevertheless, Willy's seems to generate a good deal of gemütlichkeit. Perhaps it has something to do with the high-spirited ghost of East Burke who's rumored to lodge in the building. George wouldn't talk much about him, though. Every time he's gotten interested in the subject, something has gone wrong. Now George and the ghost live in peaceful coexistence and mutual disregard.

HOURS Wed.–Sun. 5:30–9:30 pm; Bar: 5 pm–1 am. Closed Mon. & Tue.

DIRECTIONS Northbound: Take Exit 23, and at end of ramp turn right onto Route 5 North. Go 1.4 miles to a T. ■ Left at the T, one block to another T. Right, and then 0.7 mile to a fork. Bear right at the fork onto Route 114 and go 4.6 miles to the village of East Burke. It's on your left.

Southbound: (If the following sounds like too much, go to Exit 23 and follow the northbound directions.) Take Exit 24 and make a left onto Route 122S. Follow this for 1.9 miles to where the road makes a sharp left. Take this left, remaining on 122S (note the wild boar statue on a lawn here). Go another ½ mile to the junction with Route 5. Left on Route 5, and you'll soon come to a T. From there on, follow northbound directions from ■.

MISS NEWPORT DINER, *Exit 27, Newport*

The Miss Newport is a gem, probably the cleanest, prettiest, and best preserved of all the classic Worcester Car diners we've seen. So good-looking is she, in fact, that she's on the cover of *Diners of the Northeast*, the bible for those who love these wonderful anachronisms.

Born in 1944, the Miss Newport has not only the customary marble counter, tile floor, arched roof, oak woodwork, and enameled exterior, but she's even got perfect slope-shouldered '50s jukeboxes at every table. Red-checked curtains give a homey feel and drive away any hint of the dreariness that sometimes overtakes diners in their dotage.

The clientele is almost entirely local, bound to the Miss Newport by deep affection and long-standing tradition. The surface of a corner table, for example, is visibly rutted by several men who've been playing cribbage there every morning for 20 years. Good-natured teasing between workers and customers cements the bond. At times the banter becomes out-and-out pranksterism, as when the cook baked a big plastic bug into the deputy sheriff's muffin. He had his revenge a few days later when, after seeing a few coins tossed on the premises, he sent the sheriff over with a subpoena for gambling. But that story pales compared with the merriment ignited when customers draped an enormous sign over the diner: "All You Can Eat—$1.25." Or when they parked a bus out front labeled "Express to McDonald's."

There's food here too. It's generally well prepared and moderately priced. The two local favorites are a meatloaf laced with grapenuts and steak with peppers. Some of the soups are from scratch (ask the waitress), the muffins are homemade, and the coffee is quite good, "the best in town." A hamburger is $1, simple sandwiches generally less than $1.35, and two eggs with toast and coffee go for $1.50.

HOURS Mon.–Fri. 5 am–3:30 pm; Sat. 5–10:30 am; closed Sun.

DIRECTIONS From Exit 27 follow signs for Newport for 2 miles until road ends at a T. Turn right and go one block to light. Right at the light for 0.3 mile. It's on the left.

THE LANDING, *Exit 27, Newport*

One of the owners of the Landing is named Howard Johnson, but fear not, you won't find much in common between this seafood restaurant and what that name brings to mind. It's a new and nicely decorated place right on the shore of Lake Memphremagog, a 32-mile sliver of water, most of which lies in Canada. In summer, Canadians boat down for dinner at the Landing, and the cook can sometimes be seen fishing on the dock for the day's menu. Now that's fresh!

The restaurant itself is a very up-to-date place, tastefully decorated in tones of tan and blue, with lots of lightly stained oak.

Lovely place settings in the same spirit and many small-paned windows overlooking the lake complete the scheme. There's a deck for summertime dining in the open air.

Dinners run from $8.95 to $11.95 and are of the standard American seafood variety with a few beef dishes for those who won't touch fish. Mako shark at $8.95 was the only real surprise.

They've tried to make lunch more out of the ordinary by designing 20 "uncommon" lunches, none more than $3.25. Some samples: grilled salmon patty with cheese topping, deep-fried scallops on a roll with cheese sauce, and "Hawaiian toast," a ham, tomato, and pineapple concoction topped with Swiss.

Four kinds of salads are available, including a seafood special with crab and shrimp for $3.95. There are three soups at about $1.50/bowl, six deli-style sandwiches at $2.75, and a host of plain and fancy hamburgers ($1.95–$3.25).

HOURS Mon.–Sat. 11:30 am–midnight. Dinner 5–9:30 pm, with light meals available other times, either in the dining room or bar. Sun. 11 am–8:30 pm.

DIRECTIONS Take Exit 27 and bear right at end of ramp. Follow signs for Newport for 2 miles to a T. Right at the T, through the next light and then one more block to a left turn by the railroad bridge. Take the left and then another one in ½ block. Follow your nose for a few hundred feet and you're there.

MICHAEL'S, *Exit 29, Derby Line*

Derby Line is Vermont's northernmost settlement and hardly the sort of town you'd probe for haute cuisine. You'd expect to do better here with secondhand furniture or used farm equipment. We were lucklessly stalking a funky lunchroom when a bare 100 feet from the Canadian border we spotted a tiny gold-on-black sign. With the greatest of restraint it read simply, "Michael's." Not a word of explanation.

But there was no mistaking it. It had to be, and was, a classy little restaurant. Just seven tables with starched white cloths and lovely settings, hushed brown carpeting, light peach walls, a collection of framed mirrors, and a few plants was all there was to it. The effect was one of dignity and intimacy in stark good taste.

The menu, which changes daily to take advantage of whatever is freshest, was handwritten on an artist's sketchpad. Smoked trout, bluepoint oysters, and steamed mussels were among the appetizers. Some sample entrées: poached Norwegian salmon trout, bay scallops in garlic butter, blanquette of Vermont spring lamb, and swordfish Meunière.

When Michael LaCroix opened this place in 1979, some local wags in the drugstore across the street made book on how long he'd last. A lot of people must have lost money, because he's still there—doing things his own way, from the mirrors to his style of cooking. "Sometimes I tend to cook for myself," he's been quoted as saying. "I guess that's what a good meal is. You make what you like for other people, knowing they'll like it too."

Dinners at Michael's run from about $9 to $14. On Sundays you can get a continental breakfast for $1.95 or a full salmon and eggs brunch for $7.95.

HOURS Tue.–Sun. 5–10 pm; closed on Monday, and for extended periods when the mood seems right.

DIRECTIONS At the end of Exit 29 ramp turn left onto Route 5 toward Derby Line. Go 0.4 mile to center of town and look for a gray building with tiny sign, on the right, just before U.S. Customs.

ROUTES 55 AND 10

Quebec

AUX PETITS OIGNONS
LA SOURCE, *Exit 33, Magog*

Magog isn't Montreal, and rural Quebec isn't provincial France. Truth be told, we came across some pretty marginal eateries as we scoured the road to Montreal. But in Magog we turned up a few places that will probably leave you satisfied.

Aux Petits Oignons is a low-budget, five-table establishment offering good food at bargain prices. It's decorated with a Québecois sense of color—green and lavender, even down to the painted chairs—pretty floral tablecloths and small hanging lamps over each table. Charming and appealing in a homespun sort of way.

We found the menu on a piece of loose-leaf paper tacked just outside the door. Spaghetti with tomatoes was about U.S. $2.80, and soups were 80 cents to $2. Poulet vol-au-vent, a chicken-stuffed pastry, was $4, while beef Bourguignon topped the menu at $5. Clearly a good place to sample Quebec-style French cooking at very modest prices.

Just up the street from Aux Petits Oignons is **La Source,** a lovely deli/gourmet shop with a tempting selection of French pastries. You can't eat in the store, but a walk down Rue Principal while sampling one of these delights is a pleasant experience. There's a joyful sense of life and color on the street here, and lots to look at.

HOURS **Aux Petits Oignons:** Tue.–Sun. 11 am–midnight; closed Mon. **La Source:** Mon.-Sat. 10 am-5 pm; closed Sun.

DIRECTIONS From Exit 33 go right if southbound, left if northbound, onto Route 112 West (Ouest). Go about 2 miles to a T near the center of town and turn right onto Rue Principal. **Aux Petits Oignons** is just after the next light, on the left. **La Source** is also on the left, just a bit farther up.

LES TROIS MARMITES, *Exit 33, Magog*

Les Trois Marmites (The Three Kettles) is a nice, small-town restaurant, in looks and quality not a great deal different from its counterparts back home. But there are enough differences to make things interesting and maybe even to tip the scales in favor of Quebec.

The common American dishes are on the menu, from two eggs with bacon and coffee (U.S. $2.25) to steak, but here the sirloin ($10) comes with a choice of black pepper or Bordelaise sauce. Twelve crepes ($1.80–$3.75) further enliven things, as do escargots, Bar-B-Q chicken (a Quebec favorite—$5.60 for half a bird) and beef, chicken, or scallops brochette ($6.40).

A loud storefront sign, as seems to be the fashion here, announces Les Trois Marmites to the outside world, but within it's all quite pleasant, and more tasteful than its counterpart in Peoria. Subdued tones of brown and yellow set the mood. There's a wall of woodsy wallpaper and another displaying some quite nice paintings by a local artist. Curlicues of ornamental ironwork provide the French accent.

The Canadian pea soup we tried here had gusto if not subtlety, and the crepe was acceptable too.

HOURS Every day 7 am–10 pm.

DIRECTIONS Follow directions for **Aux Petits Oignons,** above, but go 0.3 mile farther up Rue Principal. It's on the right.

THE ELITE, *Exit 68, Granby*

The only thing elite about the Elite was its service, which was superb, from the elegance of the nattily dressed maitre d' to the delicate care of the waitress as she transferred the entrée from serving dish to plate—which was surprising, really, since in no other way did the place have serious pretensions to excellence. Efforts to produce a posh decor have fizzled into a campy blend of ordinariness with something on the quiet side of glitzy. And no one seemed to mistake a meal here for a dress-up occasion—the customers were either plainly dressed or even a bit disheveled.

The menu is enormous—everything from eggs and omelettes through sandwiches, soups, pizza, and cheeses to lasagne, seafood, steaks, whole roast chicken, and beef Bourguignon. And at prices that are certainly not elitist: a smoked-meat sandwich, for example, could be had for less than U.S. $1.50. A six-inch pizza is $1.80, and soup only 80 cents. Shellfish dinners begin at a bit over $6, with regular fish entrées from $3.50.

What we tasted of all this was a mushroom-packed beef Bourguignon, which was okay—maybe a hair better, but certainly no worse—a fair deal considering the $5.50 price tag. We developed an affection for the Elite that went beyond the food. Perhaps it was the feeling that this curious juxtaposition of excellent service, improbable decor, and all-right food, a combination we'd never seen before, was somehow uniquely Québecois. But our international travels were brief, and we never did find out whether our hunch was right or what we saw here was just an Elitist idiosyncrasy.

HOURS Sun.–Thu. 9 am–midnight; Fri. 9 am–2 am; Sat. 9 am–3 am.

DIRECTIONS From Exit 68 turn right if eastbound, left if westbound, onto Route 139 North (Nord). Go 5 miles and turn right onto Route 112 East (Est). Go 1.7 miles on 112 and you'll see the **Elite** on the right after passing through much that you'd do better not to stop at. (Yes, this one's a long way, but there just isn't much near the highway.)

RESTAURANT LA TÊTE DE PIOCHE, *Exit 37, St. Gregoire*

* *Color, not cuisine*

It's only a short way from here to Montreal. If you're looking for a culinary experience, you'd best keep going, but if a taste of life on the French Canadian plains tempts you, then drive the four very flat miles to this outpost of the restaurant world. You'll pass lots of small white houses that seem as starkly vertical as the grain elevators that dot the landscape, and you can have a bite to eat among the people who work this land.

Expect nothing exotic. La Tête de Pioche is just a modern, overgrown toolshed of a building beneath a good-sized Pepsi sign. It's caught between a suburban-style housing development and the immense farmlands that spread to the horizon. The name suggests fine dining only if your French is scanty. Roughly translated, it's the Pickaxe Restaurant ("The Head of the Hoe," to be more exact), which befits its function as a resting place for people who work hard.

Inside, it is absolutely clean and absolutely plain. For food you'll find nothing more exotic than French fries, chef's salad, and hamburgers (all cheap), along with a bar not much more fully stocked than your own. The people around here, however, were marvelously friendly and filled with good-natured enthusiasm. They didn't even seem to mind our crude attempts to speak their language.

HOURS Mon.–Fri. 10 am–10 pm; Sat. 10 am–2 am; closed Sun.

DIRECTIONS From Exit 37 (St. Gregoire) turn right if westbound, left if eastbound, onto Route 227 South (Sud). Go 2 miles to a light by a gas station. Left at the light, and in 1.8 miles you'll see it, off by itself, on the left.

ROUTE 3

Massachusetts

WOOD'S TAKE OUT
OTHER RESTAURANTS ON TOWN PIER,
Exit 6, Plymouth

What, we wondered, would we find to eat in New England's earliest settlement, a town world-renowned for its seaside boulder and the Puritans who first touched it? Since that eventful landing in 1620, countless thousands of less adventuresome individuals have landed in their station wagons to touch the rock and the town as well.

The famous hunk of granite is all but lost amid the tourist kitsch, and there is no shortage of big seaside eateries either. (Pilgrim's progress?) **The 1620 Restaurant, Mayflower Seafood,** and **McGrath's** are on or near Town Pier, all within a cherrystone's throw of Plymouth Rock.

However, we think that the much less imposing, lower-priced seafood of Wood's Take Out and Fish Market is more fun to eat. After a brief stop at Wood's to pick up some stuffed quahogs (large clams), lobster rolls, or seafood platters, you can sit on the pier and dangle your feet in the water, munching your meal as you watch the fishing boats unload what will be tomorrow's stuffed quahogs, lobster rolls, and seafood platters.

HOURS **Wood's:** Summer: every day 7:30 am–9 pm. Winter: every day 8 am–6 pm.

DIRECTIONS From Exit 6 turn right and go 0.8 mile to the first traffic light (not counting a blinker). Continue straight through the light, jogging right, then left, with the road until the road ends in a T-junction. **Wood's** is straight ahead, at the end of the pier, and the others are within sight. Parking may be tough.

COLONIAL RESTAURANT, *Exit 6, Plymouth*

Located in downtown Plymouth, the Colonial is all but ignored by the pilgrimage of tourists who come each summer to glimpse the town's famous rock. The Colonial Restaurant belongs to a wonderful, nearly-extinct species of homey, but in its own way classy, village restaurant. With their warm-toned, varnished hardwood booths, their friendly, chatty waitresses, and their just-folks clientele, these restaurants symbolize small-town America before the days when restaurants—or anything else—went out of their way to symbolize anything. The people who come here represent every page in the demographer's notebook—teenagers, harried shoppers, smooth-looking businessmen, moms with kids, and Norman Rockwell grandmothers. Just folks, plain and simple.

And just food. Nothing fancy, everything good. We had a chicken salad sandwich ($1.25) simply loaded with chicken chunks—tasty and satisfying, if a little bit too mayonnaisey. The minestrone soup (60 cents a cup) was also chock-full of good stuff. For $2, plump, fresh, fried haddock sandwiches put fast-food "fishburgers" to shame. Hamburgers here are $1.10, and roast beef on a bulky roll is $1.85. Complete dinners are as low as $2.75 for fried sausage, potato, vegetable, and apple sauce, or $3.85 for pork cutlets with the same fixin's. A fried sole dinner is $4.25, fried clams a dollar more. All are pleasantly and efficiently served.

We left the Colonial shaking our heads and wondering aloud how the fast-food chains ever got a foothold in the American restaurant landscape. With their impersonal service, cardboard food, and plastic atmosphere, they should have long ago been booed off the map. As we stepped out onto Plymouth's bustling Main Street, our question was answered: parking. Evidently, most Americans care more about their parking than their eating. If you would rather eat well than park well, visit the Colonial. To alleviate the problem, try to come after downtown shopping hours. Or leave your car a few blocks from the center of this small town and walk. We'd walk a mile for a Colonial.

HOURS Fri.–Wed. 11 am–8:30 pm; closed Thu.

DIRECTIONS From Exit 6 turn right and go 0.8 mile to first traffic light. Turn right and go 0.4 mile to the **Colonial Restaurant** on your left (39 Main St.).

TINKER'S DAM, *Exit 12, Hanover*

In looks, this place is much like its big brother at Exit 13, a genuinely old building that from the outside looks like a new building trying to appear old. But at Tinker's Dam, things are on a smaller scale, quieter, and more intimate. The interior renovation was pretty thorough. Although not much of the original house is still visible, is still has much of the Colonial warmth, especially in the lovely small dining room upstairs.

Dinners upstairs run $9–$15 (mostly steaks and seafood, with a few items like veal Oscar). Downstairs there's a pub, and meals there are considerably cheaper. Full dinners start at $4.95 for lasagne, moussaka, and others, and you can get two such meals for just $8.95. That's a good deal, especially when you consider that it comes with a bottomless salad bowl. Sandwiches in the pub are $2.75–$3.75.

HOURS Pub lunch: every day 11:30 am–4 pm; Pub dinner: every day 4–11 pm. Upstairs dining: Tue.–Thu. 6–9:30 pm; Fri. & Sat. 6–10 pm; Sun. 5–9 pm; closed Mon.

DIRECTIONS From Exit 12 turn right if northbound, left if southbound, and go 0.2 mile. It's on the right.

BARNSIDE TAVERN, *Exit 13, Assinippi*

From the outside, it looks like a huge new building trying to look like a bunch of old buildings. From the inside, you see that it is really a mélange of old buildings trying to be one—two old barns and an 18th century Cape, bolted together into a labyrinth of dining rooms, pubs, function rooms, bakery, raw bar, and gift shop. Each of the many eating areas has an entirely different character —the fireplace, antique chairs, exposed rafters, and old-fashioned

wallpaper of the Cape have the warming aura of a comfortable old inn, while the expansive barns feel like . . . well, like barns.

There's little question that people like this place. On an average day, the Barnside's Williamsburg-style, gingham-clad waitresses (and waiters!) serve over a thousand people. And on Thursday, Friday, and Saturday nights after 7 pm (travelers take note), customers wait two or three hours for their seats.

The cuisine is red-blooded American, and better than most of its sort. Breads, pies, and cakes are right out of the oven. The scampi we had was nicely seasoned with garlic (not drowned), and the shrimp were firm and fleshy (not wooden). The chocolate mousse was rich and velvet smooth.

Most lunch items here run from $5 to $6 (broiled fish and shellfish, liver and onions, roast prime rib), but the luncheon buffet in the tavern is an absolute bargain at $3.95—two homemade soups to choose from, salad bar, cold meats for sandwiches, and three hot entrées (lasagne, beef tips, and scrod casserole, when we visited). Dinner gets a bit more expensive, of course—from a low of $8–$9 to around $17 for the day's gourmet special (seafood in parchment, for example).

HOURS Every day 11:30 am–11:30 pm.

DIRECTIONS From Exit 13 turn right if northbound, left if southbound. Go ½ mile; it's on your right, just before the first traffic light.

ASSINIPPI EATING ESTABLISHMENT, *Exit 13, Assinippi*

Behind the spruced-up façade lies a neat little grocery store, butcher shop, and lunch counter. There's nothing very special about any of them, but all together they offer you the alternatives of either making your own or grabbing a quick, cheap meal.

The eatery is done up in lunch-stand rustic, offering about what you'd expect at about what you'd expect to pay for it. The butcher shop has a dozen or so lunch meats, cheeses, and some decent French bread for sale. Get chips, sodas, and ice cream at the grocery, and check out the Lilliputian post office within—it's a gem.

HOURS Lunch counter: Mon.–Fri. 6:30 am–2:30 pm; Sat. & Sun. 7 am–2:30 pm. Butcher shop: Mon.–Sat. 9 am–6 pm; Sun. 9 am–5 pm. Grocery: every day 6 am–11 pm.

DIRECTIONS See **Barnside Tavern,** above. It's right next door.

LA SCALLA, *Exits 20 & 25, Randolph*

La Scalla's northern Italian cuisine is celebrated among gastronomes of Boston's southern suburbs, and it has earned a reputation that ranks it among the metropolitan area's finer Italian restaurants. The decor is plain and simple with a touch of class—white walls with a few brick archways and framed portraits. There is also a Venus or two around, in case you need to be reminded that you're in an Italian restaurant.

Although it is open only for dinner, La Scalla's dinner prices might be expected at lunch. Just about all the entrées are between \$6 and \$8, and the house specialty—boneless chicken breast and eggplant with prosciutto and cheese, baked in a wine sauce—is intended for two people and costs just \$15. Veal scallopini Marsala is also very popular at \$6.25. Each month, the restaurant features a different reasonably priced Italian wine.

HOURS Every day 4:30–11:30 pm.

DIRECTIONS Northbound: Where Route 3 forks (inconspicuously labeled Exit 20), bear left onto Route 128 North. From Route 128, take Exit 67 South. Go 1 mile on Route 28 South to **La Scalla,** on the right.

Southbound: Where Routes 3 and 93 (concurrent up to this point) split, 93 goes off to the right and joins Route 128. Take this right fork (Exit 25) onto Route 128 and get off at Exit 67 South. Go 1 mile on Route 28 South to **La Scalla,** on the right.

CORY'S, *Exits 20 & 25, Dedham*

See p. 195 for a description of this fine restaurant.

DIRECTIONS From Exit 20 (if northbound) or Exit 25 (if southbound) get on I-93 South, and from I-93 get onto I-95 North (Route 128). All this takes just 5 minutes. From Exit 60N on I-95, follow directions given.

I-93

Massachusetts, New Hampshire

(Including I-293)

Massachusetts

CORY'S, ***Dedham***

See p. 195 for a description of this fine restaurant.

DIRECTIONS From I-93, get on I-95 North. Go just a few miles to Exit 60N and follow directions given.

ABOUT BOSTON

It's hard to imagine a city better situated than Boston for eating off the interstate. I-93 goes right through downtown, within blocks of Boston's many famous, good, fast, and inexpensive restaurants (and a few good, expensive ones too). There are literally hundreds to choose from in every category.

First, there's the North End, with as many Italian cafés, restaurants, pizzerias, bakeries, and groceries as anyone could want. Just blocks away, on the other side of the highway, is bustling Quincy Market, a recent restoration of the historic Faneuil Hall marketplace. It boasts a seemingly endless number of restaurants and lunch stands offering foods of virtually every ethnic group you can think of. And right across the street from the market is Durgin-Park, a New England institution all but unchanged for a hundred years, where for $2 you can get codfish cakes and baked beans served by waitresses famous for their rudeness.

The only problem with this hungry traveler's paradise is parking. It's simply impossible, and traffic grinds agonizingly along the narrow streets where you have to back in to double-park. Unless you're very patient and very forgiving, you'd do best to park in one of the nearby garages and walk.

Sometimes there's another problem: Bostonians like good food; at peak hours, being seated at a restaurant can require patience. One solution is to do your dining at Quincy Market, where many of the concessions sell their food over the counter, à la McDonald's (but worlds better).

In general, stopping downtown can take some time, but you just can't beat it for the variety and confusion of its urban delights.

A bit south of this area is the No-Name Restaurant, another wonderful and inexpensive place, this one specializing in seafood, and located right on Fish Pier, where the boats turn over their catch to the wholesale distributors. There are several other seafood places on the pier; the traffic and parking here are much easier than downtown.

We have to admit that your life will be simpler if you wait until you're out of town to eat. On the other hand, you'll be passing up some of the best food and most colorful settings to be found near an interstate highway. Somehow life's like that. If you opt for the color, read on. If you want to keep things simple, keep driving.

NO-NAME RESTAURANT, *Boston*

Fish Pier is where the boats unload the day's catch, a no-nonsense collection of busy warehouses jutting into Boston Harbor. All around are the shouts of burly men and the rumblings of trucks and pushcarts loaded with gleaming fish. Occupying an all but invisible corner of the pier is the signless, nameless, No-Name Restaurant, a Boston institution whose low profile has only fanned its fame. With good food, good prices, more local color than you can absorb, and relatively easy parking, it's a place not to be missed.

The original part of the restaurant looks more like a diner than anything else, with a long, very worn counter, cheap paneling, Formica tables, and a thorough disdain for style. A new addition is spiffier, but not really out of keeping with the original, not even in the glassed-in room at the rear which gives you a view not only of the boats unloading all of 10 feet away, but of Logan Airport across the bay and huge Navy ships to boot. The whole place bustles with a gruff, big-city cheerfulness, usually expressed in loud tones of Greek, and the customers come from every niche in the social hierarchy.

You can't spend more than $5.45. For it you get a seafood plate (fried or broiled) consisting of a good-sized piece of swordfish, a still bigger chunk of scrod, a hearty scoop of scallops, and a few mussels. With all this comes a mound of tasty garlic bread, an enormous helping of delicious coleslaw, and a little dish of vegetables. This isn't gourmet cooking. What makes it all so good is the unsurpassed freshness of the fish. To get it any fresher it would have to be cooked on the boat!

Other fish dinners are the same $5.45 or a dollar less. A meal-in-itself bowl of fish chowder is $1.50 (cup, 75 cents), a scrod sandwich, $2.65.

Unfortunately, Boston's great cheap restaurants don't remain undiscovered for long, and the No-Name has been around a long time. We arrived early at lunchtime and had no wait at all, but we were told that at peak mealtimes, especially in summer, the line goes to . . . all the way to . . . well, all the way to "there," with our informant gesturing at the Hancock Tower.

But it's worth it.

HOURS Mon.–Thu. 11 am–9:30 pm; Fri. & Sat. 11 am–10 pm; closed Sun.

DIRECTIONS Northbound: Take exit marked "Atlantic Ave./ Northern Ave.," which comes at the end of an underground section of I-93, after the Chinatown exits and before the Callahan Tunnel. At the fork in the exit bear right and you'll be fed onto a street running parallel to I-93. Make the first right onto Northern Ave. (large brick building on corner), ■ drive over a little bridge and onto the cobblestone. You'll shortly see **Anthony's Pier 4,** on the left. For the **No-Name,** continue along Northern Ave. and make the first left after you pass under a large iron walkway. Park anywhere, walk out onto the pier, and look for No. 15½, on the right. Remember, there is no sign, but everyone knows where it is.

Southbound: Take the exit marked "High St./Congress St./Downtown," which comes a bit after the Government Center exit. At the end of ramp make a left (not a U), onto Oliver St. Go one block to a T. Turn right at the T, and then left at the second set of lights. Pass over highway, and then take the first left on the other side. Go about 1½ blocks to Northern Ave. (large brick building on corner). Right onto Northern, then as above from ■.

ANTHONY'S PIER 4, *Boston*

If you like the idea of seafood on the waterfront but the No-Name sounds too rugged, consider Pier 4, a block or so away. It's one of Boston's biggest and most popular restaurants, with wonderful views of the harbor through enormous windows. New and posh, it's the kind of place that displays pictures of the owner with Nixon, Humphrey, Jack Kennedy, Carter, Tip O'Neill, Liz, and even the Pope, not to mention a steel plate of the *New York Times'* front page bearing the date of the owner's birthday.

Every kind of nautical artifact has been worked into the decor, including the aft section of a fishing boat which now serves as a raw bar. Out front there's an old steam locomotive—perhaps it once hauled oysters.

Except for prime ribs and some steaks, the menu is entirely seafood. Luncheons run from $4.95 for broiled bluefish all the way up to $26 for lobster Savannah. Dinners start at $7.95.

HOURS Mon.–Fri. 11:30 am–11 pm; Sat. noon–11 pm; Sun. 12:30–10:30 pm.

DIRECTIONS See directions for **No-Name Restaurant,** above.

THE NORTH END: AN OVERVIEW

Boston's North End has everything there is to be had in Italian food, from the most subtle gourmet cooking to pizzas (thick, thin, or deep-dish) to grocery stores with piles of colorful fruit out on the sidewalk. There's so much to choose from that no matter what we recommended we'd be slighting someone's favorite. And since the best way to enjoy this kind of neighborhood is to walk, peek, poke, and take a chance, that's what we urge you to do. Chances are, you'll be happy with what you find. If you're not, just buy a scrumptious-looking pastry from a bakery and devour it on your way back to the car, telling yourself it was an experience. It will be, no matter what the outcome.

All the same, we're going to walk into this lion's den and recommend Felicia's for gourmet Northern Italian cuisine, the European for more standard Italian-American fare, and Regina's Pizzeria for what is often called the best pizza in town. But these are only meant to give you a tentative goal. If something looks good on the way, go for it.

FELICIA'S, *Boston*

Felicia's is at 145A Richmond Street—Richmond being a narrow side street off Hanover Street, the North End's main thoroughfare. To get into Felicia's it is necessary to ascend a steep staircase, adding to the European flavor you begin to taste the moment you turn onto Richmond. For us, the foreign fantasy was shattered slightly when we found that Felicia herself—who has a reputation as an effervescent hostess as well as an outstanding cook—instead of being in the kitchen stirring sauces, was at that very moment in Palm Springs, California, catering a bash for Bob Hope.

But the restaurant, even without her presence, did not disappoint us. Not tiny, it still feels small and intimate; it is dimly lit and decorated in warm colors with some fine antique pieces. A nine-foot oil painting of pastoral Castello Amare would look more at home in the Uffizi Gallery than in most restaurants. That's what we liked so much about Felicia's—it seemed a lot more Italian than the Italian restaurants that wallop you over the head, shouting, "We are Italian."

The cuisine is of Northern Italy and, given its quality, surprisingly reasonable. Felicia's special concoction, which has received considerable acclaim from Boston's gastronomic community, is chicken Verdiccio—boneless chicken breasts, mushrooms, and artichoke hearts sautéed in butter and garlic and served with a lemony Verdiccio wine sauce ($7.50). Her cannelloni is also a treat —wide pasta tubes filled with veal and spinach ($6.75) or with scallops, shrimp, crab, and lobster ($7.75) and drenched in a flavorful cheese sauce. For dessert, try Felicia's fantastic stuffed peaches (summer only); she has made a winning match of fresh peaches, crushed macaroons, ladyfingers, and Marsala wine, which is then baked and served flambé. Memorable.

HOURS Mon.–Sat. 5–10:30 pm; Sun. 2:30–10:30 pm.

DIRECTIONS See end of Downtown Boston entries, page 145.

THE EUROPEAN, *Boston*

Back on Hanover Street, the European has been serving Italian and American food for 64 years. Now expanded to five dining rooms, it can handle over 500 people at a time. With this kind of capacity, it is not exactly intimate, but neither is it likely that you'll have to wait more than 15 minutes to be seated at even the busiest times—definitely a plus in Boston.

The decor is heavy on plastic and Formica, but the weekday lunch specials make almost any decor tolerable—soup, entreé (lasagne or manicotti, for instance), vegetable, potato or spaghetti, and coffee or tea, all for $3.25. Most complete dinners are $7 to $10, but à la carte pasta dishes are as low as $4. The European serves pizzas in three sizes ($3.15, $4.10, and $5.80, plain), with all the usual toppings.

HOURS Every day 11 am–12:30 am.

DIRECTIONS See end of Downtown Boston entries, page 145.

REGINA'S PIZZERIA, *Boston*

According to many North End aficionados, Regina's is the place to go for pizza. So successful at pleasing pizza lovers is

Regina's that it has opened a branch in the much tonier environs of Quincy Market. But the original (corner of North Margin and Thacher streets) remains a small, spirited pizza joint done up plainly but nicely with dark hardwood booths, cream-colored plaster walls, and ceiling fans (the old kind, from before they became a fad). Most important are the regal, soulful pizzas that they pull out of the oven by the dozen.

If this appeals to you, you won't be alone—be prepared for up to an hour's wait during prime pizza time.

HOURS Mon.–Sat. 11 am–midnight; Sun. 3–11 pm.

DIRECTIONS See end of Downtown Boston entries, page 145.

DURGIN-PARK, *Boston*

Noisy, bustly, frowzy, gusty, gutsy Durgin-Park was "Established Before You Were Born," as its tagline claims. We won't argue with that, since it baked its first beans before the Revolution, but we do take issue with their boast, "Where Your Great Grandfather Dined." If our great-grandfathers dined out anywhere, it was in some tumbledown Anatevka, certainly not in Boston.

We could regale you with stories of Presidents (TR, FDR, Cal Coolidge) and celebrities (Arthur Godfrey, Helen Hayes, Lillian Gish) who ate here regularly. More interesting, perhaps, are the non-celebrities, like the retired sea captain who dined on chowder, Indian pudding, and coffee every morning at 11 o'clock for 42 years. Or the fisherman who, twice a week for 23 years, dragged a large cod up the front steps and asked the broiler cook to fix it for him.

And Durgin-Park hasn't changed a bit. It is one of Boston's prime tourist spots—not because it tries to please tourists, but because it doesn't try to please anyone. And that pleases everyone.

Some time ago, *Collier's* magazine did a story on Durgin-Park. "Of all the famous eating places in America, Durgin-Park is by far the least prepossessing," declared the author. "The ancient three-story building in which it is housed makes no attempt to disguise its dinginess with an air of quaintness."

And that—especially considering some of the deliberately quaint places we've been—is what makes Durgin-Park such a delight.

The waitresses are as surly as ever. "Sit over there," they snap, pointing to a table. "Whaddya want?" they ask. The long tables, carelessly set with red-checked tablecloths, are piled with menus, and before she brings your meal, the waitress drops the necessary cutlery in front of you.

All the food is real Yankee cooking. Aside from chowder, vegetable soup, oysters, and clams, there are, for entrées, beef stew, poor man's roast beef, chicken pot pie, chicken livers and bacon, pot roast, codfish cakes and beans, fried smelts, broiled scrod, baked sausage, and much more. Believe it or not, all the above dishes cost between $2 and $2.75. (Leg of lamb, whole duck, and lobster, etc., get higher but are still a bargain.)

We tried chicken pot pie and codfish cakes with beans—huge portions of solid, tasty food that was far from subtle, but with character. A sweet crispy biscuit came on top of the pot pie; sitting unceremoniously in the goo was a bowl of mashed potatoes. Everything was fresh, made to order in the exposed, steamy kitchen.

Though stuffed, we couldn't leave without trying some of Durgin-Park's famous desserts. Made from real ground beans, the coffee gelatin was a new experience. It's only 50 cents, yet is topped with thick gobs of real whipped cream. A king-sized wedge of deep-dish apple pie came with vanilla ice cream for $1.50. Indian pudding and hot apple pan dowdy are two other specialties, but enough was enough. The total for everything we ate, including the 5% tax, was a ridiculous $7.09.

But then we had to ruin it all with a pack of spruce gum bought at the cashier's desk. Yecch! Not until we were home did we read the *Collier's* article and learn that the awful stuff is actually used for glueing broken chairs together.

HOURS Mon.–Sat. 11:30 am–10 pm; Sun. noon–9 pm.

DIRECTIONS FOR DOWNTOWN BOSTON RESTAURANTS To give precise directions to all of the above places would be more confusing than helpful. If northbound on I-93, take the exit labeled "Government Center/North End." If southbound, take exit at "Haymarket Square" (for the North End) or "Dock Square" (for **Quincy Market** and **Durgin-Park**). All these exits put you within a block or two of the North End on one side of the elevated highway, and equally close to Quincy Market/Durgin-Park on the other side. Visible from the exit ramps are two large parking garages—a white concrete monstrosity (closer to the North End) and a red brick monolith (closer to Quincy Market and Durgin-Park). We urge you to use them, although you may find a parking place on the street—it's been known to happen. Ask the parking attendant—or anyone—how to find your chosen restaurant.

ABOUT ANDOVER

This is a very handsome town that wears its dress-up clothes as if it were born in them. It probably was. Since 1778 life here has been dominated by Phillips Academy, one of the country's most prestigious prep schools, the campus of which would be the envy of most colleges. But whatever the reason, Andover's boutiques, bookstores, and general good design seem to have grown up naturally. You've seen the T-shirts, books, and bumper stickers, but if you want to find out what "preppy" really means, this is the place to come. Actually, it was kinda nice.

FORD'S COFFEE SHOP, *Exit 18N, Andover*

Let's begin with the town's unprepossessing luncheonette. It's nice enough, but hardly spectacular, with its long counter, plastic tables, and imitation brick wall. But high above the milkshake machines there's a wonderful mural of Main Street, painted in 1957 and delightfully out of perspective.

A jumbo cheeseburger here will cost you $1.39; fish chowder, 60 cents a cup, 90 cents a bowl. The only surprise, aside from the mural, was a Greek salad for $1.89.

Overheard while sampling coffee and an acceptable coconut custard pie: "Once a preppy, always a preppy!" from one well-dressed young man to another, in solemn tone of voice.

HOURS Mon.–Thu. 7 am–5:30 pm; Fri. 7 am–7 pm; Sat. 7 am–5 pm.; closed Sun.

DIRECTIONS Exit 18N puts you on I-495 North. Go 2 miles to Exit 41A, which will put you on Route 28 South. Go ½ mile to light at Route 133. Cross 133 and continue on 28 for 1.2 miles to light in center of town. **Ford's** is on left, just past the light, at 14 Main.

JUSTIN'S, *Exit 18N, Andover*

Andover just had to have a place like this. Actually it had two, but we preferred Justin's. What we found here was first-rate Northern Italian cooking in a tasteful, restrained environment of oak woodwork, handsome wallpaper, bentwood chairs, and nicely set tables. That's upstairs, where dining is something of an event. Downstairs the feel is Victorian-pubby, with sandwiches ($3–$4), soups ($1.95), five salads ($1.95–$5.95), and quiche ($4.25) at lunchtime.

Owner/manager Brian Jaymes seems to be the sort of man who really cares about the quality of his food. He makes three trips a week to Boston for the imported pasta he favors and the fresh fish that he likes to serve poached, not broiled. He waxes eloquent over the art of keeping the vegetables' color through the steaming process, and he rails against those who smother shrimp scampi in garlic. If the dish we sampled was typical, he's not just a good talker. Veal with prosciutto and mozzarella in a mustard and cream sauce, it was subtly rich, tangy, and cheesy all at once.

Full dinners at Justin's run from $7.95 for poached fish in a bouillabaisse or chicken in apricot sauce to $13.95 for filet mignon with spinach, lobster, and Béarnaise sauce. Those aren't bad prices for this kind of quality.

HOURS Every day 11:30 am–10 pm.

DIRECTIONS Follow directions for **Ford's,** above, but continue along Main St. to the next left, Park St. **Justin's** is ½ block down, on the left.

THE ANDOVER INN, *Exit 18N, Andover*

What can humble writers on highway dining say about the showpiece of a gorgeous campus built with all the stately elegance and formal symmetries that the 18th century stood for? It's a Georgian inn on the campus of Phillips Academy, where America's privileged have been educated since the Revolution. Fluted columns, velvet curtains, plushly upholstered chairs, and formally dressed waiters set the tone in the dining room.

It's certainly worth a look if you have the time, but a meal here is likely to be more than you want to take on during a highway stop. The menu is eclectic American and continental, and prices are right up there near the 20-foot ceiling.

HOURS Every day for breakfast, lunch (except Sat.), and dinner.

DIRECTIONS Follow directions for **Ford's** (p. 145), but continue up Main St. for about ½ mile. (Don't turn onto West St.) Turn left through the main gate of Phillips Academy. Second building on the left.

New Hampshire

LITTLE MEXICO, *Exit 1, Salem*

In the midst of a commercial-strip jungle and fast-food forest we found a little Mexican place that wasn't half as bad as we thought it was going to be. The taco ($1.50) was chock-full of good meat, and the chili relleno ($1.95), though smothered in Velveeta, was really all right. Not the best, to be sure, but if you're in a Mexican mood it beats Taco Bell.

The exterior is would-be adobe, and the interior has Mexican tile tables, a few saddle blankets, and lots of barnboard in small, close-feeling rooms. Full dinners aren't that cheap ($7.50–$9.95).

Too much for a place like this, but their single burrito-taco-enchilada sort of thing is ample and a fair buy at $1.40–$1.95.

HOURS Tue.–Thu. & Sun. 11:30 am–9 pm; Fri. & Sat. 11:30 am–11 pm; closed Mon.

DIRECTIONS Exit 1 automatically puts you onto a connector road that takes you ½ mile to a light. Turn right at the light onto Route 28 South. Go 1½ miles; it's on the right.

DERRY DAIRY, ETC., *Exit 4, Derry*

* *Slim pickin's*

For some reason we thought Derry was going to be a primped-up town with lots of quiche and spinach salad, stained glass and natural wood. We first suspected otherwise when we spotted the **Derry Dairy,** occupying a former Texaco station. Its high point was a terrific aquarium. Next we found the Orange Crush sign that announced the **C & K Restaurant** (inoffensively Ethan Allen, with plastic) across from **Ozzie's Fish and Chicks** (Pepsi sign, but true fresh shrimp, January to March!). A little farther downtown came **Derry Donuts** (the hole), the **Pancake House** (Pepsi sign again, not half bad within), and finally the **Hoodcroft Restaurant** (fine old house, closed "indefinitely").

Actually, it was a relief.

DIRECTIONS From Exit 4 bear right onto Route 102 East. Look sharp and you'll find them all within a mile.

NORTH STAR DINER, *Exit 5, North Londonderry*

The North Star is a small clapboard affair with a wonderfully simple 1930s-style sign out front. Absolutely invisible from the highway (which passes practically on top of it) and absolutely local in character, the North Star is a favorite with truckers hauling milk from Vermont and lobsters from Maine. Clean, homey, and pleasant, with very friendly people and decent, diner-style food. No pretensions whatsoever.

Hamburgers go for $1.25, soup for 55 and 85 cents, and most dinners for about $3. You may enjoy the homemade tables and chairs and the six old chrome stools at the counter.

HOURS Mon.–Sat. 4 am–9:30 pm; Sun. 7:30 am–noon.

DIRECTIONS From Exit 5 turn right if northbound, left if southbound. It's 100 yards from highway, on your left.

JOLICOEUR'S COUNTRY STORE, *Exit 5, North Londonderry*

Here's a place that is exactly what it says it is. Nothing's been done to make it old, quaint, or authentic, so, in an unspectacular way, it is exactly that.

And Dick Jolicoeur, a former dairy farmer, serves home-cooked food: sandwiches, pastries, cookies, and white chocolate made by two women who live down the road. Hot meals on weekdays. There's no place to sit, but no one seems to mind if you walk the aisles while you munch.

HOURS Mon.–Fri. 6 am–9 pm; Sat. & Sun. 8 am–7 pm.

DIRECTIONS From Exit 5 turn left if northbound, right if southbound, for 1½ miles until you see a small sign for the North Londonderry Business District. Left at the sign, go another mile, and you'll see it on the left.

Entering I-293

DAFFODIL'S, *Exit 3 (I-293), Bedford*

Sometimes restaurants defy classification. When we heard that a place called "Daffodil's" was one of Manchester's favorite dining spots, we didn't know what to expect: cutesy or classy, theater or good food? What we discovered was something for everyone.

Boldly commanding the top of a hill, Daffodil's looks like a cross between a Tudor townhouse and a Japanese pagoda. Inside, it is colorful, cheerful, and well designed. There are three dining areas, one of which is papered with a bright, boisterous floral print. The plush green carpet, blue designer chairs, and beautifully set tables (stoneware, fresh flowers) sparkle like a *New Yorker* ad, especially when they catch the light that beams through the big patio windows. (There is outdoor service in summer.) In another, gargantuan Indian rugs serve as elegant wall hangings; and the third, an intimate little dining room, is lushly appointed with fine modern art, nicely hung on white walls.

But also framed and hung on the walls are dozens of mock news clippings detailing the misadventures of Raoul Fenstermacher, Daffodil's fictitious chef. The menu itself devotes considerable space to a soap-opera account of the life of the cherubic "Daffodil." (If you wish to add this literature to your personal library, the restaurant sells menus for $2.) Finally, we found the *Wall Street Journal* tacked to the wall above the urinal in the men's room. (We didn't check the ladies'.)

They take the cooking more seriously. We tried a seafood crepe that was thick and flavorful, filled with meaty pieces of lobster, scallops, and fish in a Newburg sauce ($5.95). Crab quiche, at $4.50, is the least expensive lunch entrée, while broiled scallops tops the list at $8.95. A chef's salad ($5) includes chicken, Gruyère, artichoke hearts, ham, sliced almonds, Romaine and Bibb lettuce. Dinner can be light and low-priced (seafood Rockefeller, $5.95; chicken breast with cheese stuffing, $6.95), or a bit heavier and higher (sole with sliced bananas and almonds, $10.95; beef Wellington, $3.50). At both lunch and dinner hours, sandwiches are available at sandwich prices.

HOURS Mon.–Sat. 11:30 am–1 am (light menu after normal dinner hours); Sun. noon–midnight.

DIRECTIONS Northbound: From I-93 enter I-293 between Exits 5 and 6 (signs are clear). ■ Take Exit 3 off I-293 (Bedford), which puts you on a highway spur that ends at a light. Turn left onto Route 101 West. Go 2 miles; it's on your left.

Southbound: Enter I-293 between Exits 10 and 11 (signs are clear). Stay on 293 (don't let yourself get fed onto the Everett Turnpike). Then as above from ■.

ANTON'S, *Exit 4 (I-293), Manchester*

This is a pleasant enough, suburban sort of place that from the outside looks like a miniature bar-mitzvah palace. The decor is an odds-and-ends collection of Oriental rugs, Tiffany-style lamps, stuccoed white walls, colorful indoor awnings and Muzak, quite tolerable if you don't fret about things like integrity of design. But Anton's has a terrific reputation in this neck of the woods, and for the traveler it's got a lunchtime bargain that's hard to beat, an all-you-can-eat soup and sandwich bar for $4.35.

Fill up on the beautifully displayed roast beef, pastrami, corned beef, and turkey, along with various cheeses, deep-fried chunks of chicken, and corn fritters. The breads are only average, and the two soups are good, but nothing spectacular. For another $2.10, you gain access to another all-you-can-eat extravaganza, this time at the extensive and equally beautiful salad bar. Children under 10 get all this for $3.75.

Full luncheons are pricey ($6.95–$8.95), mostly American seafood, ribs, and steaks, with a few exotics. The dinner menu is similar, but the prices are higher, $10.95–$13.95.

HOURS Mon.–Fri. 11:30 am–8 pm; Sat. 11:30 am–8:30 pm; closed Sun. The sandwich bar is available until 2 pm.

DIRECTIONS Northbound: From I-93 enter I-293 between Exits 5 and 6 (signs are clear). Take Exit 4 off I-293 and turn right onto Route 3 North. Go 2 blocks and you'll see it on your left.

Southbound: From I-93 enter I-293 between Exits 10 and 11 (signs are clear). Take Exit 4 off I-293 and bear right onto Route 3 North. Go 2 blocks and you'll see it on your left.

Return to I-93

THE NATURAL SELECTION, *Exit 13, Concord*

Concord being the capital of straight-as-an-arrow New Hampshire (the governor flew the flag at half-mast when Vietnam draft-dodgers were readmitted to the country), we didn't expect the town to boast a flourishing natural foods restaurant. Also unexpected was the starched-collar lunch crowd enjoying vegetarian specialties, especially considering the restaurant's location in a wing of a three-story clapboard apartment building in a residential neighborhood. When we tasted the food, we understood. Here is a health foods restaurant where the "health foods taste" that one of us abhors is subtle, subordinated to the other pleasing flavors.

The decor is simple—a bit frowzy, but clean and cheerful. Bright yellow director's chairs line long wooden tables, and big windows with brown café curtains admit abundant light. If the worn wooden floor could use a good sanding . . . well, so what—this place is a pleasure to discover after seeing so many deliberately rustic "theme" restaurants.

Naturally, it's all very informal here. You place your order at the counter and when it's ready it is set out for you to pick up. Cold drinks, salad, and herb teas (loads of 'em) are self-service. When you leave, tell the cashier what you had, and she'll tell you what you owe.

It won't be much. Poultry and fish entrées go for $3–$4; vegetarian dishes are sometimes less. We tried cabbage stuffed with tempeh (a cultured soyfood), rice, and sunflower seeds—a savory, if irreverent, variation of Grandma Pearl Schwartz's Jewish stuffed cabbage. With a nice salad, it goes for $2.95. There's a good meal-in-itself fish chowder for only 95 cents a bowl. Another popular item is broccoli, mushroom, ricotta, and macaroni casserole. Desserts are all made on the premises. How does apple-cranberry pie with whipped tofu cream sound to you? We gave it a try and had no regrets.

HOURS Mon.–Sat. 11 am–8 pm; closed Sun.

DIRECTIONS If northbound on I-93, take Exit 13; if southbound, take Exit 13N. Either way, follow signs for Route 3 North–Downtown. Go 0.7 mile on Route 3 North and turn left onto Concord St. One block takes you to S. State, and it's on the corner.

B. MAE DENNY'S, *Exit 14, Concord*

Good food, good values, and a great decor have combined to make B. Mae Denny's the brightest star in this part of New Hampshire. The renovation job done on this 19th century carriage factory would alone make it well worth looking into. Sand-blasted brick walls support 20-foot ceilings that tower high over the multilevel dining areas. Tall arched windows brighten this grand spaciousness, and earth-tone colors warm it. Three greenhouses are part of the scheme, one so large it accommodates 15 tables. Hanging Oriental-style carpets soften the bare brick, and there are lots of nice small touches, like candles on the tables and the quietly colorful velour seats. Mexican papier-mâché animals peer out from the shrubbery here and there—a whimsical touch that keeps the mood light.

So handsome a building usually brings a heavy price tag, but at B. Mae's you get all this for no more than you'd happily pay for less. Soup and half a sandwich at lunchtime, for example, cost only $2.25, and there's a good variety of plain and fancy sandwiches to choose from, none at more than $3.50. The quiches, the crepes, the salads—they're all there too, but if you feel like something more festive, how about skewered chunks of swordfish, pineapple, and green pepper with potatoes O'Brien and a baked stuffed tomato? Quite a lunch for $4.25.

The dinner menu has been selected from the popular favorites of all cuisines. You can get spaghetti with meatballs and garlic bread for $6.50 or prime rib for $13.75. In between are Cornish game hen with apple and raisin stuffing ($8.95); chicken teriyaki ($7.95); and crabmeat and scallops sautéed in garlic butter, wrapped in pastry, and baked in a casserole ($10.95).

You won't be disappointed by the desserts either, which all come from B. Mae's own bakery (their fine chocolate mousse was written up in *Gourmet* magazine).

Another nice touch is the policy on wine prices. Most restaurants simply double what you'd expect to pay at the wine store, but here they're content with a markup that makes wine with the meal seem like something less than a grand extravagance.

Good people doing a good job at modest prices—a touch of grandeur for the day-to-day world.

HOURS Mon.–Sat.: lunch 11 am–3 pm; sandwiches only, 3–5 pm; dinner 5–10 pm; Sun.: brunch 10 am–2:30 pm; dinner 4–10 pm.

DIRECTIONS Northbound: From Exit 14 turn left. Go three lights and then left again onto Main St. ■ Go 0.2 mile on Main, and then left again onto Depot. One block down the hill brings you to **B. Mae Denny's** on the left.

Southbound: Left at end of Exit 14 ramp. Left again at second light onto Main St. Then as above from ■.

THURSDAY'S RESTAURANT, *Exit 14, Concord*

Concord was apparently a culinary Sahara until Thursday's opened its doors in the late '70s. No one seems to know how it got its species name, but there's no doubt about the genus: a brick-plants-and-oak café, low on brick but high on natural wood. Stained latticework covers even the ceiling here, and the general effect is pleasant and up-to-date, even if not altogether original.

Lunches are good and run true to type. Fancy sandwiches—roast beef with cream cheese and garlic, for example—come on homemade white, rye, dill, or whole wheat. For $3.25 you get the whole affair, but half a sandwich and homemade soup or salad (there are five kinds) can be had for as little as $1.75. Six crepes are available, including a spinach with ricotta and nutmeg version at $2.50.

The lunch menu is served all day, but if you're in the mood for more you'll find dinners that go beyond the expected for a B.P.O. Steaks, Newburgs, scampis, Stroganoffs, schnitzels, and the like are offered, along with an interesting local favorite—chicken breast wrapped in bacon with mushroom sauce, Swiss, and toasted almonds. Served with soup or salad, potato or fried rice, and a vegetable, they run from $5.95 to $9.95.

HOURS Mon.–Thu. 11:30 am–3 pm and 5–9 pm; Fri. 11:30 am–10 pm; Sat. 11:30 am–3 pm and 5–10 pm; closed Sun.

DIRECTIONS Follow directions for **B. Mae Denny's,** above, to get onto Main St. Go 0.3 mile on Main to Pleasant. Right on Pleasant. **Thursday's** is ½ block up, on the right.

THE COMMON MAN, *Exit 24, Ashland*

According to the charming hostess, owner Alex Ray just hates pretentious restaurants; he even has an abiding affection for diners. So when he opened the Common Man in 1972 he was determined to offer good, interesting food at reasonable prices—a place where everyone would be at home and no one intimidated.

Well, he's done it. Here in an 18th century building that's been nicely but not painstakingly renovated are friendly people serving veal Marsala for $7.95 and chicken Florentine for $6.95. There are ten such uncommon entrées and ten more familiar ones, all in the neighborhood of $6.95.

At lunchtime $2 will get you a good solid sandwich of ham, turkey, or beef on homemade pumpernickel, sourdough, or honey wheat. Seven fancy sandwiches, including a roast beef with mushrooms and Marsala sauce, go for only a little more. A medley of chicken, walnuts, and orange slices is but one of five salads. Quiche du jour is $1.25.

We tasted an oyster stew here that was really wonderful, and while the rest of the meal, though certainly good, was not equally remarkable, it was a very happy dining experience. The small rooms of the old building have an intimate feel. And where else will you get white tablecloths, friendly, efficient service, and good food at prices like these?

A nice final touch is the white chocolate that comes gratis after every meal.

HOURS Lunch: Mon.–Sat. 11:30 am–2 pm; Dinner: every day 5–9 pm.

DIRECTIONS From Exit 24 turn right onto Route 3 South. Go 0.3 mile and it's on your left.

THE DOWNUNDER, *Exit 26, Plymouth*

Not long ago there wouldn't have been anything to write about in Plymouth, but Mike Hanley, owner of the Downunder, has brought good cooking to this college town.

He used to work at the Common Man in Ashland (above), and with him came the Common Man commitment to good food and uncommonly good prices. Nothing's higher than $6.95, including the likes of veal Oscar and shrimp scampi.

These bargains come in trendy comfort. The place is in a Main Street basement, but everything is light and bright, with pine wainscotting and white walls. A butcher-block bar and caned stools are separated from the dining area by a lively aquarium.

Seafood is the specialty here, and Mike is especially proud of the Downunder bake, a casserole of shrimp, lobster, and scallops, simmered in butter and topped with a seafood stuffing ($6.95). But landlubbers can enjoy chicken Kiev at $4.95 or pork pie for just $3.95.

Lunch is a pleasant occasion here too. There are four kinds of salads ($1.50–$3.50), soups from scratch (we heard a customer raving about the French onion), deli sandwiches for $2.50 and fancier varieties, including crab salad on English muffin with tomato, sprouts, and Swiss, for $3.95 tops. A light quiche and salad lunch will set you back only $2.25.

HOURS Mon.–Sat. 11:30 am–9:30 pm; closed Sun.

DIRECTIONS From Exit 26 turn right onto Route 3 and go 0.8 mile to center of Plymouth. You'll see the sign on your left. Restaurant is down the small side street by the sign.

SCANDINAVI-INN, *Exit 28, Campton*

On the outside it's a modern, well-designed, condominium-looking sort of motel with a hint of ski-chalet architecture. Inside, there's a chef who once cooked at the Grand Hotel in Stockholm and a very pretty dining room done up in rough barnboard decorated with Blue Willow ware. Matching blue tablecloths and hand-painted plates make for happy final touches.

They serve breakfast and dinner only. Toast, juice, and coffee is $1.10; the same with bacon and eggs, $3.25. The dinner menu isn't especially Swedish, but features popular favorites, filet of sole for $7 to filet mignon for $10.95. Schnitzel and Hungarian goulash at $7 provide variety and good bargains. The chef's pride once won an award at a Chicago restaurant show: lobster chunks simmered in white wine with mushrooms and spices, thickened with cream, then returned to the shell and baked beneath a topping of bread crumbs. Be prepared to do some shelling out yourself—$16.95, to be exact.

HOURS Breakfast: every day 7:30–10 am; Dinner: Mon.–Sat. 5:30–10 pm; Sun. 4–9 pm. Closed June.

DIRECTIONS From Exit 28 go left if northbound, right if southbound, onto Route 49 West. First building on the right, right by the road.

MT. ADAMS INN, *Exit 32, North Woodstock*

We know no place on earth to which the phrase "home cooking" more justly applies than the Mt. Adams Inn. The inn is, in fact, home to owners Larry and Dixie Hartle, and the kitchen, with its cluttered linoleum table and ordinary appliances, looks only a hair more commercial than your own, and quite likely more down to earth.

Solid Polish cooking at very modest prices, utterly unpretentious friendliness, and Dixie's ebullient personality are the main attractions here. There's a small dining room with a low acoustic-tile ceiling and inexpensive paneling that is brightened by large picture windows in two walls. Far from elegant, but full of the warmth suggested by its homemade tables of varnished pine tops and debarked tree-limb legs.

Like the decor, the food is all homemade. Gołabki, pierogi, and kielbasa are what you get here, at about $4 for a full dinner or $5.25 for the popular combination plate that lets you sample all three. The soups are from scratch, and for the less adventuresome meat-and-potatoes fans there are American dinners, sandwiches, and breakfasts at comparable prices (95 cents for a hamburger, $3 for an enormous breakfast of juice, eggs, kielbasa, home fries, toast, and coffee). Good, solid food, all of it, even if *Gourmet* magazine won't come asking for the recipes.

The Mt. Adams Inn is true to its name. In addition to meals there are rooms—about ten of them—at a ridiculous $10 a night for a single, $16 for a double. They have the same feel as the dining room, plain and inexpensive, but with endearing touches. Dixie really cares about her guests. Like a good daughter she watches over an elderly man who lives permanently in one of the rooms. It's that kind of place—like staying with a family of friends, because that's exactly what it is.

The Hartles took over three years ago, buying the inn on savings from their milkman and housecleaning jobs in Lawrence, Mass. "We took a challenge and we made it," says Dixie proudly. You can't but admire them and be reminded of what is best about America.

HOURS July 1–Oct. 31: every day 8 am–9 pm. Dec.–Mar.: every day 8–11 am and 5–9 pm. Closed Nov., Apr., May, and June.

DIRECTIONS From Exit 32 turn right and go about ½ mile to light. Left at light onto Route 3 South. Go 300 yards and you're there, on the right.

POLLY'S PANCAKE HOUSE, *Exit 38, Franconia*

Superb pancakes and waffles made from home-ground flour plus an absolutely spectacular view of the White Mountains—that, in a nutshell, is the story of Polly's Pancake House, a place that has received a good measure of well-deserved renown.

The building, which was first a carriage house, nestles beside pine trees high on a hilltop above Franconia. This spot has been owned by the same family since 1819, and from it you can gaze across the valley to the soaring wall of mountains on the far side. Be sure to do so—it's one of the few places in the East where mountains really look like mountains.

But when the flour is not only home-ground but comes in four varieties, it won't do to dwell on the scenery too long. You can have your pancakes in buckwheat, cornmeal, whole wheat, or plain white flour, all organically grown and stone-ground. If that's not enough, Polly makes her own maple syrup, tapping the nearby sugarbush and boiling down the sap each spring. If you've never tried the real thing, stop by and find out what you've been missing.

Light, fluffy, and delicious, plain pancakes come in orders of six 3-inchers for $2.60. If you want blueberries, walnuts, or coconut in them, or if you'd prefer the more unusual flours, it's a bit more. All-you-can-eat specials start at $4.

There are simple pancakes and regular breakfasts for those who just don't feel like pancakes. But it's hard to imagine being here and not eating mountains of 'em.

Polly, by the way, is a woman in her sixties, at least, who skis in winter and may well do more than just *direct* the sugaring operation come spring. She knows what she's about and what she wants. If you can talk with her, you'll learn a lot about the character of the Granite State.

HOURS Open only from May to mid-Oct. May 1 to Memorial Day: weekends only. Memorial Day to mid-Oct.: every day 7 am–7 pm.

DIRECTIONS From Exit 38 turn left if northbound, right if southbound, to stop sign. Turn right onto Route 18, and go ½ mile to junction with Route 117. Left onto 117. Go 1.7 miles to **Polly's,** on the right.

FRANCONIA INN, *Exit 38, Franconia*

If you're an aficionado of old inns, consider this very likable one in the shadow of the White Mountains. It's extremely livable, with 28 modestly priced rooms, a lovely dining room, rustic bar, good service, tennis in summer, spectacular foliage in autumn, cross-country skiing in winter, and . . . and . . .

If you can't stay over, the Franconia Inn still makes a fine break from the drive at dinnertime, and on weekends and holidays you'll find a simple lunch available in the lounge.

The dinner menu is more or less continental, with an accent on veal. There's veal Oscar (sautéed with butter and shallots, topped with crabmeat, white asparagus, and sauce Maltaise), $12.95; Cordon Bleu (sautéed and stuffed with ham and Swiss cheese in sauce suprême), $11.95; and Viennoise (schnitzel-style with lemon slices), $10.50. But shrimp scampi ($11.50) and chicken Florentine ($10.95) are great favorites too.

These delights are served in a wonderful dining room, surrounded on three sides by small-paned windows. It's a perfect blend of formality and simplicity, sure to make you forget you've spent the whole day driving.

Lunch is harder to find at the inn. It's served on weekends and holidays only, and then only in the bar, which is done up in remake-rustic, ski-lodge variety. And they don't go all-out over it—just simple, but generous, sandwiches ($2) and some good chili ($2.25). But even that makes for a nice diversion.

HOURS Dinner: Sun.–Fri. 6–9 pm; Sat. 6–10 pm. Lunch: weekends and holidays only, noon–3 pm. Closed Oct. 20–Dec. 20, and from April to June.

DIRECTIONS At end of Exit 38 ramp go left if northbound, right if southbound, to stop sign. Go straight across Route 18 onto Route 116 South. Go 2.3 miles. Inn is on your right.

LITTLETON DINER, *Exit 42, Littleton*

Left to their own devices, north-country locals and urban émigrés prefer not to mix, but like oil and vinegar, when shaken together the combination has a flavor all its own. You can taste it in Littleton, where, side by side, two restaurants feed opposite ends of a socio-dietary spectrum.

There's no question which end the Littleton Diner caters to. The building has been here, feeding the local populace, since the twenties. With its maroon and yellow enamel exterior and antique lettering, it's a classic diner, but the sign above the door looks like someone's idea of modernization. Inside, it's the same story—some true diner features, but also a display-case counter loaded with knickknacks for sale. On the walls is a lot of inexpensive paneling, and in back is an added dining area that looks like a finished basement.

But the fact is that we found here the best corn chowder we've come across yet. It was loaded with bacon, crunchy corn, and hefty hunks of potato. At 80 cents for a good-sized bowl, or with a decent toasted cheese sandwich and a nice bread pudding for $2.25, you've got yourself a deal.

We asked owner-cook Joe Howe for the recipe, but failed to learn the trick. "I just throw things together," he said with humility, "and fortunately it always comes out the same." Whether he was telling the truth or just guarding his secret, we'll never know.

Like the chowder, the other soups are made from scratch; about 75 percent of the dishes here are really homemade. Ask the waitress before ordering if you want to check. Dinners are from $3.95 for spaghetti with meat sauce to $8.95 for a T-bone with sautéed mushrooms. The usual sandwiches are all there, along with barbecue beef and a full breakfast menu at modest prices.

HOURS Summer: Mon.–Sat. 6 am–8 pm; Sun. 6 am–noon. Winter: Mon.–Sat. 6 am–7 pm; closed Sun.

DIRECTIONS See **Byblos,** below.

BYBLOS ORGANIC OASIS, *Exit 42, Littleton*

Next door to the Littleton Diner, the Earth children gather. Byblos is a natural foods restaurant of the most "spiritual" sort. Try this gem of menu prose and we think you'll get the idea: "We hope to awaken and surprise conventional palates to the uninhibiting and exciting superior protein succulents. Mimicking at best the Awesome Aesthetics and utilitarian beneficiense of Nature." (That gets one big *SIC*!)

Literary matters aside, we found here a combination health foods shop and restaurant, set in an old, delightfully cluttered store complete with a gorgeous oak counter displaying canisters of dried fruit and an old apothecary case supplied with an up-to-date arsenal of vitamins and supplements.

We were surprised to find any meat here at all, but Byblos was serving turkey sandwiches (organic, free-range, granola-eating turkeys, no doubt). The meat was juicy and tasty. There was also an absolutely stunning salad bar ($3.95 for all you can eat) loaded with fresh spinach, Romaine and red-tip lettuce, hummus, tabouli, baba ganoosh, chunks of Vermont cheddar, raisins, sesame and sunflower seeds, brewer's yeast, sprouts, coconut, several toothy breads, and Arden's rice cakes. Although neither of us is usually a tabouli booster, we found it most palatable—moist and perky, with a hint of cayenne.

There are three kinds of soup each day—seafood, split pea, and chilled cucumber-mint-avocado ($1.20/cup, $2/bowl, and up). The split pea was rich, thick, and mildly spiced with curry and a hint of brewer's yeast.

Byblos also serves fish ($5.95–$10.85), described on the menu as "24 hours fresh, broiled in the blessed olive oil, fresh lemon & faint flame via the Mediterranean (South Seas & Oriental) Delicate Art of Fish Savory." There is whole wheat pizza ($1.25 a slice), half a dozen types of quiche ($5–$6, with salad), and a wide selection of sandwiches, including a vegetarian club made of "tomatoe (*sic*), avacado (*sic*), sprouts, onion and cheddar" ($3.95).

Top all this healthy eating with Byblos's own "High on Health" ice cream. For an organic dessert, it is the crême de la crême—made in ten flavors with honey and other goodies, and without sugar, eggs, or other baddies. If you want to know more about it, they'll hand you a fact sheet, but we must warn you: it seems our "creative" menu writer is trying her hand at poetry.

HOURS Mon.–Sat. 11:30 am–8 pm; Sun. 11 am–3 pm.

DIRECTIONS From Exit 42 turn onto Route 302 East (right turn if northbound, left if southbound). It's about 0.2 mile to the downtown area. Both **Byblos** and the **Littleton Diner** are on your right.

THE CLAM SHELL, *Exit 42, Littleton*

The odds-on local favorite here is the Clam Shell, a very American sort of seafood restaurant in a low white clapboard building with porthole windows. The interior is a familiar blend of barnboard, green carpeting, Ethan Allen furniture, fishnets, and aquaria. Hardly indigenous to the mountains of New Hampshire, but pleasant enough in a just-folks way.

Lunch offers four salads, with lobster and tunafish specialties; three crepes, including a lobster-and-shrimp Newburg version for $3.95; lobster, clam, scallop, and tuna rolls ($2.10–$4.75); and a few non-seafood sandwiches.

For dinner there's a wide variety of seafood dishes, broiled or fried, starting at $5.50 for clam strips and topped off at $11.50 for the captain's platter—a sampling of deep-fried scallops, haddock, sole, shrimp, oysters, and clams. There are prime ribs, six steaks, three chicken dishes (around $6), and no fewer than five versions of surf 'n turf.

Not our kind of place, in all truth, but a good bet in its class.

HOURS Lunch: Mon.–Sat. 11:30 am–4 pm. Dinner: Mon.–Thu. 5–9 pm; Fri. & Sat. 5–10 pm; Sun. noon–9 pm.

DIRECTIONS From Exit 42 turn right if northbound, left if southbound, onto Route 302 East. **The Clam Shell** is only 100 feet from the exit, on your left.

I-95

Connecticut, Rhode Island, Massachusetts, New Hampshire, Maine

(Including I-295)

Connecticut

ABOUT GREENWICH

Greenwich is loaded—and loaded with restaurants. Although traffic can be sticky, the highway puts you not far from the center of town. You might enjoy parking a few blocks away and walking to your destination—or discovering it along the way. You'll find places to eat of every style, from lunch counter to haute cuisine, from bagel deli to patisserie. We've picked out a pastry/light-lunch café, a fancy (spectacular, even) bank-turned-restaurant, a bagel joint, and a chowder house. But don't feel limited by our choices. Explore.

VERSAILLES PATISSERIE, *Exit 3, Greenwich*

The Versailles Patisserie is not the kind of opulent spectacle you might expect from its name. It isn't even named after the palace of Louis XIV, but after the owner, Maurice Clos-Versailles, who after 15 years in this country finally fulfilled his dream of establishing a reasonably priced, informal, but pleasant place where customers could meet, sip espresso, discuss *The Times,* and sample his delicious pastries. The room's soft textures and understated brown and cream color scheme put you in the mood for just that—it's got a touch of elegance, but nothing stuffy.

The pastries—croissants, palmiers, pain du chocolat, raisin and apple rolls, and many more—are light, buttery and, best of all, not too sweet. Maurice makes them (and everything else) himself, and when the kitchen door swings open, a bounty of French aromas wafts out. Pastries, espresso, cappuccino, regular coffee, and tea are available whenever the Patisserie is open, but lunch items, described on a porcelain menu, are also served from 11:30 to 3:00.

In addition to spinach and seafood quiches ($2.50/$2.95), there are soups and several unusual salads. The Versailles' seafood salad ($3.75) consists of shrimp, scallops, and mussels glossed with vinaigrette; a large opera salad of Swiss, ham, capers, and greens will get you all the way through the third act of *Aïda* ($4.95). Maurice's delectable specialty is his Tourte Milanaise ($3.95). With onion soup, it's about as civilized a lunch as you can find anywhere.

HOURS Lunch: every day 11:30 am–3 pm. Pastries and coffee only: Mon.–Fri. 7:30–11:30 am and 3–5 pm; Sat. & Sun. 8–11:30 am and 3–5 pm. Take-out only: Mon.–Sat. 5–7 pm.

DIRECTIONS See end of Greenwich entries, p. 167.

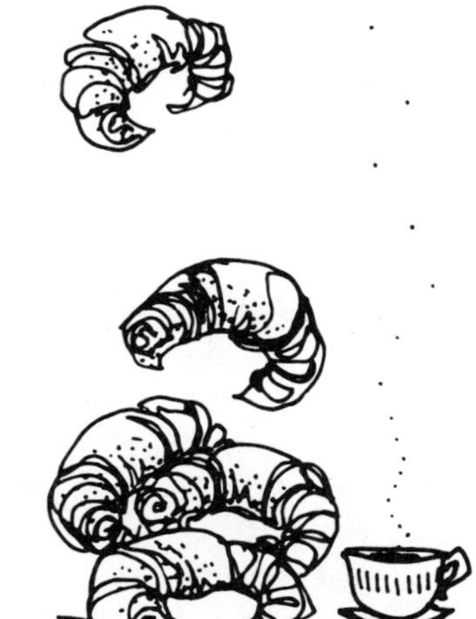

GREENSTREET, *Exit 3, Greenwich*

Located one block from Versailles Patisserie, Greenstreet comes closer to being the palatial extravaganza that the patisserie is not. In this case, though, the architect and the architecture are Italian. Greenstreet was once a bank building, and its wide-open interior soars high overhead, in vaulted ceilings of amber-colored tile. The bank president's office is now one of two dining balconies, a choice spot for regular guests who love to look across the expanse of tiled columns and arches, wide staircases, brass banisters, bentwood chairs, and abundant (though not overbearing) indoor foliage, all illuminated through skylights.

The dinner menu matches the decor—it's extensive and expensive, with entrées in the $12–$17 range, largely French (sole Meunière, chicken tarragon, veal Cordon Bleu) and Italian (veal piccata, veal and chicken Marsala), with some steaks and American-style seafood dishes as well. Lunch, a bit surprisingly, leans toward burgers, sandwiches, and salads (most $3–$5), the same kind of "nouveau cuisine" found in less spectacular brick-plants-and-oak cafés—right down to the carrot cake.

HOURS Sun.–Thu. 11:30 am–3 pm and 6–9 pm; Fri. & Sat. 11:30 am–3 pm and 6–11 pm; Sun. noon–4 pm.

DIRECTIONS See end of Greenwich entries, p. 167.

BAGEL PLUS, *Exit 3, Greenwich*

The "Plus" at Bagel Plus is that you get to watch them make the bagels in front of you. First the dough is shaped in a special device, then it's dropped into a vat of steaming water. Finally, the white doughnut shapes are browned in a great stainless-steel oven, pulled out, and deposited in one of eight bins—plain, poppy, sesame, onion, etc. (25 cents each). It's the dual cooking—boiling and baking—that makes a bagel a bagel.

To turn a bagel into a meal, Bagel Plus slices it and smears the halves with chicken, tuna, egg, or shrimp salad. There's lox, of course, sliced or in a spread, and sliced meats as well. Most bagel sandwiches are $1.99; the portions are ample, but the spreads are commercially made and their quality falls short of the bagels themselves.

It's clean, well lit, and sanitary white in here, and next to the simple tables there's a self-service cooler with milk, orange juice, and sodas (including Dr. Brown's Cel-Ray).

HOURS Mon.–Sat. 5:30 am–6 pm; Sun. 5:30 am–2 pm.

DIRECTIONS FOR GREENWICH RESTAURANTS Northbound: From Exit 3 take the first left (Arch St.) and go through three lights to city parking lot on right (0.3 mile from the exit). Park here and walk through the lot to Greenwich Ave. at the opposite end. You'll be right near **Greenstreet** (253 Greenwich Ave.), **Versailles Patisserie** (315 Greenwich Ave.), and **Bagel Plus** (335 Greenwich Ave.).

Southbound: Same as northbound, except turn right from Exit 3 to get onto Arch St. Parking lot will be on your right, after two (not three) lights.

BOBBY VALENTINE'S SPORTS GALLERY CAFÉ, *Exit 7, Stamford*

Good afternoon, sports fans . . . This one is for you.

What happens when local high school athlete makes good, signs on as an outfielder with the Dodgers, breaks his leg in his first season, never completely recovers, gets traded around both leagues, quits playing, and comes home to Stamford? He starts a restaurant, of course.

Bobby Valentine's is at the same time a monument to the former ballplayer's ego and an utterly fascinating museum of sports memorabilia. Along with dozens of old letters offering Valentine athletic scholarships at practically every university in the nation, a 10-foot effervescent mural of our hero in mid-swing, and the framed jerseys from five of his major league clubs, the restaurant has an overwhelming display of old baseball cards and gate tickets, Hall of Fame profiles, *Sporting News* covers, team photos, old-time programs, and the like. Above the bar, a sports ticker tape keeps you informed of the latest action all over the country.

Here you can expect to find, in addition to the man himself (when he's free from his busy schedule of scouting and sportscasting), big leaguers who happen to be in town, local jocks who dream they were big leaguers (but instead come here to put on everything they just took off at the Nautilus machine), corporate customers from nearby IBM and Xerox, and teenagers who hope some of the fame will rub off. Weekday evenings after eight and all day Friday are loud and beery—you might want to wear a batter's helmet—but Saturdays and Sundays are quieter, as are weekday lunches and early evenings.

The food is brick-plants-and-oak café fare, and the menu looks like the sports page of the New York *Daily News*. There are "Hall of Fame" sandwiches ($3–$4), "Burger League" burgers (same), and "Runners Club" salads ($2.25–$4). We didn't strike out with the Monte Cristo sandwich we sampled. It was quite good, a tasty hybrid of ham, turkey, and French toast. As a warm-up item, nachos ($2.50) are a big scorer here; they come in five varieties—bean, jalapeño and bean, chili, spicy beef, and the grand slam (all of the above). And for brawny—but not beefy—lads there are veggie fries—onion rings, zucchini, eggplant, mushrooms, and artichoke hearts.

HOURS Mon.–Thu. noon–10 pm; Fri. & Sat. noon–11:15 pm; Sun. 5–10 pm.

DIRECTIONS Northbound: From Exit 7 go straight to the second light and turn left onto Washington Blvd. ■ Turn right at the fourth light (Main St.). It's ½ block down, on your right (225 Main).

Southbound: From Exit 7 go straight, turning right at the third light, onto Washington Blvd. Then as above from ■.

HUNAN 95, *Exit 9, Stamford*

Chinese food is "in," especially Hunan and Szechuan, and it is true that the restaurants serving these cuisines tend to be, as a reviewer for *The New York Times* has said, "clones of one another." Further, this particular clone happens to be situated in a motor inn —not usually the most auspicious sign for a restaurant of any sort. And to make matters worse, its cantilevered, glass-enclosed dining room offers a stupendous view—of the Connecticut Turnpike.

But we'll stop complaining and admit that it's a pleasure to find quality Chinese food so close to the highway. At Hunan 95, the short-range view of what's on your plate is certain to be more memorable than the panorama out the window. Almost every dish is dressed up with baby corncobs, red or green peppers, chili pepper pods, black Chinese mushrooms, or some combination of vegetables that creates a medley of bright colors and varied textures. Only fresh ingredients could look so good, and the food tastes as good as it looks.

Surviving the hot and sour soup (95 cents) may require many water chasers. Lamb Hunan style ($8.95), chicken with pine nuts ($5.25), Szechuan sesame beef ($7.95), eggplant in garlic sauce ($4.25), and about 20 other Hunan and Szechuan dishes are equally fiery. Moo Goo Gai Pan ($5.25), Mu Shu Pork ($5.25), shrimp with cashews ($6.75), and other Cantonese and Peking standbys are milder. At lunchtime, entrées are about $1 less, and a luncheon special, including soup, entrée, rice, dessert, and tea, goes for an affordable $4.75.

The view may be less than an inspiration, but at least you won't have any trouble finding your way back to the highway.

HOURS Mon.–Thu. 11:30 am–11 pm; Fri. & Sat. 11:30 am–midnight; Sun. noon–11 pm.

DIRECTIONS Northbound: At the bottom of Exit 9 ramp, look left —it's in the Stamford Motor Inn.

Southbound: From Exit 9 turn left for 1 block. It's on your right, in the Stamford Motor Inn.

CAPT'N HENRY'S SEAFOOD, *Exits 11 & 12, Rowayton*

* *Color, not cuisine*

If you're a lover of tiny places with local color, then Capt'n Henry's is for you. The food at this seven-stooler is decidedly fried and the decor is decidedly funk, but it's right on Long Island Sound. Inside, everyone's talking about boats, from the yachtsman types who hold the place in campy affection to the local fishermen for whom it's just a place to eat. Outside, the lobster traps are piled high on the dock, just like it's s'posed to be.

A fried clam roll is $2.30 for strips (Ho-Jo style) or $2.95 for whole clams. Shrimp, oyster, and scallop versions are $3.75. You can get a two-egg breakfast here, with home fries, for $1.25. The rest of the menu is scattered about the walls on various pieces of posterboard. If you don't see what you want, ask the waitress; it's easy to miss a fragment. But if the place is busy—and it doesn't take much to fill it to the gunwales—you'll have to move fast to catch her.

HOURS Tue.–Sat. 7 am–8:30 pm; Sun. 8 am–8:30 pm; closed Mon.

DIRECTIONS Northbound: Turn right at the end of the Exit 12 ramp and continue 1.7 miles through the town of Rowayton. It's on the right.

Southbound: Take Exit 11 and turn right onto Route 1. Go 0.3 mile to Route 136 and turn right, following signs for Rowayton. Go about 2 miles, through Rowayton, and it'll be on the right.

ABOUT WESTPORT

At the eastern edge of Connecticut's "Gold Coast" is Westport, a New England–style Beverly Hills with all the earmarks of vogue: seaside setting, trendy shops, resident celebrities (Paul Newman and Joanne Woodward), restored buildings, and restaurants galore. **Chez Pierre** and **Le Chambord** are toney, pricey, and French. **The Mooring** is woody, planty, and airy, with an unbeatable view of the Saugatuck River. **Viva Zapata** is a popular spot for Mexican food, and **Pearl's Restaurant** is a tiny tea parlor of a place serving salads, sandwiches, pasta dishes, and fondue. All of these, and other fine restaurants, are easy enough to find, but we have chosen to feature two quality dining spots that are especially close to the highway.

DE ROSA'S, *Exit 17, Westport*

In a well-heeled town like Westport, it's surprising to find a highly regarded restaurant located in a small utilitarian building perched on an embankment and sandwiched between the elevated highway and a nest of huge oil tanks. Inside, De Rosa's is equally surprising; you'll find wooden floors and tables, walls embellished with steamboat prints, a watercolor of Harvard University, and a Toulouse-Lautrec print—a far cry from the Italian restaurant stereotype.

Well, who wants glitzy Italianate statues anyway? We were happy to find De Rosa's money invested where we could taste it —in fine Italian food, carefully prepared with the best ingredients. Everything—bread, sandwich rolls, pasta, desserts—is made daily on the premises.

Lunch here is not necessarily true to type. To be sure, it can be Italian, with appetizers like baked clams oreganato ($3.25) and pasta dishes like fettucini Alfredo ($4.50) or linguini with zesty Italian sausage ($5). But it can also lean toward the modern American cuisine of spinach salads ($3.50), tuna melt on rye ($3.25), or a seven-ounce hamburger ($2.75).

Dinner, however, is the real thing. Any of a dozen Italian appetizers can start your meal; we found the caponata—a cold eggplant relish served on lettuce ($2.50)—to be outstanding. Of the eight pasta dishes (most $4.75–$6), we chose linguini with white clam sauce and found it very satisfying. De Rosa's is especially proud of its veal dishes ($8.95), using only the tenderest cuts, which are sautéed and served as veal Florentine, Marsala, or piccata.

There are only 35 seats here and so, understandably, demand exceeds supply on Friday and Saturday nights. Phone ahead, (203) 227-7596, or come with a book to read while you wait.

HOURS Lunch: Mon.–Sat. noon–3 pm; Dinner: Mon.–Sat. 5:30–10:30 pm; Sun. 5:30–9:30 pm.

DIRECTIONS Northbound: From Exit 17 go straight through two traffic lights to a stop sign at a T. ■ Turn left here onto Riverside Ave. In 0.1 mile, it's on your right.

Southbound: From Exit 17 turn right to first light. Left here and straight through one light to a stop sign at a T. Then as above from ■.

DAMEON, *Exit 17, Westport*

Dameon is a warm and comfortable little restaurant with surprisingly reasonable prices for an altogether pleasing, eclectic cuisine. The color scheme is a restful chocolate and cream, accented with brown-checked table runners laid diagonally across coffee-colored tablecloths. Light jazz, played in the bar on piano and bass, adds an aural component to the somewhat sophisticated atmosphere.

Every day there are pasta, fish, and quiche specials ($3.50–$5 at lunch; $6–$10 at dinner). All dishes, and even sauces, are cooked to order. Desserts are made from scratch daily, and they include cranberry-apple pie, three-layer lemon cake, pear tarts, and—a new one on us—kiwi tarts.

For our lunch we turned down the regular sandwiches, salads, and omelettes, as well as several tempting specials like Bombay chicken (a curried chicken salad served on freshly baked apple-nut bread) and Marquis salad (tuna with red cabbage, onion, garlic, and olives). Instead, we went for the house special, Dameon's Viennese meatloaf with a slice of hard-boiled egg dead center. It was full-flavored, redolent with seasoning but short of overspiced. So that's what meatloaf is supposed to be!

Hearing that linguini with clams, shrimp, mussels, and crab in white wine sauce ($8.95) was slated for that evening's meal, we thought about hanging around until dinner, but duty called. We were satisfied that you'll like it here, any time of day.

HOURS Lunch: Mon.–Fri. 11 am–3 pm; Sat. & Sun. noon–3 pm. Dinner: Mon., Tue. & Thu. 5:30–10:30 pm; Wed. & Fri. 5:30–11 pm; Sat. 6–11 pm; Sun. 5:30–9:30 pm.

DIRECTIONS Northbound: From Exit 17 go straight through two lights to a stop sign at a T. ■ Turn right here, go one block to another stop sign, and right again onto Railroad Place. It's three doors down, on the right.

Southbound: From Exit 17, turn right to first light. Left here and straight through one light to stop sign at a T. Then as above from ■.

DOGWOOD'S, *Exit 21, Fairfield*

The affluent towns along Connecticut's western coast pride themselves on Colonial charm, trendy shops, and resident celebrities. While possessed of all of the above, Fairfield also has a more modest claim to fame: dogwood trees, about 30,000 of them planted all over the town's roads, a tradition that dates to the Revolutionary era. Each May, Fairfielders hold a Dogwood Festival to celebrate the graceful trees.

Dogwood's Restaurant also celebrates the trees with its woodsy wallpaper and a few blossoms on table and menu. It's spacious and pleasant inside, though a little on the Ethan Allen side. Dogwood's prices are reasonable, its menu varied, and its food quite respectable. There are a dozen variations on hamburger ($2.65–$3.50), each with a provoking name like Siberianburger (sour cream and onions) or Mediterraneanburger (feta cheese and olives). For $4.70, you can get half a sandwich with a bowl of homemade soup. The soups, including seafood chowder, are all made here from scratch (around $2.50), as is the French bread that accompanies them. Entrées include steak, goulash, fish of the day, stuffed cabbage, and tortellini, all served with garden salad and French bread (most $4–$7). Five full-meal salads should satisfy the grazers among you, and tasty desserts, the indulgent.

HOURS Sun.–Thu. 11 am–11 pm, sandwiches until 1 am; Fri. & Sat. 11 am–11:30 pm, sandwiches until 2 am.

DIRECTIONS From Exit 21 turn left if southbound, right if northbound, and go about 0.2 mile to U.S. 1. Right on U.S. 1, and go 0.2 mile to South Pine Creek Rd. **Dogwood's** is on the right, just before the light, opposite an Arco station.

THE SHELL STATION, *Exit 32, Stratford*

It's not a gas station; it's a converted railroad depot, and it hasn't been made over as a theme restaurant—semiphores hanging from the walls, yellowed pictures of spewing locomotives, and a menu with sandwiches called "The Engineer" or "The Caboose." Steve Wang—owner, manager, and chef—passed all that by and produced a charming restaurant by keeping everything simple, pretty, and tasteful. Especially the food.

Primarily a seafood restaurant, the Shell Station serves meals that have the look and taste of sophistication but are in reality deceptively simple. After ten years' experience, Steve believes—and we agree—that the secret to superb fish cookery is contained in three words: "fresh, fresh, fresh." With a light touch and just a few basic ingredients—flour, egg, butter, lemon, garlic, herbs, and wine—fish speaks for itself.

Early each morning Steve combs the nearby fish markets to stock up for the day. The most beautiful catch he can find ends up as the day's special, and his inspiration for how to prepare it often comes to him right there on the wharf.

Because sautéeing affords him such control of the cooking process, it is Steve's favorite technique. Clams and chicken in garlic ($9.50) has received the plaudits of local restaurant reviewers more than once; it is very popular with Stratford's Shakespeare Theater patrons. Served in a huge bowl, saffron-seasoned paella—a Spanish shellfish stew—has not yet been finished in one sitting. Try to set a record, if you like, but bring an accomplice, for the $30 price tag is meant for two people. It will probably satisfy three.

Steve also makes fresh pasta, and tops it with a glorious red sauce thick with clams, mussels, and shrimp ($8.95 at dinner, $4.95 at lunch).

There is no bar, not even a liquor license. Steve provides a complimentary glass of Chablis with every meal; if you come prepared, you can refill it yourself.

HOURS Mon. & Wed.–Fri. 11:45 am–2 pm and 5–10 pm; Sat. & Sun 5–10 pm; closed Tues.

DIRECTIONS Northbound: Exit 32 feeds you into a rotary. Follow it three-quarters of the way around and head under the highway bridge. Turn right at the light and go one block to stop sign. ■ Turn left and go under the bridge. Take your first right and go one block (0.1 mile) to another stop sign and a T-junction. Look across the road and a little to your left, and you will see a driveway. Pull into it, and the restaurant will be on your right.

Southbound: From Exit 32 make a sharp right immediately at the bottom of the ramp. Go one block (0.1 mile) to stop sign. Then as above from ■.

INTERNATIONAL HOT DOG RANCH, *Exit 34, Milford*

We weren't overly enthusiastic about even entering this low-slung, dilapidated yellow shack of a building, but its garish sign showing a giant hot dog impaled by four international flags pricked our curiosity. Tentatively, we walked into the dingy, smoke-filled room.

We were amused but still a bit skeptical when we learned that here are served five sizes of hot dogs, each available in any of 30 "international" versions. There's the Italian hot dog, topped with tomato sauce and mozzarella cheese, the Greek frank with feta cheese, the Hawaiian dog doused in crushed pineapple, and the English version with Piccadilly relish. The Dutch dog, with melted Gouda cheese, is set in potato skins instead of a roll, while Mexico's sits in a taco shell, appropriately garnished with lettuce, tomato, onion, and cheese.

But best of all, we found that the hot dogs were not only gimmicky, but good!

"We're the only one in the whole world," exclaimed Phil Garozzo, emperor of this hot dog kingdom. (He's probably right—we doubt there'd be another.)

His hot dogs are indeed a cut or two above the bonemeal tubes you get at ballgames. Most are Roessler's brand, but there are exceptions in keeping with the international theme: the Swedish hot dog is a bockwurst (veal and pork), and the Polish frank is kielbasa. The Israeli variety? Hebrew National, of course.

The biggest seller here is the Belgian dog—bacon and cheese. But Phil's favorite is the Russian—pastrami and sauerkraut with melted cheese and Russian dressing. We tasted it and were astonished at just how tasty it was. "It's important to grill the kraut," Phil explained diligently. It took him ten years, he claims, to work up a chili recipe that would work on a hot dog. "What country?" we foolishly asked. "Chile, of course."

There have been some failures, though. The crepe-wrapped French frank was a flop. Why? His customers didn't know what a crepe was, or how to pronounce it.

The International Hot Dog Ranch also serves a few items that are not tube-shaped, particularly in the morning. Two pancakes, two eggs, two slices of bacon, and coffee or tea costs $2.29; one egg, one pancake, three slices of bacon, and coffee is $1.29.

Hot dogs, by the way, run from 75 cents for the smallest American (plain) to $2 for a foot-long Russian. Frankly, they're worth it.

HOURS Mon.–Sat. 6 am–8 pm; Sun. 7 am–5 pm.

DIRECTIONS From Exit 34, the ramp takes you to a traffic light. Turn left onto Route 1 and go ½ mile. It's on your right.

MAYFLOWER DINER, *Exit 40, Milford*

Once a showpiece American diner, the Mayflower has been completely done over to look like a low-lying Crystal Palace. With terrazzo floor, pawnbroker light fixtures, ersatz brick, and Roman-weave window shades, it now earns its berth in Americana as a herding ground for 18-wheelers and the cowboys who drive them. Here, in truckers' heaven, you can get a haircut or a shave, do the laundry, take a shower, watch TV, pick up some souvenirs for the kids, fix your rig, or buy a new one altogether. And, in case you've worked up an appetite attending to those matters, you can feed yourself silly. We don't need to describe the food—it's got no surprises. Order one of the specials—it's fresh. Prices are reasonable—$3.60 for dinner à la carte, $5 complete. For just over a dollar, you get a big bowl of chunky soup—not subtle, but good and filling.

Unlike some truck stops, the Mayflower doesn't segregate professional drivers from us mortals, so if you have any repressed fantasies of truckerdom, here's the place to act them out. Just don an appropriate headpiece (we noticed that cowboy hats outnumbered baseball caps by about three to two, with lumberjack hats a distant third), pull out one shirttail, and start griping about Smokies. And before you leave, you'll want to visit the showroom out back. We looked at two muscle-bound Kenworths—one at $78,000, the other at $88,000. We inspected the $88,000 model and found the mattress somewhat flimsy for the price. A peremptory kick at the tire, however, resulted in one very sore toe.

HOURS 24 hours, every day of the year.

DIRECTIONS Northbound: From Exit 40 turn left at stop sign. Go 0.2 mile; it's on the right.

Southbound: From Exit 40 turn left, pass under highway, look right.

ABOUT NEW HAVEN

Until the wrecker's ball and Wooster Street's apartments met face to face, this thoroughfare and nearby side streets were New Haven's Little Italy. In the wake of urban renewal, the Italian community has dispersed, but Wooster Street remains Restaurant Row. All kinds of Italian food can be had in all kinds of Italian atmosphere, at all kinds of American prices. Walk the streets and take your pick. We feature two—a moderately priced lunch and dinner spot, and a wonderful little pastry shop—and we mention a few others.

With only a one-mile detour onto I-91, the Greek food of Basel's, and the modern American cuisine of Annie's Firehouse Soup Kitchen are also accessible from I-95 in New Haven.

CASA DELLA PASTA, *Exit 46, New Haven*

Casa della Pasta is more than a pasta house. Certainly it is that—you can watch gleaming machinery extrude the stuff in the little glass-enclosed pasta factory—but it is also a very pleasant restaurant with a varied menu and high-quality food.

Ida Giemei, hostess, bookkeeper, and odd-jobs lady, greets you at the door and, unless it is exceptionally busy, spends some time chatting at your table. She makes you feel at home right away in this airy, bright, very up-to-date dining room enhanced by skylights that show off the tile floor, polished mirrors, and basket lamps. On the walls, Italo-Restaurantesque paintings show wheat fields and windmills instead of the expected Roman ruins—a welcome change, certainly appropriate for a pasta restaurant.

It comes as no surprise that pasta dishes excel here. Fettucini Alfredo comes in all its creamy grandeur, but there are five other fettucini dishes as well, including fettucini della chef (artichokes, mushrooms, cheese, and cream) and fettucini matrigiana (bacon, onion, tomato, and ham). Spaghetti, linguini, ziti, pappardella (wide ribbons), cannelloni (rolled tubes), gnocci (small dumplings), manicotti, and ravioli are also offered with a winning assortment of sauces and toppings, such as broccoli, tuna sauce, pesto, seafood, and cream sauce with peas and prosciutto. Pasta dinners run $4.25 to $7.25 at lunch, $5.95 to $9.50 at dinner.

It was nice to find good pasta-less dishes too. The escarole-with-bean soup was smoky and delicious ($1.50). Red snapper was sautéed in a delicate herb sauce ($5.95 lunch/$7.25 dinner), while the tender veal Francese ($5.50/$9.75) was dipped in egg, sautéed, and served in a sprightly white wine and lemon sauce.

There is an all-you-can-eat spaghetti special here for $2.50 on Tuesdays. On any day, a children's menu is available.

Only the Muzak and the flat-tasting bread detracted from an excellent meal at Casa della Pasta. We skipped dessert, and instead skipped over to Libby's Pastry Shop next door, where the Casa's cannoli are made. Read on.

HOURS Mon.–Thu. 11 am–11 pm; Fri. & Sat. 11 am–11:30 pm; Sun. 1–11 pm.

DIRECTIONS See directions for New Haven restaurants, p. 181.

LIBBY'S ITALIAN PASTRY SHOP, *Exit 46, New Haven*

Libby's Pastry Shop served its first cannoli in 1922. No one knows how many have been sold since then, but no one will deny that the pastries emanating from Libby's have been a predominant sight—and smell—on Wooster Street for the past 60 years.

Cannoli (65 cents) is the biggest seller. Fortunato Dell'Amura, whose father, Liberato, founded the shop, uses pistachio nuts in the creamy ricotta filling. Heaven! A close second to the cannoli were the sfogliatelle (80 cents), shells of flaky puff pastry leaves filled with ricotta and orange-flavored farina. Libby's pastry case also flaunts rum babas, Napoleons, bigne (cream puffs), eclairs, almond tarts, Italian cheesecakes, and a dozen other caloric creations, many of them originals.

Fortunato recently added a continental-style coffee shop to let customers linger in a hedonistic stupor over his pastries and any of twelve kinds of coffee, from espresso con ànice to decaffeinated cappuccino. He also serves Italian ices, all made with fresh fruits and nothing artificial. Lemon is the big seller, but consider pomegranate, tamarind, almond, wild cherry, or mint.

If you want to see Fortunato launch into an impassioned tirade right out of a Fellini flick, ask him about spumoni. Americans have come to regard spumoni as ice cream dotted with a meager dose of fruit, and Fortunato bristles at the thought. His authentic spumoni is a rainbow of ices and ice creams flecked heartily with fruit and nuts: vanilla, chocolate, coffee, strawberry, and lemon ices in the outside ring, vanilla ice cream, fruit, and nuts within. To distinguish his product from the impostors, Fortunato has trademarked the name "Capriccio Italian." His eyes danced as he served us a slice. "You've hit the moment of truth for spumoni," he announced, beaming.

Believe us, it's good. Go find out what spumoni can be.

HOURS Mon., Wed., Thu. 4–11 pm; Fri. & Sat. 11:30 am–1 am; Sun. 2:30–11 pm; closed Tue.

DIRECTIONS See directions for New Haven restaurants, p. 181.

Also on Wooster Street

Pepe's Pizza (157 Wooster St.) is a New Haven institution. Its devotees are many—too many if you are in a hurry. Be prepared to wait in line, but also be prepared for the "best pizza in Connecticut" if 30 years of committed followers are to be believed.

Salvatore Caffè, on the corner of Wooster and Brown streets, is also a New Haven favorite, but of a different sort. Under skylights and beautiful arched walkways, high mirrors, and a huge schefflera tree, dine business people and jet-setters, the well-to-do and the up-and-coming. Italian ices between the courses. Maybe too much for a highway stop.

Tony and Lucille's, next door to Casa della Pasta, is a fast in-and-out sort of place. Calzone (dumplings filled with mozzarella cheese and pizza toppings) are big here. Prices are not.

DIRECTIONS FOR NEW HAVEN RESTAURANTS Northbound: From Exit 46 go to the stop sign and turn left. Go ¼ mile to first light and then left, under the highway. At the light on the other side turn right. ■ Follow curves in road for 0.4 mile to next light. Turn right here and go 2 blocks to next light. Turn left. Bear right around the curve onto Franklin. The first light you come to is at the foot of Wooster St., on your left. All the restaurants mentioned are two blocks up the street, but Wooster is one-way, the wrong way. Park and walk, or drive around the block, but don't turn right or you'll be fed onto the highway against your will.

Southbound: From Exit 46 turn right at light and go through the next light (in front of Armstrong Building). Continue straight, as above from ■.

ANNIE'S FIREHOUSE SOUP KITCHEN

BASEL'S, *I-91 Interchange, New Haven*

See pp. 77 and 78 for descriptions of a fine Greek restaurant and a good brick-plants-and-oak café.

DIRECTIONS Go north on I-91 about a mile to Exit 5. Then follow directions given.

THE HAPPY WOK, *Exits 57 & 58, Guilford*

Among the many theorems of restaurantology that we developed in our travels is the one that says you can't find a decent restaurant in a shopping center. The Happy Wok, a Vietnamese and Chinese restaurant, challenged that hypothesis, and we will concede that it was the exception that proved the rule.

If our visit was typical, you can expect to be much happier with the cooking than the service; the Happy Wok's food, once it arrived, was indeed good. The Vietnamese specialties were collages of interesting flavors, some of which seemed to spill over into the Chinese standbys. The won-ton soup, for example, had an uncommon punch. Ga Xao Sa is chicken sautéed with lemon grass (a Vietnamese green vegetable), chili peppers, and a "special sauce"; it is spicy and well prepared ($6.75). In another Vietnamese dish, Bun Thit Nuong, marinated pork is broiled and served with pickled vegetables, delicate rice-stick noodles, and another "special sauce." We're not sure what goes into these sauces, but they do manage to impart a delightful pungency.

The menu also offers stir-fried crabmeat or chicken with cellophane noodles ($6.45/$5.25), some spicy spring rolls served with fish sauce ($1.25 for three), shrimp chips, and, for dessert, a tart lime pie that was popular, we were told, in Saigon's French pastry shops back when French pastry shops were popular in Saigon.

Luncheons at the Happy Wok run $3.45 to $5.95 and are strictly Chinese.

HOURS Tue.–Sat. 11:30 am–3 pm and 5–9 pm; Sun. 4–9 pm; closed Mon.

DIRECTIONS Northbound: From Exit 57 turn right onto Route 1 North. Go about 2 miles. It's on the left, in Guilford Plaza.

Southbound: From Exit 58 turn right. At the first light, turn right onto Route 1 South (Boston Post Rd.). It's in Guilford Plaza, about ½ mile down, on the right.

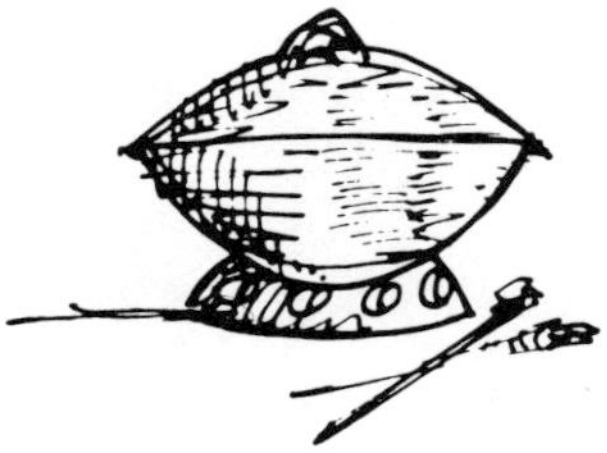

THE PLACE, *Exits 57 & 58, Guilford*

Unlike the Happy Wok, the Place isn't in a shopping center. In fact, it isn't even in a building. It's out behind a small red cottage on the Boston Post Road. Every summer since 1948—it was known as "Whitey's" then—this locally famous institution has been roasting clams over a 20-foot-long barbecue pit. The people who come here represent every age, class, and style. Whether their workaday garb is pin stripes or hard hats, at the Place they happily sit on tree-stump seats, order from wooden menus nailed to a tree, and set their plates on slab tables. There are 32 such tables, yet on July weekends as many as 50 people patiently wait for a place to sit.

The director of this backyard operation is Vaughn Knowles, a math teacher for 10 months of the year. Vaughn has worked here every summer since he was 14 years old. When his old boss, Whitey, moved to Florida, Vaughn took over and changed nothing.

A dozen roasted clams dabbed with butter and cocktail sauce cost $3.85; plain roasters are $3.75, and steamers a dime less. Shrimp, also bathed in sauce, go for $5.90 a dozen.

Corn on the cob (roasted, of course) is also sold here, as are cheesecake and carrot cake. But if you want anything else, you'll have to bring it yourself. Customers in the know regularly do, toting ice chests fairly overflowing with salads, bread, desserts, and libations of every sort. You don't have to be quite so well prepared, though—there's a large shopping center right across the street.

Hardwood roasting imparts a very special flavor to shellfish, and we know of nowhere else to try it. For a modest price, the Place gives you a whole new experience.

HOURS Memorial Day to Labor Day: Mon.–Fri. 5–11 pm; Sat. & Sun. 1–11 pm.

First weekend in May to Memorial Day and Labor Day to mid-Oct.: Sat. & Sun. only, 1–11 pm.

DIRECTIONS Northbound: From Exit 57 turn right onto Route 1 North. It's just before the sixth stoplight, about 1¾ miles down, on the left.

Southbound: From Exit 58 turn right. At the first light, turn right onto Route 1 South. It's on the right, about 1 mile down, just past the first light.

THE FISH TALE, *Exit 63, Clinton*

There is no shortage of greasy fish joints along Connecticut's shoreline, but here's a little place that goes out of its way to do things differently. From the outside, the Fish Tale looks like a wooden version of Arthur Treacher's, and the inside is not a great deal better. But there the comparison stops.

Every day of the year, the Fish Tale prints a different menu, "to reflect weather, market conditions, and fishing luck," says Joe Goldberg, who runs the place with his brother Lenny. When they can get striped bass, salmon, swordfish, or bluefish, you'll read about it on the menu; otherwise scrod and native sole are pretty sure bets.

The kitchen would just as soon broil your fish in butter, but if you prefer it fried, you'll find the surface soft and flaky, not clothed in a coat of greasy sandpaper. The secret is in the batter. "The real purpose of batter is to let heat, not oil, penetrate the fish," says Joe. "We've worked out a batter that is just thick enough to protect the fish but not so heavy as to give it a bready taste." Instead of preparing and stacking a hundred filets each morning, Joe and Lenny batter each one to order. It takes a little longer, but we could certainly taste the difference.

For all this love and attention, a scrod dinner with new potatoes, coleslaw, and bread goes for only $3.95. Sole is $4.95 and a double portion costs about 1½ times as much.

There's a complete seafood menu here—scallops, clams, shrimp, crab, littlenecks, etc.; dinners average about $5. Sandwiches are $2–$4, seafood salads $4–$7.50. The clam chowder we tried was nicely flavored, but on the chewy side. Wednesday is fish-fry day—all the fried scrod you can eat, with potato and coleslaw, will set you back $3.95.

Children's portions are available. Beer and wine are served, and there's Häagen Dazs ice cream for dessert.

HOURS Summer: Sun.–Thu. 11 am–10 pm; Fri. & Sat. 11 am–11 pm. Winter: Wed.–Sun. 11 am–9 pm; Mon. & Tue. 11 am–8 pm.

DIRECTIONS Northbound: From Exit 63 turn left to traffic light, then right onto Route 81. ■ Take Route 81 for 0.6 mile, through twists and turns, to Route 1. Left onto Route 1; go 1.3 miles. Look right.

Southbound: From Exit 63 turn right onto Route 81. Then as above from ■.

THE MUFFIN KORNER, *Exit 65, Westbrook*

With restaurants of every conceivable sort—and some inconceivable—springing up on the culinary landscape, it's always nice to find a plain old village lunchroom still standing right where it's supposed to be, doing what it's supposed to do, and looking as it's supposed to look.

Which is not to say that the Muffin Korner, in tiny Westbrook, has stood still for 30 years. In fact, it's even been modernized in its own homey way. Blue-checked tablecloths (though plastic) and dark paneling (though Masonite) give the room a warm feel. And the menu has also moved with the times. Quiche Lorraine ($1.75) and spinach salads (95 cents and $2.25) are lunchtime favorites. Also available are tuna melt ($2.95) and eggs Benedict ($3.25).

Aside from these and a few other items you might expect to find in a brick-plants-and-oak café, the Muffin Korner grills up mundane sandwiches, egg breakfasts, and pancakes, all very reasonably priced. And, as its name suggests, it serves very good homemade muffins—corn, bran, blueberry, and "muffin of the day." If you want yours toasted, they'll slather it with butter and sizzle it on the grill for a few minutes. Not bad, but the muffins stand up better on their own.

Despite its flirtation with the times, the Muffin Korner is still an old-style neighborhood luncheonette; you can see it in the friendly local faces and hear it in the gentle banter. When we were there, the morning's topic was an aphrodisiac cookbook that had found its way into the waitress's mailbox. The fellows at the counter all pleaded innocent.

HOURS Mon.–Fri. 6 am–3 pm; Sat. & Sun. 6 am–1 pm.

DIRECTIONS From Exit 65 turn right if northbound, left if southbound. Follow signs for Route 1 and in ½ mile you will be in the center of Westbrook. Turn left at light, and look left.

HIGHLINER CAFÉ, *Exit 65, Westbrook*

* *Untried, but likely*

Here's another entry for the unconfirmed rumor department. The Highliner Café, within sight of the interstate, is said to have the best chili this side of New Haven. Unfortunately, the place was closed up tight for vacation when we tried to verify the report.

You'll have to check it out for yourself, but we promise that you won't lose much time finding it.

HOURS Winter: Lunch, Mon.–Fri. noon–2:30 pm; Dinner, Fri. & Sat. only, 6–9 pm; closed Sun. Summer: every day, noon–2:30 pm and 6–9 pm.

DIRECTIONS From Exit 65, turn right if northbound, left if southbound. Norris Rd. is the first right turn you can make, and on it you'll see the **Highliner** in an old depot.

SAYBROOK POINT, *Exits 67 & 68, Old Saybrook*

The Connecticut River meets Long Island Sound at Saybrook Point, and this restaurant was situated to take every advantage of the fact. It's built right out over the water with walls of windows facing both directions. On a clear day you can see . . .

Seafood, of course, is the thing in this large, light, and airy restaurant, suitably bedecked with decoys and sailing ships, but not overdone. The view is excellent and the food is good to very good. A lunch of baked bay scallops au gratin ($5.95) was very fine indeed, while the crabmeat in Mornay sauce with pasta was a trifle bland. There's a good, spicy house dressing and an excellent mocha layer cake.

They downplay the fried dishes here, offering a good number of baked and broiled versions along with a large selection of non-seafood items, mostly in the American vein. Full lunches are $5–$6.50, with some very generous sandwiches from $2.75 to $4.75 for a Monte Cristo. Dinners are $8–$14.

On Sundays there's something really unusual—a full hunt breakfast with chicken livers, kidneys, smelts, eggs, meats, chipped beef, etc., all for $5.95, and free for children under six.

If Saybrook Point is pricier than you want to go, you'll find many small seafood restaurants in the village of Old Saybrook.

HOURS Lunch: Every day 11:30 am–2:30 pm; Dinner: Sun.–Thu. 5–9 pm; Fri. & Sat. 5–10 pm.

DIRECTIONS Northbound: Take Exit 67 and bear right twice onto Route 154 (to U.S. 1). Stay on 154. The road turns left at a light 0.4 mile from the exit. Take this left and go 2 miles farther, through Saybrook Point. Restaurant is on the left at the end of the road.

Southbound: Take Exit 68. Follow signs to U.S. 1 and bear right onto it. At first light (½ mile), turn left onto Route 154 South. Go 0.3 mile to light in the village of Old Saybrook. Turn left and go 2 miles to end of road. It's on the left.

THE GRISWOLD INN, *Exit 69, Essex*

The Griswold is as rich in history as any museum, but it isn't frozen in the past. It lives and breathes. Less than a block from the mouth of the Connecticut River, here the Revolution, the War of 1812, steamships, and riverboats all came and went, and that heritage is still treasured, but not held in awed reverence. If your boots are muddy as you tramp through two centuries, no one's going to mind.

The Griswold was Connecticut's first three-story frame structure when it was built in 1776. Except for one small alteration, the main building is structurally unchanged. The front foyer leads you into the dark and pubby Tap Room. It's welcoming and restful, with ancient woodwork, handsome bar, and huge cast-iron stove. Next comes one of the dining rooms, just as charming but lighter, and decorated from floor to ceiling with steamboat prints, many of them Currier and Ives originals.

The problem you'll have at the Griswold is to avoid getting carried away by the building. There are many other dining areas, smaller and more intimate. One is a library, one houses a fine collection of 18th century firearms, another is made from a covered bridge, and finally there's the Steamboat Room, with its mural of 1890s Essex as seen from the stern of a departing ship. Flick a switch and the whole thing starts swaying with the waves. Corny, but endearing. And kids love it.

The "Gris" is an eclectic collection of historical odds and ends, to be sure, but therein lies its charm. It's a place not just for looking, but for living.

And eating! The Griswold serves New England country cooking, as befits its spirit. Not a word of French on the menu. "We call fish fish, and beef beef," says owner Bill Winterer, who rails against what he calls the "planned arrogance" of so many New England inns.

Lunch here runs from $3.95 for overstuffed "steamboat sandwiches" to $5.50 for broiled filet of bluefish, served with fresh vegetable or potato. There are also omelets, roast meats, cold platters, and three varieties of the Griswold Inn's own sausage. The sausage, which can be bought for home consumption, is based on traditional recipes that Bill and his family dug out of dusty old cookbooks found in the inn and nearby.

Dinner is along much the same lines as lunch, with the emphasis on fresh seafood and roast meats. Steak and kidney pie, roast duckling, braised lamb shank, gingered game hen, and fried oysters are representative examples ($8–$12). Children's portions are available.

The gastronomic highlight of the week is Sunday's hunt breakfast, when, from 11:30 to 2:30, the kitchen's talent is unleashed and out come scrambled eggs, ham, bacon, sausage, smelts, perch, chicken livers, lamb kidney, creamed mushrooms and ham, hot cornbread, English muffins, and whatever else the morning has inspired. As the story goes, the hunt breakfast dates back to the British occupation of the inn during the War of 1812. We don't know what they charged then, but today all you can eat is only $5.95 (free for children under 6). One problem: not surprisingly, reservations are advised; phone (203) 767-0991. It's worth planning for.

HOURS Lunch: Mon.–Sat. noon–2:30 pm; Dinner: Sun.–Thu. 6–9 pm; Fri. & Sat. 6–10 pm; Sunday hunt breakfast: 11:30 am–2:30 pm.

DIRECTIONS From Exit 69 enter directly onto Route 9 North. Go about 3 miles (highway driving) to Exit 3. At bottom of ramp turn left, following signs for Essex. The road curves, but continue watching for signs to Essex. In center of town (0.7 mile from Exit 3), take sharp right. Go 2 blocks to inn, on your right.

THE BOOTLEGGER, *Exits 85 & 87, Groton*

The food here is excellent and the atmosphere pleasantly informal, with a marvelous view of the Thames River and New London

on the far shore. But your politics may get in the way of your pleasure—this area is a focal point for the military-industrial complex. Not only does the wall of windows overlook a refueling station for nuclear submarines, but the restaurant is adjacent to the sprawling General Dynamics complex where they build them to begin with. Not 300 yards from your table stands the mammoth unfinished hull of the multi-billion-dollar *Poseidon.* It's an awesome sight, whether or not you approve.

The food we found here was among the best we discovered: baked ham in a superb sweet-and-sour mustard sauce; an enchanting sweet-and-sour-curry house dressing, blended with cucumbers and apples, and a spicy bouillabaisse, crammed to the gills with shellfish, topped with an entire lobster, and served in an antique tureen (it's $17.95, but without a doubt enough for two, and sharing is allowed). Other entrées are pretty much straight American, running $9 to $13.

For lunch there are salads from $2.50 to $4, clam chowder at $1.75, sandwiches ($3.50–$4.25), and the likes of beef kabob for $5.75 or a small sirloin for $7.50.

Plain oak tables, chrome-and-rattan chairs, and knotty pine make up the decor, which inevitably has nautical touches (the menu comes on a float), but not too many.

HOURS Lunch: Mon.–Fri. 11:30 am–3 pm; Dinner: Sun.–Thu. 5–9:30 pm; Fri. & Sat. 5–10:30 pm.

DIRECTIONS Northbound: Take Exit 85 (Bridge St.). At end of ramp turn right and follow road 1 mile. It's on the right.

Southbound: Take Exit 87, which is a left-lane exit marked "Groton Industrial Area." Follow signs for Industrial Park, which will effortlessly lead you to a right turn at 1.8 miles from the highway. Take this right and go ½ mile to the end of the street at the Thames River. Turn right again onto Thames St., left at the next light, and then 0.3 mile to the restaurant, on the left.

Rhode Island

WOOD RIVER INN, *Exit 3B, Wyoming*

In the 19th century the town of Wyoming was called Richmond Switch because it was where you switched stagecoaches midway between New York and Boston. Across from the coach house was a large general store, which has since been a rough-and-tumble barroom, the County Democratic Club, and now, the Wood River Inn.

Not so perfectly preserved as to be prissy, nor so rough as to be uncomfortable, Wood River is agreeably in-between. The food is family-style American cooking: roast beef dinner ($5.95 with salad bar) is easily the biggest seller, except on Sunday, when roast turkey is available at the same price. Owner Frank Limpert roasts his meats in the kitchen and makes his own gravies. Fish and chips and thick meat sandwiches are the mainstay of the lunch menu ($2.25–$3.50). Children's portions are available.

If you are game for a culinary adventure and you plan to be in town on the third Sunday of January, phone well ahead, (401) 539-2862, to reserve a seat for the annual game dinner. Raccoon, woodchuck, and bear are just appetizers; you're likely to eat hippo or rattlesnake before dessert.

HOURS Tue.–Fri. 11 am–9 pm; Sat. & Sun. 8 am–9 pm; closed Mon.

DIRECTIONS From Exit 3B bear right onto Route 138 West for ½ mile to village center. **Wood River Inn** is on your left.

DOVECREST, *Exit 3B, Wyoming*

Dovecrest is an American Indian restaurant run by two full-blooded Narragansetts. Although four miles from the interstate—usually beyond this book's striking range—we include Dovecrest for travelers willing to venture out of the way for an out-of-the-ordinary menu that includes buffalo steak ($17.95), venison steak ($14.95), pot pies of venison, buffalo, oysters, or quahogs ($8.95), succotash, Indian meal pudding, and Rhode Island's indigenous favorite, jonnycakes.

Jonnycakes are stone-ground cornmeal pancakes invented by the Indians and later packed by white men embarking on long coach trips; hence the name "journey cakes." Whether jonnycakes should be wide and lacy or small and thick is the subject of an undying, if amicable, debate among devotees, but both schools participate actively in the Society for the Preservation of the Jonnycake Tradition in Rhode Island.

Dovecrest serves the little, fat jonnycake version; it comes, if you wish, in lieu of a potato with your entrée, or on their own with an apple ring and apple sauce (six for $2.25). You may bathe your cakes in maple syrup, if such is your habit, but owner Ferris B. Dove, whose tribal name is Chief Roaring Bull, is likely to inform you that neither Indians nor "swamp Yankees" ever bothered with the sweet stuff. Swamp Yankee or not, you can pick up a recipe and a bag of jonnycake meal as you leave.

HOURS Every day 11:30 am–9 pm. Closed Feb.

DIRECTIONS Follow directions for Wood River Inn, above, continuing along Route 138 past the inn and bearing left where it joins Route 3. Go 100 feet and turn right onto Bridge St. Bear right at the fork and in 3½ miles you will be in the village of Arcadia. Go 200 yards past the fish hatchery; **Dovecrest** is on your right.

RUE DE L'ESPOIR, *Exit 20, Providence*

See p. 224 for description of this excellent, modestly priced restaurant with an informal atmosphere.

DIRECTIONS Exit 20 on I-95 will put you on I-195 heading east. Go about 1 mile to Exit 2 on I-195 and follow directions given from that point.

ANGELO'S CIVITA FARNESE RESTAURANT, *Exit 21, Providence*

We were still 30 miles from Providence when we started hearing tales of Angelo's, and when we got there our local informants confirmed the rumor. Angelo's is *the* place in town for a great, cheap meal and local color.

It's a 60-year-old trattoria, bursting with life, and all but devoid of decoration. Your dinner companion is whoever takes the next seat at the long stone table, and friends shout greetings over your head. You request spaghetti ($1.65) from an aproned waiter and watch him unceremoniously boom your order to the kitchen.

We'd have loved every minute of it even if the food hadn't been surprisingly good. We got a wonderful eggplant parmigiana with fine Italian bread for all of $2.25. Veal parmigiana is tops at $5.25, veal and peppers a mere $3.25. Antipasto is only $1. If this is your kind of place, don't miss it.

But if it isn't, don't fret. Angelo's is but a dot on the freckled map of Providence's Little Italy, which stretches for blocks along Atwells Avenue. Nearby you'll find dining that is far more—or less—genteel.

Whatever your choice, do check out the arch that serves as an entryway to this part of town. It's a minor wonder. Two thin, stone arches, supported by squat little Corinthian columns, intersect high above the street, and from their junction dangles a bronze pine cone—homage, we like to think, to that gem of Italian cooking, the pignola nut.

HOURS Mon.–Sat. 11 am–8:30 pm; closed Sun. and holidays.

DIRECTIONS Northbound: Exit 21 (Broadway, Downtown). At end of ramp go straight ahead and through the first light. Left at the second light, over the bridge and under the arch. This is Atwells Ave. You'll see **Angelo's** 1 block up, on your right. Other Italian places will be all around you.

Southbound: Exit 21 (Atwells Ave.). Right at end of ramp onto Atwells. One block to **Angelo's,** on the right (141 Atwells Ave.).

HAVEN BROTHERS, *Exit 21, Providence*

* *Color, not cuisine*

Would you be interested in a stainless-steel diner that parks each night next to City Hall and plugs itself into a street light? Any night between 5 pm and 2:45 am, you can walk up three steps into the closest living relative to the world's first diner. It's called Haven Brothers, a portable lunch wagon like the one that a certain Walter Scott (who never wrote poetry) rolled onto this same city's streets back in 1872, thereby starting the craze for "night owls," later called "dog wagons," and eventually—when their wheels had been removed—"Diners."

But Haven Brothers never lost its mobility. We couldn't determine how old the actual wagon is—nobody seemed to know, or else they're wary of busybodies with notepads—but nowadays it's pulled by a V-8 pick-up, and it looks as if it would fit better next to a circus tent than a city hall. It is indeed a strange feeling when you slide open the door and enter the eccentric world of Haven Brothers.

In front of you is a narrow counter that wraps around half the room. You can't see the grill right away because most of the diner's space is occupied by a motley throng of customers awaiting their food. It comes on a paper plate, passed from hand to hand through the crowd. Once served, you can sit on a stool at the counter (if one is available) or eat standing up. Or you can elbow your way back through the crowd and out the door for dining al fresco.

The orchestration of activity between the customers and the cook is in the able hands of the man behind the cash register. In his broad Rhode Island accent he calls out your order in slang to his grillman who adroitly juggles burgers, beans, and buns. "Bloody bull," he shouts, meaning a hamburger with ketchup, or "Reds, cut up two" for franks and beans. Nothing seems to ruffle our man up front, despite the brisk pace. "You didn't want mayo? No problem." Then, to his grillman: "Give me another, high and dry."

Whether you need a break from roadway boredom or some new characters for your novel, a stop at Haven Brothers is worth the time it takes to park the car, even if you aren't especially hungry. In fact, it's better if you're not. You weren't really planning on coming here for the food, were you?

HOURS Every day 5 pm–2:45 am.

DIRECTIONS It sounds complicated, and you do have to go through about 10 short blocks of downtown traffic. Even though there are many turns, the road will carry you in the right general direction and the distance is not great. If confused, just go with the flow and you won't come out too far wrong. Or ask—everyone in Providence knows **Haven Brothers.**

Northbound: Exit 21 (Broadway, Downtown). At end of ramp go straight to second light (Atwells Ave.). Right onto Atwells. Go 1 block and then left onto Broadway. ■ Broadway will soon swing to the right, carrying you with it. The first light after this swing rightward is Fountain. Left on Fountain, and go three more lights to a gentle right turn onto Dorrance (a park on the left, the Biltmore on the right). Two lights on Dorrance, which angles a bit to the right, brings you to City Hall and the corner of Dorrance and Fulton, where Haven Brothers plugs into the corner lamppost.

Southbound: Left at end of Exit 21 ramp onto Atwells Ave., over bridge, and straight through the light. One block more straight ahead and then left onto Broadway. Then as above from ■.

STATE HOUSE RESTAURANT, *Exit 23, Providence*

* *Color, not cuisine*

It's not uncommon to find restaurants where the architecture far surpasses the cooking. This must be the ultimate example.

You walk up an expanse of marble steps, through a pillared portico, and into a huge rotunda. Three hundred feet above you towers a vaulted, unsupported dome, the second highest in the world! Only St. Peter's in Rome is higher. The Taj Mahal comes third.

We're cheating of course. This couldn't be simply a restaurant, and it is not. It is the Rhode Island State Capitol.

Come here for the building, which is simply awesome. Walk

into the stately Senate chamber and peruse the collection of historic paintings, battle flags, and guns, and gaze at the staggering dome. When you've had your fill, head downstairs to the lunchroom. There, under plain yellow walls and fluorescent lighting, you can file through the line and pile your tray with doughnuts, muffins, bagels, yogurt, sandwiches or full dinners, all prepared and served by the culinary arts students of William M. Davies, Jr. Technical High School. The food is decent (no better) and cheap ($1 for sandwiches, $1.75–$2.50 for full meals). Admittedly, it's a letdown after what you've just seen upstairs, but you get to walk through all that splendor again on your way out.

HOURS Mon.–Fri. 8 am–3:30 pm; closed weekends.

DIRECTIONS Northbound: From Exit 23 (State Offices) turn right. Go ½ block and turn left (sign for State Offices). ■ Take next left onto Davis. Go 2 blocks to parking area on left in shadow of Capitol.

Southbound: From Exit 23 (State Offices) bear right at end of ramp. Take first left (almost a U) under highway and bear right around Marriott Hotel. At second light turn right onto Orms St. Go 1 block on Orms, and turn left at sign for State Offices. Then as above from ■.

Massachusetts

CORY'S, *Exit 60N, Dedham*

It's all but impossible to find good restaurants when the road passes through the local suburban tangle, but Cory's is a place that would please you in any circumstances.

Don't be put off by its architecture. It's a roofy, low, shapeless sort of thing in brick and barnboard, and it looks distressingly at home among the car dealers and shopping centers. But once inside you'll find as tasteful an environment as you could hope for —and food to match.

Cory's main dining room is airy and pleasant, quiet and relaxing. Oak tables set with cloth placemats and real flowers blend nicely with the textured plaster walls in cream yellow. There are old paintings and a few quality antiques, but nothing is overdone.

No themes or gimmicks—just good taste, comfort, and friendly, efficient service.

And the food is first-rate. We tasted a hearty, full-flavored beef and vegetable soup that was crammed with fresh vegetables. Rare roast beef, freshly cut, on excellent French bread with horseradish sauce made a terrific sandwich, and since it came with a turmeric-flavored rice and orzo pilaf, it felt festive enough to be dinner. With everything else so good, we could not resist trying the chocolate layer cake with walnuts and fudge frosting. As expected, it was moist and rich, but not too sweet. With the excellent coffee it concluded a very happy highway lunch.

The roast beef sandwich is $3.50, as is the salad bar. Soup and salad are $4.25, and there are eight full luncheons from $4.95 to $5.75.

The dinner menu offers mostly solid, popular favorites. Steaks are the house specialty ($10.95–$13.95); other entrées start at $8.95. The most unusual are veal in a vermouth and lemon sauce, veal Marsala, chicken breast on spinach with ricotta, and a scallop casserole.

There's an upstairs dining room here and a lounge. While nice, they are not nearly so special as the main dining room. So if you're tempted enough to stop in, ask for the front room.

HOURS Lunch: Mon.–Fri. 11:30 am–2 pm. No lunch on weekends. Dinner: Mon.–Thu. 5–10 pm; Fri. & Sat. 5–11 pm; Sun. 4–9 pm.

DIRECTIONS Exit 60N puts you on Route 1 North. Go 1 block past the traffic light and you'll find **Cory's** on the right.

THE MILL FALLS, *Exit 55E, Newton Upper Falls*

Nature, architecture, a maitre d' who believes in old-school service, and a chef devoted to his sauces have combined to make the Mill Falls an experience unto itself. If formal dining on the banks of the Charles River is your mood, don't miss this place.

Since 1688 there has been a mill of some kind here to take advantage of the 30-foot waterfall. From the late 1880s the business was silk, but now the whole complex has been renovated to make room for the Mill Falls Restaurant and various specialty shops. The dam and the river with its steep, wooded banks, now freed from utilitarian drudgery, are illuminated at night to provide a setting for gracious dining.

You enter the restaurant through leaded-glass doors into as beautiful an old paneled lobby as you'll find anywhere. The dining room itself is luxuriously formal, set in tones of deep, hushed red with touches of soft pink. The place settings are elegant, and scalloped valences cap the many windows that overlook the river. Off to one side is an equally luxurious lounge with soft leather chairs, and there's a piano bar from Wednesday to Saturday nights.

Classic French cuisine dominates the menu, with a few items like prime rib for domestic tastes. The ribs, veal piccata, and sole Bretonne are the favorites, the latter being a lightly sautéed filet topped with diced shrimp and capers in white wine sauce. These delights run from around $10 to $15 and come with a salad, vegetable, potato, fresh-baked bread, and a crock of cheese with crackers. The wine list has 60 entries.

The Mill Falls is not so formal as to disdain hamburgers and sandwiches for lunch, however. There's a good variety in the $4–$5 range. Quiche, four salads, eggs Benedict, appetizers, and a dozen or so entrées are all available at a comparable price.

HOURS Lunch: Mon.–Fri. 11:45 am–3 pm; Dinner: Mon.–Thu. 5:30–9:45 pm; Fri. & Sat. 5:30–10:45 pm. Closed Sun.

DIRECTIONS Exit 55E (Brookline, Boston, Route 9) will put you on a limited access road, Route 9 East. Leave this at the first exit (Chestnut St.). At end of ramp make a right and then take the next two rights. This will put you at the parking lot, on the right. The restaurant itself is tucked within the complex. Total distance is only ½ mile.

PILLAR HOUSE, *Exit 54E, Newton Lower Falls*

Here's a place that would be hard to miss even at 60 mph. Its four thick Greek Revival columns rise a majestic 40 feet above a sea of asphalt, where they are crowned by a diminutive gable that looks like Charlie Chaplin's bowler hat atop Paul Bunyan. Highways and exit ramps surround the place like spaghetti around a meatball.

You enter it by a noble flight of steps that lead to the side door. A red carpet, the kind that Agamemnon got in trouble on, leads from the door, down the steps, under the awning, and across the sidewalk.

Inside, everything is done to suggest opulent luxury. The menu is American and continental and the food is good, even if it's no bargain. Dinners are $9–$15; luncheons, $4.75–$8.25.

HOURS Mon.–Thu. 11:30 am–9 pm; Fri. 11:30 am–10 pm; closed Saturday, Sunday, and the first two weeks of July.

DIRECTIONS Absolutely unmissable. Southbound, it's directly off the Exit 54E ramp, on the right. Northbound, take a left at the end of the ramp and go 0.2 mile over the bridge to first left, at the light. Restaurant is on left, just after the turn.

HELEN'S RESTAURANT, *Exit 49, Waltham*

* *Color, not cuisine*

It wasn't the most subtle cooking we came across, but breakfast at Helen's was nearly the cheapest: two eggs, sausage, home fries, and toast for $1.45. For some reason scrambled eggs are 5 cents more, but if that puts a dent in your purse, consider the 80-cent hamburgers, the spaghetti special for $1.25, and the meatloaf and peppersteak dinners at $2.10.

Perhaps these nostalgic prices have something to do with the fact that the phone number on the menu is pre–all-digit-dialing vintage (TW 3-9675), but in any case not much has changed here for a long time. It's a workingman's restaurant with a decidedly weathered feel. At breakfast time the huge, horseshoe-shaped counter is filled with construction workers and delivery men en route to the day's work. Orange plastic booths line both side walls, while a few tables sit by the front window keeping watch on Main Street.

Down-to-earth local life and great prices. No more, no less.

HOURS Mon.–Fri. 6 am–7 pm; Sat. 6 am–2 pm; closed Sun.

DIRECTIONS From Exit 49 follow signs for Route 20 East into Waltham. **Helen's** is 1.4 miles from the exit, on the left.

ABOUT LEXINGTON

Lexington is a very handsome little town, as rich in restaurants as it is in history. And though it can claim to be the birthplace of the American Revolution, the cuisine here is decidedly international. Within a few blocks of Depot Square, right in the center of town, you'll find excellent French, German, Italian, and Chinese places, as well as a less distinguished sandwich shop with an Italian accent.

In fact the one thing we didn't find was the expected Lexingtone Inne. We can't imagine why some entrepreneur hasn't seized this opportunity, but we aren't sorry. In any case, you'll find a meal in Lexington a delightful break from the drive.

We've featured the two restaurants that local people spoke of most enthusiastically; for the others we just give the basics. Don't consider this a ranking—we doubt that any of these places will disappoint you.

BEL CANTO, *Exit 44S, Lexington*

Bel Canto is a style of operatic singing, and you may break into song yourself in praise of this delightful place. For light Italian eating you're just not going to do much better anywhere.

The opus major is a deep-dish pizza that won five "Best of Boston" awards. You can get it with whole wheat or white flour, tomato or ricotta sauce, and there are no fewer than 19 add-ons, from artichoke hearts to zucchini. This beauty starts at $4.30 and will feed two or three.

If you're tired of sandwiches but still partial to the general idea of meat and wheat, there's a new twist for you at Bel Canto. They serve calzone, fresh-baked turnovers stuffed with customary and not-so-customary sandwich fillers ($2.85–$3.65). The traditional version comes with pepperoni and three cheeses, but here you can get a "club" calzone, bursting with turkey, ham, bacon, and Swiss.

With two soups ($1.60), four salads ($1.65–$3.95), and a few appetizers (around $1.85), it's hard to go wrong here at lunchtime. But if none of the above tempts you, consider the cook's pie, the contents of which change daily, and salad for $2.95. There's a full bar and a good selection of imported beers.

The feel of things is modern, crisp, light and informal. One wall is sand-blasted brick, the others white, hung with pictures by local artists. The staff is friendly and the crowd cuts nicely across all age groups.

HOURS Sun.–Thu. 11 am–10 pm; Fri. & Sat. 11 am–11 pm.

DIRECTIONS See end of Lexington entries, p. 202.

YANGTZE RIVER, *Exit 44S, Lexington*

Boston Magazine, the *Boston Phoenix*, and TV's "Evening Magazine" have all given the Yangtze River their highest ratings, and no wonder: not only are the food and decor excellent, but the prices are moderate.

The restaurant is laid out in good modern design, uncluttered by bric-a-brac. Tan colors, natural wood, and subtly textured materials predominate, setting a light and relaxing mood. The Orient is merely suggested, more by the general tranquility than anything else.

The menu is eclectic Chinese, drawing on the cuisines of four provinces for its 120 entries. You'll find Mandarin sliced jumbo shrimp ($8.50), Szechuan pork ($6), Hunan beef ($7), Cantonese chicken with straw mushrooms ($5.75), and even chow mein ($4). All the familiar favorites are there, next to such exotics as lychee- or plum-flavored duck and fried bean thread topped with a spicy meat sauce.

About a third of the dishes are spicy, but whatever your taste in Chinese food, you're sure to find something here to your liking. The truly famished should consider the $9 all-you-can-eat special, Sunday through Thursday nights. It could turn a mere meal into a banquet.

HOURS Sun.–Thu. 11:30 am–9:15 pm; Fri. & Sat. 11:30 am–10:15 pm.

DIRECTIONS See end of Lexington entries, p. 202.

LE BELLECOUR, *Exit 44S, Lexington*

This is a charming, living-room-like French restaurant that manages to be pretty and elegant at once. The light pink tablecloths, sofa, and bentwood chairs lend the charm, despite the somewhat out-of-place barnboard paneling. But ask for the front room. The rear is not so nice.

There are ten luncheon entrées between $4.50 and $5.75 and appetizers like oysters baked in a piperade sauce and topped with Hollandaise ($4.75).

Dinners at Le Bellecour are interesting. You'll be tempted by such treats as sole with salmon mousse in Hollandaise ($14.50), chicken breast filled with spinach and garlic butter, served with mustard sauce ($11.95), and roast leg of lamb with a garlic mayonnaise ($12.95).

HOURS Mon.–Fri. 11:30 am–2 pm and 6–10 pm; Sat. 6–10 pm.

DIRECTIONS See end of Lexington entries, p. 202.

GUENTHER'S CAFÉ RESTAURANT, *Exit 44S, Lexington*

The specialty here is Viennese cooking in a handsome, modern setting. There are interesting and unusual lunch offerings, like asparagus tips rolled in ham and served on a bed of Viennese salad ($3.95), and more common items like clam chowder ($1.95). Dinners seem to be strictly Viennese, at $10–$15.

HOURS Mon.–Fri. 11 am–2 pm and 6–10 pm; Sat. noon–3 pm; closed Sun.

DIRECTIONS See end of Lexington entries, below.

GRACIE'S RESTAURANT, *Exit 44S, Lexington*

Hardly in the same class as the others and decidedly on the plasticky side, Gracie's nevertheless does have the virtue of serving breakfast. It also has simple sandwiches, omelettes, and charcoal-grilled dinners ($5.45 tops).

HOURS Mon.–Sat. 7:30 am–9 pm; Sun. 9 am–1 pm.

DIRECTIONS FOR ALL LEXINGTON RESTAURANTS Exit 44S will put you onto Routes 4 and 225 South. If you go 1.1 miles you will pass the village green on the left and then see Depot Square, also on the left. The **Yangtze River** faces the square in the far left-hand corner. For **Le Bellecour,** turn right onto Muzzey St.; it's ½ block up. **Guenther's** is 1 block straight ahead on the left side of Massachusetts Ave., and **Bel Canto** is 1 block beyond Guenther's, also on the left. For **Gracie's,** make a left turn onto Merriam St., just after the green, *before* Depot Square; it's on the right, ½ block up.

THE NEW MONTROSE RESTAURANT AND DRIVE-IN, *Exit 32, Wakefield*

This is one of those exits mysteriously labeled FOOD, and if you follow the signs you'll find they lead straight to a huge chain motel/restaurant. Totally ignored by the blue sign that points directly away from it is the neat and tiny Montrose Drive-In, with only a humble Coke sign to make its presence known. (Sometimes we wonder just who the Highway Department works for.)

The fact is that this place has been a family operation for 32 years and has quite a local reputation for its ice cream. It's all made right here, with natural flavorings, fresh fruit, and 16 percent butterfat—every bit as good as what you get at the fanciest ice cream emporium.

Admittedly, the atmosphere is nothing special and neither are the meals. Everything is sparkling clean, but the new dining area is done up in modified McDonald's. The corned beef sandwich we tried wasn't half bad, but if you love corned beef you'd probably be happier sticking to ice cream. A hamburger with pickle and fries or potato salad is $1.90. There's a Greek salad for $2.50 and a bowl of soup du jour for $1.10. The seafood is all fresh, with dinners around $4. Spaghetti with salad and roll is only $2.50.

HOURS Mon.–Fri. 6 am–8 pm; Sat. 7 am–8 pm; closed Sun.

DIRECTIONS From Exit 32 turn left at end of ramp, then about 0.2 mile straight ahead, on the right.

VILLAGE BAKERY AND DELI, *Topsfield Road Exit, Topsfield*

* *Slim pickin's*

Unless you are looking for superb food or a cushy atmosphere, you can find something you'll like here: freshly baked bread, bagels, quiche, pizza by the slice, subs, deli meats, homemade cookies and cake, hamburgers, egg breakfasts, hot cider, homemade pretzels, and the unchallenged favorite among teenagers—fried dough.

You walk right up to the Coke sign menu, tell the woman what you want, take it to one of the little tables with white ice-cream-parlor chairs, and eat under fluorescent lights. It's no competition for Zabar's, but it's not bad either—cheaper, more variety, and more fun than McDonald's. And we bet that you'll pop up to the counter at least three times before you're out the door.

HOURS Mon.–Fri. 6:30 am–6 pm; Sat. 7 am–5 pm; Sun. 8 am–1 pm.

DIRECTIONS Take the exit labeled "Topsfield Road"—it's not numbered, but it's the one just south of Route 97. At bottom of ramp turn right if northbound, left if southbound, onto unmarked road. Go about 1½ miles to the village green (you'll know you're there when you see a church on your left, town hall on right). Turn right and go 1 block to Topsfield Village Shopping Center on right. Therein lies the bakery/deli.

ABOUT NEWBURYPORT

This is a fine old brick town, right on the water. It has undergone extensive restoration in recent years. The result is charming but also a bit precious, as often happens with such projects. Still, the restaurant scene is varied and happy—everything from a Danish bakery and a 1930s drugstore lunch counter to continental fare in elegant surroundings, not to mention the inevitable brick-plants-and-oak cafés that seem to spring up at renovation sites like dandelions on a June lawn.

FOWLES NEWS STORE AND SODA SHOP, *Route 113 Exit, Newburyport*

Right out of a Norman Rockwell painting, Fowles has stood here since well before the *Saturday Evening Post* took its plunge. All around this classic soda fountain, Newburyport has been spiffing itself up, putting on a new face meant to look old. But Fowles is the real thing, with tile floor, marble counter, and gleaming wooden booths and walls. It even has an inlaid mural behind the counter, but to judge from the attitude of those who work here, they don't want to make much of a fuss about it. "We make our money from the local people who sit here and read the paper," they told us.

The menu *has* changed with the years. Fowles offers frozen yogurt as well as ice cream. Frappes or sodas are $1.95, and you can get such novelties as "Tahiti Sweetie" (pineapple juice, orange sherbet, and strawberry syrup, $1.50) or "Fowles Flamingo" (a parfait of strawberry and vanilla ice cream, pineapple and strawberry toppings, and whipped cream, $1.65).

There's a large selection of herb teas (honey available) and sandwiches that Norman Rockwell never heard of: cukes or avocado and sprouts ($1.95/$2.25) or chicken salad melt ($1.95), for example. But there's also traditional fare: sandwiches of the ham-and-cheese variety ($1.50–$2) and good old two-eggs-over-easy breakfasts ($1.75–$2.95), available till late afternoon.

HOURS Mon.–Thu. 6 am–7 pm (grill closes at 4 pm); Fri. 6 am–9 pm (grill closes at 4:30 pm); Sat. 7 am–7 pm; Sun. (breakfast only) 6 am–1 pm.

DIRECTIONS See end of Newburyport entries, p. 207.

SCANDIA, *Route 113 Exit, Newburyport*

You won't find Scandinavian cuisine at Scandia. But what it does have to offer is some of the most innovative—and most outstanding—seafood we've found, and it is served in a handsome, intimate setting.

There's elegance here, even a hint of opulence. A large gilt mirror and ornately framed paintings, Oriental carpet, chandeliers, and a Victorian sideboard dominate the landscape. Yet the simple black wooden chairs, dark wood tables set with blue napkins, and friendly service give it a comfortable sense of controlled informality.

"Creative Dining" is Scandia's tagline, and indeed owner Gordon Briedenbach loves to concoct. Although the cuisine is basically continental, it is splashed with Scandia originals. When Briedenbach's inventions work well as specials, they earn a berth on the daily menu. His haddock and scallop mousse, for instance, is a gorgeous stratification of fish filet stuffed with puréed scallops, layered with filo dough and butter, baked, inverted, sliced like a cake, and served with white wine sauce ($10.95). As an appetizer, chilled shellfish mousseline is the same idea on a smaller scale ($4.75).

Another Scandia original is veal and lobster sauté ($13.50). Veal marinated in Galliano and lemon juice, then grilled, is Scandia's version of veal piccata ($12.95), and its New England fish stew ($12.50) is a stunning mélange of saffron-scented fish, clams, scallops, and lobster.

Though not quite as exotic, lunch here also has the Scandia touch. Sandwiches and full-meal salads are in the $4–$5 range, entrées a bit more. Seafood Mornay, for example, a blend of fish and shellfish in wine sauce, is served with tossed salad and French bread for $5.50. Just think—you could spend that much at HoJo's.

HOURS Every day 11:30 am–3 pm and 6–10 pm.

DIRECTIONS See end of Newburyport entries, p. 207.

STEAKE AND STEINN, *Route 113 Exit, Newburyport*

We figured a place called "Steake and Steinn" would be another beefhouse with ye olde goode cheere of the worst sort. But there were no Styrofoam half-timbers or spackle stucco. Instead, we found a nicely designed brick-plants-and-oak café.

The menu, however, is the steak-and-seafood sort of thing we had originally anticipated, with quiche and a few chicken dishes thrown in as an afterthought. And, as every proper steak house knows, there must be a large salad bar (free with entrées, $3.95 on its own). Dinner entrées run $7–$12.

Sandwiches, a bit more in keeping with the B.P.O. trend, are available all day. Most are $5–$6, a bit high perhaps, but the price includes French fries (sorry, "steake fries"), coffee and salad bar. If you are an avowed carnivore and avoid anything green, you can deduct $1 and shun the salad. Children's portions are available on some items.

The menu reaches its trendiest heights in the dessert section ($1.85–$2.45), with carrot cake, strawberry cheesecake, and hot Amaretto cake with vanilla ice cream.

HOURS Mon.–Thu. 11:30 am–3 pm and 5–10 pm; Fri. & Sat. 11:30 am–3 pm and 5–11 pm; Sun. 12:30–10 pm.

DIRECTIONS See end of Newburyport entries, below.

EBENSEN'S DANISH BAKERY, *Route 113 Exit, Newburyport*

Newburyport is famous for more than just its restoration. The town is the jumping-off point for Plum Island, New England's prized birdwatching spot. And Ebensen's Bakery, on the road to Plum Island, probably serves more pastry to binocular-wearing customers than any other shop in the world. To most birders, a trip to Plum Island without a stop at Ebensen's would be almost as unthinkable as forgetting the Peterson guide. Ebensen's kringle, like the people who bake it, is as Danish as anything out of Hans Christian Andersen, a sweet feast for eye and tooth.

HOURS Wed.–Sun. 7 am–5 pm; closed Mon. & Tue.

DIRECTIONS FOR NEWBURYPORT RESTAURANTS Take exit labeled "Newburyport–Route 113" (no number). Follow Route 113 toward Newburyport for 2½ miles, turning left at blinking light (sign: Newburyport Center). Go to T junction, then turn right. Drive the short distance to Market Square, turn right onto State St., and park (except for Ebensen's; see below). It's all within one block: **Fowles** and **Scandia** on the left (20 and 25 State St., respectively), **Steake and Steinn** at 1 Threadneedle Alley, off to the right. For **Ebensen's,** do not take the right onto

State St. but continue along Water St., heading out of town (signs for Plum Island). Go about ½ mile; it's on your left.

New Hampshire

ABOUT PORTSMOUTH

Now being dubbed "the San Francisco of the East," Portsmouth is home to a still-bustling waterfront, aggressive historic restoration, and a slew of excellent restaurants scattered among the boutiques and trendy shops. What's more, the interstate brings you into the middle of all this quickly and easily.

THE BLUE STRAWBERY, *Exit 7, Portsmouth*

The Blue Strawbery (single "r" spelling, as in the town's old name) is one of New England's most celebrated gourmet restaurants. However, reservations are always required, and meals (prix-fixe at $25) are served only at two seatings, making the Strawbery less than convenient for travelers on their way to other places. If, however, Portsmouth is your evening's destination, you would do very well to call ahead and dine here; phone (603) 431-6420.

HOURS Summer: Mon.–Sat., seatings at 6 and 9 pm; Sun., seatings at 3 and 6 pm. Winter: Wed.–Sat., seatings at 6 and 9 pm; Sun., seatings at 3 and 6 pm. Closed Mon. & Tue.

DIRECTIONS See end of Portsmouth entries, p. 212.

CLARENCE'S CHOWDER HOUSE, *Exit 7, Portsmouth*

Clarence's shares a building with the Blue Strawbery. It was opened in 1970 by the exclusive restaurant as a less formal lunch spot with a limited menu. The two are different in every way, but they have an important thing in common: the restrooms! So, without having to make a reservation, and at much lower cost, you can eat at Clarence's and use the Blue Strawbery's plushly carpeted powder room.

Before chowder issued forth at Clarence's (or escargots at the Blue Strawbery), the building was a ship's warehouse and later a hardware store. The sand-blasted brick interior bespeaks its history, as do the tables, which were cut from the store's thick oak counter, and the eight-sided nuts-and-bolts cabinet that stands sentinel at the door. These days, it serves as cash register.

Named after the amiable hardware-store clerk who first thought up the idea of a chowder house in this spot, Clarence's is now a center for feminism and anti-nuke politicizing. It's not strictly politics here, however. In fact, "Dining for Fun" is engraved on the menu, and men are certainly welcome. Many come. But we suspect that a conservative, pro-nuke, meat-eating male would feel about as comfortable here as a clam in a starfish's embrace.

Mary Jane Moulton took over Clarence's ten years ago and has been experimenting with chowder recipes ever since. What she has finally come up with uses heavy cream and fish or clam stock in equal proportions, and is unthickened—as an authentic New England chowder should be. Hers are as fine as they come—the fish firm, the clams tender. Chowder is always on the day's menu, but the rest is left to Mary Jane's whim and what the season suggests: in summer there are cold soups, in fall and winter hot and hearty ones, like pumpkin, chicken with rice, or miso ($1.25–$1.95/cup; $2.35–$3.50/bowl).

Mary Jane also comes up with fabulous sandwiches on her home-baked bread. When we were there she served ratatouille with Jarlsberg, and langostinos with herb cheese ($1.70–$2.50/half-sandwich; $3.50–$5/whole). Many of her guests make a filling lunch out of half a sandwich and a cup of soup. There is also quiche, salad, and several desserts that—we are surprised to report—include neither carrot cake nor cheesecake, but bread pudding, mincemeat and cream cheese pies, and Clarence's trifle.

Mary Jane is almost as proud of her coffee as she is of her chowder. The blend is her own; the beans are ground daily and brewed in spring water. Tea drinkers will be equally pleased; there are seven black and nine herbal teas to choose from.

HOURS Every day 11:30 am–2 pm. Closed Sundays in winter.

DIRECTIONS See end of Portsmouth entries, p. 212.

THE DOLPHIN STRIKER AND SPRING HILL TAVERN, *Exit 7, Portsmouth*

First, the name: Dolphins must be more powerful than we thought. In the days of sailing ships, it was necessary to protect a ship's bowsprit with a spar that warded off the blows of the breaching cetaceans; this piece was called a dolphin striker.

The schooners are gone from Portsmouth harbor now, but the fire-engine-red tugboats and recreational vessels that have taken their place can be seen from the rear dining room of the Dolphin Striker restaurant. It's a very comfortable, warm place. Low ceilings with heavy beams, pine floors, wooden tables, and four small-paned bay windows just above sidewalk level put you in an 18th century frame of mind. When we visited, flickering candles and graceful curves of snow accumulating in the windowpanes lent a feeling of Christmas-card cheer.

Downstairs, there's a stone-walled tavern. Except for the tavern's raw bar, the menu is the same on both floors. The "Striker Lunch" may strike your fancy: it's a huge bowl of haddock chowder served with a small loaf of bread—white, sourdough rye, or pumpernickel ($3.95). The most popular midday meal, though, is a cup of chowder with half a sandwich—roast beef, turkey, smoked ham, or tuna ($3.50 for the combination). "The Reuben James" is a hefty seafood-salad sandwich consisting of lobster, crabmeat, and shrimp ($3.95, half; $5.95, full—good luck finishing it).

The dinnertime favorite is Hannah Mariner's Pie—lobster, crab, shrimp, scallops, mushrooms, and chives in a brandy and sour cream sauce. Other seafood specialties, such as shrimp Rockefeller, trout and crabmeat with Hollandaise sauce, and broiled haddock, range in price from $7.95 to $10.95. Chicken breasts layered with apples and almonds in an apple brandy and cream sauce is the least expensive entrée ($8.75), while filet mignon tops the list at $13.95.

HOURS Lunch: Mon.–Fri. 11:30 am–2 pm; Sun. 11:30 am–3 pm; no lunch Sat. Dinner: Mon.–Sat. 5:30–9 pm; Sun. 3–9 pm.

DIRECTIONS See end of Portsmouth entries, p. 212.

KAREN'S ICE CREAM RESTAURANT, *Exit 7, Portsmouth*

Moving up the hill, we find another kind of restaurant as different from Clarence's and the Dolphin Striker as they are from each other. A great local favorite, Karen's Ice Cream is small, airy, colorful, and altogether delightful, just as a little ice cream parlor with at-home atmosphere should be. It is so "at home," in fact, that the workers learn your first name; if you come more than once, you might be surprised to find yourself remembered.

Karen Wiese began in business five years ago selling just a few flavors of her wonderful homemade ice cream—and that was all. Now she's expanded not only to 20 flavors (mint oreo and almond joy are the reported favorites), but to two—and in summer, three—meals a day. For breakfast, two eggs, home fries, toast, and coffee cost $2.25; three-egg omelettes of various kinds go for $2.45.

Big sandwiches at lunchtime—roast beef, turkey, ham, or veggie, on a Boursin spread—run to only $2.25, while quiche and salad make a meal for $2.95. There are stews and chili, ratatouille, soups, and cornbread, all made from scratch. Daily dinner specials like spanakopita and lasagne with salad are colorfully announced on a blackboard in rainbows of chalk; they average only $3.25.

HOURS Winter: Tue.–Thu. 7 am–3 pm; Sat. & Sun. 8 am–3 pm; closed Mon. Summer: 7 am–9 pm seven days a week.

DIRECTIONS See end of Portsmouth entries, p. 212.

Other Portsmouth Restaurants

There are literally dozens more good restaurants in Portsmouth, many with fetching nautical names like **The Oar House** (Ceres

St.), **The Codfish Aristocracy** (The Hill), **Joseph's Riversmere** (37 Bow St.), and **The Old Ferry Landing** (10 Ceres St.). **The Library** (401 State St.) is a theme restaurant set in a 19th century hotel—books on the wall and stone lions on the steps are its motif. **Strawbery Court** (20 Atkinson St.) is another gourmet affair that borrows the town's old name.

DIRECTIONS FOR PORTSMOUTH RESTAURANTS From Exit 7 turn right if northbound, left if southbound, following signs for Market St. Go 0.7 mile and turn left onto Market St. into the heart of the restored waterfront district. Continue 1½ blocks to **Clarence's** (111 Market), on the left. For **The Dolphin Striker,** take the next left and you'll see it immediately on the left (15 Bow St.). **The Blue Strawbery** is ½ block down Ceres St., which runs up alongside the Dolphin Striker. To get to **Karen's Ice Cream** from the Dolphin Striker, continue along Bow St. for 1 block, turn right on Chapel and go up the hill 1 block to Daniel. Turn right on Daniel. It's a few doors down on the left at 105 Daniel (directly opposite City Hall).

Maine

KEVIN'S VILLAGE RESTAURANT
THE SPICE OF LIFE
JIMMY'S ALL SEASONS, *York—The Berwicks Exit, York*

Kevin's Village Restaurant is an unimposing little lunchroom recently opened by a young man with big plans to make major changes. We only hope it will be as pleasant when you get there as it was for us.

We found everybody friendly and happy to accommodate our whims. Without knowing we were researching a book, they gladly served us two half-portions even though the menu listed no such option. The chili was chock-full of beef—not memorable in taste but not in price either ($1.45 a bowl; 95 cents if meatless) and certainly adequate. The beef stew was similar. A hamburger here costs $1.15. Quiche is $2.99, and a clam dinner—the most expensive item on the menu—goes for $3.98. Both come with "village fries"—unpeeled potatoes, sliced and fried.

We enjoyed listening to two local women—one middle-aged, the other, wearing heavy field boots, about 70 years old—discussing the merits of the new restaurant in town. "It's really nice that there's a place to come for a cup of coffee." "Yea, they've got honest food, and you can't beat the prices." We agree.

But if this isn't what you're looking for, **Jimmy's All Seasons** and the **Spice of Life** are just around the corner. Jimmy's is a tiny breakfast and lunch place with prices to match, while Spice of Life is a full restaurant with complete bar, knotty pine paneling, and cotton print tablecloths. Dinners at the Spice of Life, mostly American, are $8.50–$11. At lunch, pastrami with melted cheese on rye is $2.75; baked scallops in casserole, $4.95.

HOURS **Kevin's Village Restaurant:** Sun.–Thu. 6 am–8:30 pm; Fri. & Sat. 6 am–9 pm, or later.

Spice of Life: Lunch: Mon.–Fri. 11:30 am–3 pm; Dinner: Mon.–Sat. 5–9 pm. Closed Sun.

Jimmy's All Seasons: Every day 6 am–2:30 pm.

DIRECTIONS From exit labeled "York–The Berwicks," follow signs for York Village. Turn right at first light onto Route 1 South and go 0.3 mile. Left at the light for 0.9 mile. Just as you come into the village, **Kevin's** is on your left. **Jimmy's** and **Spice of Life** are around the corner.

THE KENNEBUNK INN, *Exit 3, Kennebunk*

If you think you'd like to spend some time at an inn that radiates good cheer and feels more truly like home than any place we've come across, you ought to know about the Kennebunk.

It was 1978 when Arthur and Angela LeBlanc left good jobs in the city to chase a dream. They bought a "classic flophouse" and poured three years of sweat and tears (mostly Angela's tears, by her own account) into the renovation. What they've produced feels so much like home because that's exactly what it is for them. Who wants to live in a museum? they figured. Instead of history, what you get here is a sense of life, in the warmth and rich color that Angela worked into every detail.

The dining room, for example, is a felicitous blend of color and restraint, neither gaudy nor severe. Floral drapes and tablecloths spice up the tan carpet and light walls. With pleasant place settings, candles, and a few unobtrusive stained-glass panels in the windows, it's a delightfully eclectic scheme, colorful and relaxing all at once.

The dinner menu is continental, with steak and lobster for the less adventuresome. Chef Bob MacIntosh lets the fresh fish speak for itself ($7.95–$13.95). The beef, veal, and chicken dishes ($8.95–$13.95) are more heavily spiced, but never overpowering. One especially tempting specialty is shrimp stuffed with scallop dressing ($10.95), and the sour cream pie got a rave review from Joan Mondale (there's a letter on the wall).

Lunch here is a simpler matter, making it the perfect break from the drive. Soup is 95 cents a cup/$1.65 a bowl; chowder, $1.95/$2.50. There are six sandwiches from $2.95 to $3.95, quiche, chef's salad ($3.95), a fruit plate, and a daily special.

If you have a meal or stay over in one of the 40 rooms, do try to chat with the LeBlancs. Like all who have weathered a major renovation job, they love to talk about it, and will bring out the before-and-after pictures. You'll no doubt find yourself swept along by Angela's irrepressible energy and charm.

HOURS Memorial Day to Labor Day: Breakfast, 8–10 am; Lunch, 11:30 am–2:30 pm; Dinner, Mon.–Thu. 5:30–9 pm; Fri. & Sat. 5:30–10 pm. No dinner on Sunday.

Labor Day to Memorial Day: Same as above, but no breakfast, and closed all day Sunday.

DIRECTIONS From Exit 3 follow signs for Kennebunk. At 1.3 miles bear left at fork (sign says Kennebunkport). Go 0.3 mile farther, to Kennebunk, and turn right. Inn is 1½ blocks up, on the right.

KENNEBUNK RESTAURANT, *Exit 3, Kennebunk*

Right across the street from the Kennebunk Inn is a simple village restaurant open seven days a week. You'll find decent food, friendly people, and moderate prices.

HOURS Mon.–Sat. 6:30 am–5 pm; Sun. 6:30 am–1 pm.

DIRECTIONS Follow directions for **Kennebunk Inn,** above.

Entering I-295

ABOUT PORTLAND

Downtown Portland stands high on a crest above Casco Bay. Depending on your mood and point of view, the high-rise buildings look inviting or foreboding as you leave the highway in search of a meal. You can head up the hill and into the teeth of downtown traffic (not bad by some cities' standards). If you do, there's great Chinese food as your reward. Or you can avoid the city altogether and settle into one of the mahogany booths of a well-preserved diner.

HU SHANG, *Exit 6A (I-295), Portland*

Portland has never been known as the culinary capital of New England, but ever since Hu Shang appeared on the scene two years ago the city's gastronomes have been cheering and reviewers' typewriters have been clacking. At least four publications have raved about the recent epicurean eruption on Brown Street.

To begin with, Hu Shang is a renovation wonder. Converted from what appears to have been a high-ceilinged warehouse, the multilevel restaurant is capacious and beautiful, combining the best of modern American decor with hints of Oriental tranquility. Subtle textures, light colors, and vast amounts of brick have been integrated gracefully and in some places—like the bold arched windows—spectacularly. Handsome, if simple, wooden tables contrast nicely with Chinese rugs and a few well-spaced orange trees.

Hu Shang specializes in the fiery sauces and sautéed vegetables of Szechuan and Hunan cuisines, but for uncalloused tongues the kitchen produces other items from the milder ginger and scallion-flavored styles of Shanghai and Peking. The menu includes some unusual entrées such as Hunan crispy whole fish, "Buddha's delight" (a dieter's plate of fresh Chinese vegetables and mushrooms), and quite a few dishes in orange sauce. We enjoyed the excellent orange-flavored shrimp; the tangy sauce dazzled the tongue.

Aside from meat and seafood specialties (generally $6–$8), Hu Shang puts together a large variety of vegetarian plates ($4.50–$5.50) using fresh Chinese vegetables including straw mushrooms, wooden ear (a fungus), Chinese cabbage, and lily flowers. Bean curd (tofu) shows up in seven different dishes. The nutrition-conscious will be delighted to know that all of Hu Shang's fried rice dishes ($3.25–$4.50) use brown rice.

If you are inclined toward dessert, lichee nuts, pineapple chunks, loquats, or fried bananas will send you on your way. It's a nice way to go.

HOURS Mon.–Thu. 11:30 am–9 pm; Fri. & Sat. 11:30 am–10 pm; Sun. noon–9 pm.

DIRECTIONS Northbound: Exit 6A on I-95 feeds you into I-295. Take I-295 to Exit 6A (Forest Ave.). ■ Head straight for downtown; turn left on Congress St. at top of the hill. Go three lights to Brown St., turning right onto Brown for ½ block. Restaurant is on your left, at 7–13 Brown, just before a parking lot you may wish to use.

Southbound: Driving south on I-95, follow signs for I-295/Portland. Take I-295 to Exit 6A (Forest Ave.), then as above from ■.

MISS PORTLAND DINER, *Exits 6A & 7 (I-295), Portland*

If it weren't for the outsized sign atop the Miss Portland, she would be a perfect gem of a Worcester Lunch Car diner. The Gothic script that announces "Miss Portland—Booth Service" is all but eclipsed by the building's garish crown, obviously meant to attract the traveler. But don't let it deter you. Inside, the Miss Portland is as pretty as can be, and almost everything on the menu is homemade. In fact, she recently won the *Portland Chronicle*'s award for the best diner in the area.

Most dinners here, which include two vegetables and potato, are under $3. Grilled ham steaks, and fish and chips are representative examples. Hamburgers are $1.10, sandwiches slightly more. Wednesday is fish chowder day—$1.50 a bowl.

Breakfast at Miss Portland is a low-priced event: three large eggs, toast, and home fries go for $1.45, as a sign nailed to the telephone pole outside proudly attests.

HOURS Mon.–Thu. 6 am–3 pm; Thu. 11 pm–Fri. 3 pm; Fri. 11 pm–Sat. 1:30 pm; Sat. 11 pm–Sun. 1 pm.

DIRECTIONS See **Hu Shang,** above, to get from I-95 onto I-295. Northbound: Exit 7 on I-295 brings you to a traffic light. Turn right onto Marginal Way. Diner is on your left, at 49 Marginal Way.

Southbound: Exit 6A on I-295 puts you on Forest Ave. Turn left at first light onto Marginal Way. Diner is on your right.

Return to I-95

ABOUT BRUNSWICK

Brunswick seems to combine all the pluses a Maine town could boast—easy access to the Atlantic, a rich history, a prestigious New England college (Bowdoin) with all its attendant culture, and some good restaurants.

THE OMELETTE SHOP, *Exit 22, Brunswick*

Everything at the Omelette Shop, even the cooking, takes place in one small, rough, but pleasant room with big windows that look out on Brunswick's Federal-style Maine Street (pun intended, but not by us). Half the menu is a varied selection of delicious omelettes. You have your choice of cheese (sharp cheddar, Swiss, cream, or feta) and other fillings that include the expected (bacon, ham, mushrooms, onions, peppers), the not-so-expected (sprouts, avocado, broccoli), and the completely unexpected (strawberries, bananas, jams).

The Greek omelette is stuffed with feta cheese, black olives, and tomatoes. The Hawaiian? Pineapple, of course, but also ham, cherries, and blanched almonds. They're all made with three eggs and are served with bread and a large portion of very good home fries ($2.35–$3.75).

On Friday, Saturday, and Sunday nights, the Omelette Shop serves pizza omelettes! With pepperoni, mushrooms, and other pizza toppings, they sound like fun, but we didn't time our visit right.

The Omelette Shop also serves sirloin sandwiches ($4.95) and bulky burgers ($2.10–$3) with your choice of toppings. Texas burgers, served with a mandatory glass of water, come topped with sharp cheddar and scorching jalapeño peppers. Watch out!

HOURS Every day 7 am–9 pm.

DIRECTIONS See end of Brunswick entries, p. 219.

THE INTOWN PUB, *Exit 22, Brunswick*

College students and café intellectuals frequent the Intown Pub. Half of it is a quiet bar (weekend evenings excepted), the other half a sandwich restaurant on two levels. Newspapers (including *The New York Times)* await you by the door. Old, dark wood contributes to the pubby feel of things, but an equal amount of plywood and dark-stained four-by-fours are nailed up where beams ought to be. Still, it's a pleasant, informal place with captain's chairs and tablecloths, and it doesn't really seem plastique.

There are a dozen different sandwiches available on half a dozen types of bread. They're thick as you'd want them, and they run $1.75 to $2.65. The Pub's Special is lettuce, tomato, and tangy lemon and garlic dressing in pita bread. It's available plain ($2.10), with cheese ($2.50), ham and cheese ($2.75), or roast beef and cheese ($2.95). There are also a few salads, deli-style side orders, and desserts.

HOURS Every day 11 am–9 pm.

DIRECTIONS See end of Brunswick entries, below.

THE BOWDOIN, *Exit 22, Brunswick*

* *Untried, but likely*

We can't tell you much more about this establishment than you can learn by peeping in the window, which, since it was closed that day, is exactly what we did. But some sophisticated-looking folks in the bookstore across the street (yes, we always ask in bookstores) said it was the best in town, which might mean only that it has a menu in several languages, or might mean just what it says. But we thought you'd want to know about this old hotel, with its continental menu and dignified (so far as we could tell) interior.

Looked interesting. Let us know.

HOURS Lunch: Tue.–Fri. 11:30 am–2 pm; Dinner: Tue.–Thu. 5–9:30 pm; Fri. & Sat. 5–10:30 pm. Closed Mon.

DIRECTIONS FOR BRUNSWICK RESTAURANTS From Exit 22 follow U.S. 1 toward Brunswick for about 2 miles. Look for green Interstate-style signs saying "Brunswick, Routes 201 and 24." Exit here and at end of ramp turn right onto Maine St. In 0.1 mile you will be in front of the **Omelette Shop** and **The Bowdoin,** next door to each other on the left. For the **Intown Pub,** take the next right, Town Hall Place, and you'll see it shortly on your left.

JUDY AND DON'S ON THE SQUARE, *Exit 25, Bowdoinham*

We missed this one ourselves, but our friend Dave Shorey, a resident antique-flute dealer and restaurant lover, says that Judy and Don's is a grocery-luncheonette with good plain cookin', good plain prices, and good plain folks. Dave ought to know, he's a devotee of down-home things.

HOURS Mon.–Sat. 6 am–9 pm; Sun. 6 am–8 pm.

DIRECTIONS From Exit 25 turn right if northbound, left if southbound toward Bowdoinham. In 1.3 miles you'll reach a blinking light. It's right there.

GIBERSON DINER, *Exit 28, Gardiner*

We have scrutinized diners from the outside and from the inside, but this is the first one we've gotten to look at from below. This is also the first restaurant of any kind that we've found perched on stilts. It stands 40 feet above the Cobbeesee River, and if you are so inclined—we were—you can descend a steel staircase to admire the tangle of ducts and pipes that feed the diner and circulate its essential fluids.

But the Giberson's underparts aren't all that is to be admired. It's really a little beauty, a 35-year-old Worcester Lunch Car in mint condition. The people who work here are friendly, the food is tasty, and the view is great. Inside, there's so much mahogany that, for a diner, it's actually mellow. Complementing the ruddy wood is a light-blue barrel ceiling, tan marble counter, oak window sashes, and some other delightful touches: the oddly shaped window in the side door, the stained-glass ceiling vents, the sunbursts behind the counter.

The food is what you'd expect at a well-kept diner—simple but good, with two idiosyncrasies. One is that many of the meats are hickory smoked. A hickory-smoked beef sandwich can be had for $1.89, and not much more buys a complete dinner of smoked chicken or spare ribs. The other quirk, which seems to be a regionalism, is the use of vinegar as a condiment. This isn't the only place it's done, of course, but when you shake the vinegar bottle over your corned beef and cabbage dinner, you *know* you're in New England.

HOURS Mon.–Sat. 5 am–7 pm; Sun. 7–11 am.

DIRECTIONS From Exit 28 turn right if northbound, left if southbound, following Routes 126 and 9 to Gardiner. Turn left after 2.6 miles, at the first light. It's on your right.

ABOUT AUGUSTA

Augusta is Maine's capital and, for us, the end of a gastronomic journey along I-95 that began in faraway Greenwich, Connecticut. We searched Augusta, street by street, alley by alley, hoping for a fitting finale to our journey. Zilch! Nothing, not even mediocrity of minor merit, except perhaps the **Augusta House of Pancakes,** which, despite its too-familiar-sounding name, is not part of a chain. Trouble is, it looks like it's trying to be. The menu, food, and decor all seemed familiar. We'll say one nice thing about it, though—the service was friendly and fast. Our waitress even brought us a newspaper. Also, it's right near the highway (for directions, see p. 223).

Looking further, we were given a hot tip: "Try the town of Hallowell, two miles down the road." We did, and we weren't disappointed.

SLATES, *Exit 30, Hallowell*

Slates is a brick-plants-and-oak café, funky, heavy on brick, and frowzy around the edges. Even though Slates is only five years old, it seems to date back to the early days of this restaurant style—before it became chic to put a plant in every window and polished hardwood trim over the rough spots. The folks here seemed a little on the tousled side too, or "northwoodsy," at any rate. Sitting around large tables in the bar room was a crowd of regulars swapping tales, we imagine, of antique trading (Hallowell is full of shops), snowmobile legislation (it's the hottest issue at the State House, just up the road), or whatever else people talk about in northern Maine.

In restaurants of this sort it is unusual to find breakfast, but Slates serves three meals a day. At breakfast, you have some pretty enticing possibilities, like pear pancakes ($2.25), avocado and sour cream omelettes ($2.95), and lovely cranberry yogurt bread, as well as your basic two eggs, home fries, and toast (good bread) for $1.70.

Lunch is standard B.P.O. fare: sandwiches (Reubens, vegetable pocket, grilled cheese with mushrooms), big salads, homemade soups, and carrot cake–style desserts, all fairly reasonable (sandwiches, $1.55–$2.95; salads, $1.75–$3.50). There is no dinner menu at Slates—the day's specials are written on blackboards ("the slates"). Running from $4.95 for quiche to $8 or $9 for fish and beef dishes, dinner comes with candlelight atmosphere. For the tea connoisseur, a fitting end to all this is the basket of Twining's and Celestial Seasonings teas that is brought to your table on request.

HOURS Mon.–Fri. 7 am–9 pm; Sat. 8 am–9:30 pm; Sun. 9 am–2:30 pm.

DIRECTIONS From Exit 30 follow signs to Augusta along Route 202. In 1.1 miles you will see **Augusta House of Pancakes** on your right (100 Western Ave.). For **Slates,** continue for 0.6 mile to traffic circle. Take first right in circle, Route 201 South, to Hallowell. It's 1.8 miles from the circle to the center of town. Slates is on your right.

I-195

Rhode Island, Massachusetts

Rhode Island

ANGELO'S
HAVEN BROTHERS
STATE HOUSE RESTAURANT, ***Exit 1, Providence***

See pp. 192–195, for descriptions of these colorful places, especially Angelo's, with its good, inexpensive Italian food.

DIRECTIONS From Exit 1 (I-195) enter I-95 North. A mile or so will bring you to Exits 21 & 23 in downtown Providence. Then follow directions given.

RUE DE L'ESPOIR, ***Exit 2, Providence***

Owners Deborah Norman and Grace Kohn bristle when Rue de l'Espoir is compared with a Left Bank bistro. "We're not trying to be Left Bank anything," declares Deborah. "We're just trying to serve the best food we can."

Still, the Left Bank flavor cannot be denied. As Left Bank cafés fringe the Sorbonne, so Rue de l'Espoir is in the shadow of ivy-clad Brown University. With aproned waitresses scurrying about carrying cheeseboards and long loaves of crusty bread, with "Mesdames et Messieurs" on the single restroom door and Toulouse-Lautrec prints on the walls, with animated chatter and *joie de vivre* simply filling the multilevel room, we can understand how the Left Bank analogy came to be.

Whatever they were aiming for, the owners have done a bang-up job. We loved the ambiance, and the food was no less a delight.

Every day, there are meal-sized salads with interesting dressings (around $4), three kinds of quiche (the same), and several entrées ($6–$7.50). Pork tenderloin with Dijon Hollandaise, boneless breast of chicken in sherry and port wine sauce, and baked scrod in light lemon Mornay sauce all sound luscious enough, but the one most lusted after is Macadamia chicken—boneless breast with Macadamia nuts, heavy cream, and white wine.

All soups and sauces are uncompromisingly prepared from meat stocks cooked on the premises. The full flavors of the black bean soup in beef broth ($1.75) were still with us when we dug into two large whole wheat crepes generously stuffed with chunks of chicken peach puree, a most surprising but well-matched complement. The two crepes came as a single portion for only $3.95 (lunch or dinner). *Bon marché!* If peachy chicken doesn't appeal, there are four other, less radical but still interesting, crepes.

Another excellent bargain is the cheeseboard. For $4.95 you get a hunk of cheese (there are 12 to choose from), water crackers, fresh fruit, excellent French bread, and a house salad, all presented with a flourish on a wooden cheeseboard.

You can finish off all this good eating with any of several sinful desserts, or end on a less guilty note with fresh fruit and cheese. Or, if the craving for ice cream gets the better of you, you can mosey across the street to **Big Alice's Ice Cream,** where the flavors are as interesting and the quality as good as the crepes at Rue de l'Espoir.

HOURS Lunch: Tue.–Sun. 11:30 am–2:30 pm; Dinner: Sun–Thu. 5–10 pm; Fri. & Sat. 5–11 pm. Closed Mon.

DIRECTIONS From Exit 2 (Wickendon St.) turn left and go straight up the hill for 0.2 mile to Hope St. Left on Hope for 3 blocks. **Rue de l'Espoir** is on the right (99 Hope).

Massachusetts

THE GANGPLANK, *Exit 5, Fall River*

Architecturally, the Gangplank is from the Suburban Nautical School. Its expansive southern windows offer an impressive view of the Taunton River and a minor flotilla of World War II–vintage fighting ships, including the battleship U.S.S. *Massachusetts*. For $4 you can tour the ships or, for the same amount, take a tour of the Gangplank's deli board—your choice of turkey, corned beef, pastrami, or roast beef sandwich, a bottomless soup bowl, and a similarly refillable plate of salad.

This bargain is available at lunchtime only, but dinner has its own special value—the Gangplank's raw bar. Technically, it's misnamed—not everything is raw—but nevertheless a bargain. For $7.95 as a meal in itself ($5.95 with an entrée), the "raw" bar includes unlimited helpings of steamers, mussels, cherrystones, oysters, and shrimp, along with salad or soup, and bread.

If you prefer a more conventional dinner, look at the menu—it has three pages, each in a different typeface to correspond (very roughly) with three cuisines: French, Italian, and American. Shrimp scampi ($9.95) is the favorite Italian dish; steak Bordelaise, crackling and sizzling as it comes to your table ($10.95), is the biggest French seller; and the American broiled fisherman's platter is a filling and attractive presentation ($9.95).

Haute in neither cuisine nor style, the Gangplank is nevertheless a comfortable and pleasant place with some good buys to be had. And, if you like battleships, you'll love the view.

HOURS Mon.–Sat. 11:30 am–3:30 pm and 5–10 pm; Sun. noon–10 pm.

DIRECTIONS Northbound: Exit 5 puts you on a long ramp that soon forks. Bear right onto Routes 79/138 North. ■ Take first exit (it comes up quickly) onto Route 6 East/Davol St. From this exit take the first left onto Route 138 South (signs for Battleship Cove), pass under the highway, and turn left again. It's on your right.

Southbound: From Exit 5, the ramp forks; bear right for Routes 79/138. Then as above from ■.

LUSITANO RESTAURANT, *Exit 5, Fall River*

We knew that Fall River had a large Portuguese population, so we suspected that somewhere in town there just had to be a Portuguese restaurant. We turned to two policemen in a cruiser for enlightenment, and they offered to lead the way. During the ensuing tour of Fall River's labyrinthine streets, we feared more than once that the cops were simply going about their rounds, having completely forgotten the two hungry travelers on their tail. Finally, they delivered us to Lusitano's. It seems they had been changing their minds about which restaurant was the best, and changing direction accordingly. But in this working-class neighborhood of clapboard apartment buildings, they pointed to one that had been studded with glass-block windows and stuccoed over at street level, and assured us we'd come to the best in town.

Portuguese food is different, at least as it is prepared in this part of New England. It's got a lot of zing and a lot of salt, more sharp than hot. For the uninitiated, it'll take some getting used to.

The house specialty at Lusitano is marinated pork, which you can get at lunchtime Alentejana-style (with littleneck clams) for $3.95, Lusitano-style (littlenecks plus fried potatoes) for $4.95, or as a sandwich for $1.60. The chourico plate (chourico is a Portuguese sausage) comes boiled in wine or fried for $3.75, and bacalhau, which is salted codfish that has been soaked for several days before preparation and then baked with potatoes or in a tomato sauce, is $3.95. There's a nice kale soup for $1, flan and pineapple rings in port for dessert, and hamburgers for those who don't want to take a chance. Full dinners are $6–$10.

The decor here is one of laid-on Iberian atmosphere—imitation beams, heavily textured ceiling and walls, dark furniture, guitars, wine bottles, and oil paintings of bullfight scenes. The place is small and clean, charming even, especially on weekends when the crowd is almost entirely Portuguese and there is dancing to live entertainment (a one-man band who tapes his own background music at home, and then accompanies it on stage).

HOURS Lunch: Wed.–Sat. 11:30 am–2 pm; Dinner: Wed.–Fri. 5–9:30 pm; Sat. 5–10:30 pm; Sun. noon–9:30 pm. Closed Mon. & Tues.

DIRECTIONS From Exit 5 follow signs for Route 138 South (Broadway). Go along Broadway for about 1½ miles (there will be some traffic). Look for Benjamin St., next to a Texaco station. Left onto Benjamin and then next right. Go 1 block and **Lusitano** will be on the left at 820 King Philip St.

GABE MOURA'S ORCHID DINER, *Exit 13A, New Bedford*

"He insults you every day, and if he don't insult you it means he don't like you." That's what a regular at Gabe Moura's Orchid Diner told us about the garrulous owner. Gabe's benevolence was evident enough, but to drive the point home, he made it known that when he was hospitalized for an operation he received over 250 get-well cards from his customers. "And find me a McDonald's where that'll happen," he added, with no pretense of modesty.

This is a little chrome O'Mahoney dining car, built in 1951 and still in mint condition. It really does look like a railroad car—you can almost feel it sway. The silver and pink color scheme is bright and cheerful, the Venetian blinds endearing, but we were especially curious about the ceiling mirror that runs the entire length of the diner. We came up with a few kinky speculations, but Gabe pointed out that people like to have a bird's-eye view of the grill man, and the mirror gives them that perspective. "You can always see what he's doing to your food, even from the booths," said Gabe, and we recalled stories of an earlier age when you really had to worry about what went into your meal.

Gabe is a member of New Bedford's sizable Portuguese population, but he puts Portuguese specials on the menu only occasionally. However, linguica—a Portuguese sausage that tastes like a cross between pepperoni and kielbasa—is always available at breakfast time ($2.50 with two eggs, home fries, toast, and coffee). Without linguica, a two-egg-plus breakfast costs $1.45. Lunches and dinners vary from day to day. Most—baked stuffed haddock or sole, Yankee pot roast, roast pork with dressing, for example—are $2.95 à la carte, $3.95 as full dinners. Stuffed quahogs (large clams), an unusual appetizer for a diner, are 75 cents apiece.

For many of Gabe's devoted clients, the best thing on the menu—or at least the thing they look for first—is the quote of the day. We glanced at the bottom of the mimeographed sheet, and there it was: "Enough research will tend to support your theory."

Having come upon Gabe and his diner in an effort to prove that decent dining is still available to travelers, we had to agree.

HOURS Mon.–Fri. 5 am–7 pm; Sat. 5 am–2:30 pm; Sun. & holidays 5 am–noon.

DIRECTIONS Exit 13A puts you on Route 140 South. Go about 1 mile and turn left at the first light, onto Route 6 East. In about 0.3 mile you'll see it on your left, at the second light.

CAFÉ AND RESTAURANT PORTUGAL, *Exits 14 & 17, New Bedford*

New Bedford gives you a choice. You can drive an easy 1½ miles to the waterfront historical district, or you can stay right by the highway and explore the ethnic part of town. Since the town is half Portuguese, if you opt for the latter take a look at the Café Portugal, by all accounts the best of its kind hereabouts.

Virginia de Sousa came from the Azores, worked in New Bedford's woolen mills until she learned English, and then, with her husband Marcilio, opened a small pastry and coffee shop. Now they've moved across the street and added a restaurant. It looks like the beginnings of a classic American success story; we can only hope the ending is a happy one.

Azorian cooking, we learned, is stronger and sharper than its mainland progenitor. We tried fried quail, a Portuguese favorite, in a vinegary tomato sauce ($4.50), and *bacalhau a braz,* a casserole of salted cod, potatoes, onions, and eggs ($4.25). (While the cod came out surprisingly mellow, we probably won't go out of our way for Portuguese fried quail again.) Some other interesting possibilities were roast stuffed kid ($5.25), rabbit, and chopped liver with onions ($3.95).

At prices like these you shouldn't expect the plushest decor. All the same, Café Portugal is pleasant enough—new and spanking clean, with blue carpets and Spanish tile partway up the stuccoed walls. The room is bigger than you might expect, and has something of an empty feel to it, at least at off-peak hours. And you'll have to put up with a radio, commercials and all. But Virginia's friendliness and willingness to explain Portuguese cuisine make up for any such drawbacks.

HOURS Coffee shop (sandwiches and pastry): Tue.–Sun. 9 am–midnight. Restaurant: Tue.–Sun. noon–10 pm. Both closed Mon.

DIRECTIONS Eastbound: Exit 14 to stop sign and turn left onto County St. Go 0.2 mile and turn right onto Cogshall St. (no sign, but J & J lunchroom on corner). Go two lights on Cogshall to Acushnet Ave. Left, and then about 2 blocks to restaurant, on the right at 1280 Acushnet Ave.

Westbound: Exit 17 to stop sign. Left onto Cogshall St. Right at second light onto Acushnet Ave. It's on the right, 2 blocks up—1280 Acushnet Ave.

DOWN TO EARTH RESTAURANT, *Exit 15, New Bedford*

Richard and Catherine O'Berry are vegetarians who got tired of driving to Providence whenever they wanted to eat out. So they opened their own little place in downtown New Bedford. Now they've got a thriving business that is converting businessmen and secretaries to natural foods, but their lives are so tied to it that they still have to drive to Providence in order to eat out.

The Down to Earth is true to its name, but it's rather more nicely finished than most places of its kind, and not so militantly organic. Painted white chairs and white tablecloths, floral table runners, and matching curtains mitigate the unabashed earthiness of the exposed kitchen with its woks and cast-iron frying pans.

Lunch here consists of dishes like tofu, lettuce, and tomato in pocket bread ($1.95), apple, nut, and hummus mushroom melt ($2.25), pita pizza ($1.50), and maple-walnut-almond pie made with real maple syrup. There are two soups from scratch every day (90 cents/$1.30), and homemade whole wheat bread.

Dinners are equally reasonable. Salmon croquettes is the most expensive item and it's only $4.95 with potato, vegetable, and salad. Stir-fried vegetables on brown rice is $3.95, as is spanakopita and a large Greek salad.

No liquor license here, but a beer and wine permit is hoped for soon.

HOURS Lunch: Mon.–Sat. 11 am–2:30 pm; Dinner: Thu.–Sat. 5–9:30 pm. Closed Sundays and last week of August.

DIRECTIONS Exit 15 puts you on Route 18 South, a limited access road. Get off at "Downtown" Exit (about 1½ miles) and bear right onto Elm St. Take third left (6th St.) and go 4 blocks to Spring St. Turn left onto Spring and then take the very next left onto Pleasant. It's ½ block up, on the right, at 522 Pleasant St.

FREESTONE'S, *Exit 15, New Bedford*

This beautiful 1880s-bank-turned-1980s-restaurant is named for the Longmeadow freestone that constitutes its gorgeous façade. On the outside it is almost baroque, and within it's stately and dignified, a brick-plants-and-oak café of the highest order. Except that in this case the oak has been replaced by mahogany. The old, finely crafted mahogany doors and paneling set the tone here, while ceiling fans, brass rails, and frosted glass add the finishing touches. The best we've seen in this category, hands down.

New Bedford is the scallop center of America, and scallops scampi is one of Freestone's most popular specialties, served on rice pilaf for $6.95. Other fish entrées (sole Florentine Dijon, for instance) are in the same price range; chicken and vegetarian dishes dip a bit lower. Good prices for so fine an environment. Typical B.P.O. sandwiches (Reuben, Monte Cristo, tuna melt) and salads (spinach, chef's) run from $2.50 to $3.50. We especially enjoyed the creamy fish chowder ($1.50 cup/$1.95 bowl), thick with scrod, potatoes, and onions. Swamp Yankees may tell you that authentic New England chowder should be milky thin, but we liked it fine the way Freestone's served it.

HOURS Mon.–Sat. 11 am–1 am; Sun. noon–11 pm.

DIRECTIONS Exit 15 puts you on Route 18 South, a limited access road heading straight downtown. Leave Route 18 at "Downtown" Exit and head up Elm St. (signs clear). Make the third left turn off Elm, go 1 block and turn left again. Another block brings you to **Freestone's,** on the left, at 41 Williams St.

THE GALLEY DELICATESSEN AND BAKERY, *Exit 20, Marion*

A terrific place to put together your own simple meal, and in the summer there are picnic benches under the trees.

This is a family operation, located in a nice, shingled old house right by the road. Since the Forants also do catering, they offer so many items that a complete list would overrun the page. Here's a sampler: breads, sausages, meatballs, spaghetti sauce, frozen casseroles and pies, pasta, clam chowder, quiche, and Lebanese meat pie. There are salads to go, and for variety, pickled ricotta (even pickled quail eggs!) and many other unusual treats scattered around the tiny shop.

If nothing already concocted pleases you, make your own. You can choose from almost any lunch meat you can name, a gourmet selection of cheeses, and five kinds of bread, including French. If you come up with a new combination that appeals to the owners,

they may name it after you and put it up on their already extensive sandwich menu ($1.35–$2.95).

Dessert won't be a problem either. Cookies, pies, and cakes aplenty, Häagen-Dazs and Hershey's ice cream, along with exotics like Italian nougat candy. And a great lemon cheesecake.

If you do stop here, be sure to drive a little farther into town. It's a charming place, and the road skirts the sea.

HOURS Memorial Day to Labor Day: every day 8 am–10 pm. Labor Day to Memorial Day: every day 8 am–8 pm. Closed in February.

DIRECTIONS From Exit 20 turn right onto Route 105 South. Go 0.6 mile. It's on the right, just before intersection with Route 6.

HARRIET'S, *Exit 20, Marion*

* *Untried, but likely*

Harriet's was closed for the season when we came through, but it looked like a good bet, and the folks at the Galley (above), who ought to know, praised it highly. It's a Victorian carriage house that was converted in the 1920s to an ice cream parlor, and it still has the original oak paneling and booths as well as the gold-leafed ice cream signs. We peeked in the windows, and what we saw looked clean, light, and very pleasant.

There are tales of huge salads (four or five of them) and superbly prepared entrées. Continental (mostly French) dinners, we were told, are a reasonable \$5–\$8. Lunch sandwiches run \$2–\$3.50 and entrées up to \$4.50

Patty Nicholson ("Harriet") is rumored to be a great experimenter who loves to do interesting things with wine and herbs. Italian, German, Greek, Middle Eastern, Mexican, Polish, Scandinavian, and regional American cooking have been featured on Thursday's International Night at Harriet's. On any night, the superrich chowder is a favorite.

Sunday brunch has eggs as you like 'em, including Benedict, Florentine, and Sardou. Sounds good to us.

HOURS Open April 1 to mid-December. May–Sept.: every day 11 am–10 pm.

Apr. and Oct. through mid-Dec.: Mon. & Wed. 11 am–3 pm; Thu.–Sat. 11 am–9 pm; Sun. 11 am–3 pm. Closed Tuesdays during these months.

DIRECTIONS From **The Galley** (above), continue 1 mile farther on Route 105. Turn right on Cottage St., and you'll see **Harriet's** a bit up, on the right, dressed in blue.

INDEX OF RESTAURANTS AND TOWNS